Not Tonight, Josephine

A Road Trip Through Small-Town America

George Mahood

Not Tonight, Josephine

A Road Trip Through Small-Town America

George Mahood

This edition published 2016 by George Mahood

LIKE George on Facebook
www.facebook.com/georgemahood

FOLLOW George on Twitter
www.twitter.com/georgemahood

www.georgemahood.com

1

It was a series of bad decisions that led to me being alone in the dark, pushing a bicycle through a ditch alongside a busy highway in the middle of Delaware. Only a couple of weeks previously, I had been putting the finishing touches to a grand plan to fly to New York with a friend, buy a car and drive across the USA, all the way to California. Instead, I was on my own with a broken bicycle in a dark ditch in Delaware. Things had not gone to plan.

I carried on pushing. I was unlit, dressed in impractical clothing and there was no space on the edge of the highway to safely push a bike. The ditch was the only option. My back tyre had exploded at the worst possible moment, darkness had fallen, and I was left stranded many miles from my hotel in the neighbouring state of Maryland.

I continued walking in the hope that a building would materialise. Someplace where I could get some sleep and worry about the bike in the morning. Or somewhere with a telephone where I could at least call for help. Who I would call, I wasn't sure, but at least it would be a start.

I decided to try and hitch a lift. I had never hitch-hiked before, and being accompanied by a huge bicycle on a road with no stopping places was probably not the best place to start. I was left with little choice.

I climbed out of the ditch, stood on the roadside and stuck out a thumb.

I was unfamiliar with the etiquette of hitchhiking. Should I keep walking? Should I just stand still and try to make eye-contact with the drivers? I tried a combination of the two with disastrous consequences. I shuffled backwards, stumbling every few metres as I caught my legs on the pedals. Almost every other car that passed gave a loud blast of the horn. Who was I kidding? I didn't look like the most inviting prospect for passing motorists. I certainly wouldn't have picked me up.

It was time for me to take the bike out of the equation. I tossed it into the ditch, so that it was hidden from view of the road, and stuck out my thumb again.

Ten minutes passed and all I received was a barrage of angry car horns. I suddenly hated America. I cursed my idiotic idea to pack a backpack in England to come and travel this stupid country. I could be back home eating home-cooked meals and experiencing America on television from the comfort of the sofa instead.

Twenty minutes passed. I became aware just how cold it was. It was October, but I had foolishly set off in a pair of shorts and a t-shirt, tricked by the bright blue American sky.

Just as I was in the process of writing off an entire continent, an old brown battered station wagon came to a stop a few yards further up the road. There was a brief lull in the traffic and I ran towards it.

'You need a ride somewhere, boy?' said a man sat in the passenger seat.

'Yes please.'

'Hop in,' he said, with a mouth containing no more than three teeth.

He looked to be in his 70s, had long grey hair tied in a ponytail, patchy stubble and a blue chequered lumberjack shirt.

'Well, boy, what are you waiting for?' said the other man, ducking his head so that he could see me from the driver's seat. He looked almost identical to his passenger, except his shirt was red and he had a couple more teeth.

'Thank you. Thank you, that's really kind of you. I have a bicycle. Is there any chance I could throw that in the back, too?'

'You can bring the goddamn kitchen sink for all I care. Just get in.'

I rushed back up the road, heaved my bike out of the ditch and then with a bit of manipulation and brute force, squashed it into the back of the station wagon. I dived prostrate on top of the bike, catching my balls painfully on the pedals in the process.

'You in?'

'Yes,' I squealed, as I tried to readjust myself. 'Thank you so much for stopping. You have no idea how grateful I am.'

'Where you from?' said the driver.

'England.'

'Oh, gee I'm very sorry about that.'

They both looked at each other and laughed.

'What the hell you doin' out here in the dark in Delaware?'

'It's a long story,' I said.

2

We had it all planned out.

My friend Mark and I had plane tickets booked for New York. We would buy a cheap second-hand car and set off on a road trip for 6-9 months, driving every inch of the United States. We wanted to explore the parts of America no buses, trains or tour groups stopped at. We wanted to visit the America you don't see in sit-coms. We wanted to see the real America.

Mark's visa application was rejected days before we were due to leave. My application had been accepted. A little further delving suggested that my credit card debts had bizarrely worked in my favour. Apparently, this debt formed some sort of unofficial bond with the UK. It meant I would have to return home at some point to repay my debts. Mark had no such burden. He was a free-spirit. A maverick. He had no financial restraints tying him to home and could, quite happily, begin a new, illegal life in America, if he chose.

We both agreed that I would go on ahead. Mark would reschedule his flight to give him time to try and resolve his visa situation. I suggested that he go on a mad shopping bender and max out a few credit cards to try and create some ties to the UK, but he wasn't convinced by the idea.

Rather than getting a taxi from the airport, I decided to lug my heavy rucksack and guitar case to the subway. I thought that the subway would be a cheap and cheerful way to arrive in Manhattan and I could experience the famous New York City skyline from a different perspective. I forgot the crucial detail that the subway runs underground, therefore hindering the view of the city somewhat.

Like A-grade dicks, Mark and I agreed we would take our guitars with us to America. It seemed like a great idea at the time. We had played in a band together for many years and we had this romantic notion of busking our way across the country. The reality proved to be very different.

I had visited New York before but it felt very different on my own. I had forgotten just how exhilarating it is to walk the streets of Manhattan. The senses become overloaded immediately with an explosion of colours, smells and sounds.

Alexis, the older brother of one of my friends, had lived and worked in Manhattan for many years and he kindly offered Mark and me a sofa-bed at his apartment for a few days at the start of our trip.

'Make sure you take a pair of smart leather shoes with you for when you go to stay with Alexis,' my friend had said.

'Why do we need smart shoes?'

'Because I'm fairly sure he will take you and Mark out for a nice steak while you're there.'

'But why do we need smart shoes to eat a steak?'

'Some of the restaurants he goes to are very posh and you won't be allowed in without decent shoes. They might even make you wear a jacket.'

'Well I'm not taking a bloody jacket backpacking across America with me.'

'They can lend you a jacket, but you have to take the shoes.'

It seemed a bit excessive considering we were supposed to be backpacking and I would have absolutely no use for a pair of smart shoes. But I didn't want to offend our host, and I'd do pretty much anything for a free meal, so carrying an additional pair of shoes seemed like a fair sacrifice.

I reached Alexis's apartment building near the bottom west corner of Central Park just before 8pm. I managed to get myself stuck in the revolving door with the rucksack on my back and the guitar strapped to my front. I gave the door a heave and stumbled awkwardly into the large marble-floored lobby.

'Good evening, Sir. You must be George,' said the night porter who emerged from behind his desk.

'Hi… yes... I... how…?'

'Alexis from apartment 24 told me to expect a bedraggled looking student-type by the name of George.'

'Right, well, yes, that sounds like me. What's your name?'

'Frank.'

'Very nice to meet you, Frank,' I said, shaking him by the hand.

'Alexis said to tell you he's had to stay at work later than planned. You are welcome to leave your bags here if you want.'

'Thanks, that's great. Can you recommend anywhere cheap and cheerful for a bedraggled looking student type to get some food?'

'There's a great pizza place just around the corner. Tell them Frank sent you.'

'Perfect, thanks Frank.'

I ordered a giant pepperoni pizza (mentioning Frank got me a free soda), and sat on a bench on the southern corner of Central Park, under the glow of a streetlight. I was a young man, fresh out of university, and felt both tremendously excited and somewhat apprehensive about the possibilities that this road trip promised.

Travelling to The United States had been Mark's idea. He had spent three years studying American History at university and was keen to visit some of the places he had read so much about.

I too was keen to travel. I decided against taking a gap year before university, knowing that I would have found it hard to summon the enthusiasm to slot back into a life of education. Now I was finished with education, I was finding it hard to summon the enthusiasm to slot into a life of work. Taking some time to go travelling seemed like the ideal way to delay the inevitable.

The United States is not a traditional destination for backpackers from Great Britain. Most tend to choose Australia, South-East Asia, India or South America. Americans speak the same language and the culture is so familiar to people in Britain, that to travel in America is perhaps considered too easy.

I had been to America on a couple of occasions before and spent a little time in New York and San Francisco. I had grown up on a diet of American films, television, books and music and felt extremely familiar with the culture.

But it wasn't the hustle and bustle of the American cities I wanted to see. It wasn't even the popular east and west coasts. It was the places in between that intrigued me the most; the towns with almost non-existent populations and the back roads that connected these towns together.

I asked Mark if I could tag along with him and he gladly agreed. We would both spend the summer months in England earning as much spending money as we could, before heading out to the USA in early October.

My recently changed relationship status had complicated things somewhat. Rachel had been my closest female friend since the age of 16. I had known for some time that I wanted to be more than just friends, and although she too said she felt the same, Rachel was reluctant to commit to a relationship when we were both going to be studying at different universities, several hours apart.

I continued to ask her out at regular intervals throughout our three years at university but her response was always the same. She had a succession of different boyfriends during those years, and I gradually learned to accept the fact that we may never be together.

A few weeks before we graduated, I asked Rachel – as I had done routinely over the previous three years – if she wanted to be my girlfriend. This time, she surprised me by saying yes.

Travelling plans were immediately thrown up in the air. Mark assumed I would no longer want to go away with him now that Rachel and I were together. I think Rachel also assumed I would no longer want to go away with Mark now that we were together. Not that I am suggesting in any way that Rachel's timing was a deliberate attempt to sabotage the trip and stop me from going to America. It was, of course, a complete coincidence. *winky face*

It was a dilemma I wrestled with constantly over the following few weeks. We already had our flights booked and I decided that I needed to go on this adventure with Mark. I knew I wanted to be with Rachel, but this trip to America was something that I felt I had to do without her.

Having spent three years waiting for Rachel to commit to a relationship, the selfish part of me also felt like it was her turn to wait for me. I didn't want to let Mark down, and believed that if Rachel and I were destined to be together then our relationship would survive this challenge too.

I woke early on my first full day in America. I had a coffee with Alexis before he headed off to work, then I phoned Mark and learned that he was still busy trying to negotiate his visa and wouldn't be flying over for a couple more days.

As I had some time to kill, I decided to go on a mini-break. I packed a few clothes into a smaller rucksack, left a note for Alexis, and then made my way to the Greyhound station.

Greyhound buses are basically the equivalent of Britain's National Express. Except buses in America still have an air of adventure and excitement about them. There is something romantic about boarding a long-distance bus in America. There is nothing romantic, adventurous or exciting about National Express. Remember that classic Wrigley's advert with the girl and the guy sharing a single stick of chewing gum on a bus in the middle of the American desert? Now imagine that same advert filmed on a National Express bus in Wolverhampton. Wrigley's sales would have plummeted.

I scanned the giant *departures* board looking for a destination. It was a fantastic feeling knowing I had the freedom to travel anywhere I liked.

I settled on Baltimore, Maryland. Baltimore sounded familiar to me. I had heard it mentioned in a song. A song that at that particular moment I couldn't quite remember. I bought my ticket and boarded the Greyhound: destination Baltimore.

It was about 8pm when the bus pulled into Baltimore. It was dark, cold and raining heavily. I left the bus station and wandered the streets looking for somewhere to stay.

All of the hotels in the local area were full. Baltimore was hosting some big international conference and staff in two of the hotels told me I was unlikely to find a room anywhere in the city. I began to wander a little further afield.

The HBO television series *The Wire* had not yet been broadcast, so I was unfamiliar with the notorious 'corners' of Baltimore depicted in the show. Try to imagine a scene in *The Wire* and add a white, middle-class boy from England into the scene. It would have made a damn good episode. I approached a group of youths standing at one of these infamous corners.

'Hey, check out this dude,' one of them said to the group gathered around him.

'Excuse me,' I said. 'I'm looking for a hotel or a motel to stay tonight. Do you know anywhere around here?'

'Huh?' one of them said, and they all turned and faced me.

'Are there any hotels or motels nearby please?'

'Da fuck you doing out here, homeboy?' said another.

'You picked the wrong neighbourhood, man. Ain't no hotels or motels round here.'

'Oh well,' I said jovially. 'Apparently there's some big conference on at the moment so all the hotels are booked.'

'If you say so, bro. If you say so.' They all laughed at me as though I was the strangest thing to ever set foot in the neighbourhood.

'Thanks anyway,' I said. 'Cheerio.'

I regretted saying cheerio the moment it left my lips. I never ever say cheerio. But the moment I became self-conscious of sounding posh and British, I instinctively came out with the most posh and British phrase imaginable.

I could hear their laughter echoing down the street for several blocks as I retraced my way back to the bus station. I decided to spend the night there and explore Baltimore by daylight the following morning.

I was soaking wet by this point, having not thought to bring a waterproof with me to America. I sat on a cold metal chair in the bus station and started thinking about Rachel. Had I made the wrong choice leaving her back in England? At the time, it seemed like I was doing the right thing. Yet now, as I sat alone and soggy in a gloomy depressing bus station in downtown Baltimore, I felt like I had made one of the worst decisions of my life.

I suddenly remembered the context of the song that had referenced Baltimore.

It was called *Raining in Baltimore* by Counting Crows and the lyrics could not have been more pertinent to my situation.

'It's raining in Baltimore....
I need a phone call
I need a raincoat
I need a big love'

If only these lyrics hadn't escaped me during that crucial moment as I scanned the *departures* board back in New York City, then I might not have found myself at such a low point.

Because of the time difference, I couldn't even make that phone call to tell Rachel how I was feeling. I needed to pull myself together. I had made my decision and would have to live with it. Things would turn out ok, I told myself, and our relationship would be better off in the long run.

The Baltimore bus station was fairly grim, but there are plenty of worse places I could have chosen to spend the night. It did, however, have one of the most amazing inventions that I had ever seen, which did help in some way to improve my mood. There were a couple of rows of chairs in the waiting area, and each chair had a small coin-operated television attached to the arm. For 25c you could watch 10 minutes of a grainy black and white TV with barely audible sound. It really was revolutionary. It felt so futuristic, yet these chairs looked like they had been there since the 1970s. America was almost too clever for its own good. Why was nobody else in awe of these chairs like I was? I spent a couple of hours pumping in quarter after quarter watching episodes of Seinfeld. I was just beginning to doze off when I was interrupted by a *FINAL CALL FOR OCEAN CITY. FINAL CALL FOR OCEAN CITY.*

Ocean City? That sounded incredible. A city, by the ocean. It had to be nicer than Baltimore bus station. I felt like I had 'done' Baltimore anyway during my short night-time ramble.

I hurried from my seat and asked at the ticket desk what time the bus arrived in Ocean City. The lady confidently advised me that it reached there at about 6.30am. It was 10.30pm which meant I could have a full night's sleep on the bus and wake up in the morning in a new town, sorry, I mean a new CITY, by the ocean.

I waved goodbye to Baltimore – forgetting that I would have to come back in a couple of days as that was where my return ticket to New York departed from – and climbed aboard the Greyhound. I soon drifted off to sleep.

3

I was woken by the announcement that we had arrived in Ocean City. I looked up at the digital clock mounted above the front windscreen. It read: *01:55am.*

I staggered clumsily down the aisle of the bus past the other sleeping passengers.

'Is this really Ocean City?' I asked the driver.

'It sure is, my friend. Is this your stop?'

'Er... yeah, I guess so. I thought it was due to arrive at 6.30am?'

'I'm a cautious driver, my friend, but I ain't that slow. I'll be home in bed by 6.30.'

'Ok then. I guess this is me. Thanks, have a good night,' I said as I climbed down the steps into the cold, breezy night.

'You too, my friend. Take care.'

And with that, the Greyhound pulled away leaving me on the side of an empty, unlit highway in a town that I had not even heard of until a couple of hours previously.

Despite being alone, cold and slightly scared, it was a real thrill to be able to smell the sea air and hear the faint crash of the waves a short distance behind me.

I had planned to arrive in Ocean City as morning broke. I would maybe walk straight into a seaside cafe and treat myself to a coffee and huge cooked breakfast before taking in the sights. Now Ocean City was to be my home for most of the night.

I headed towards a few lights in the distance and strolled down what appeared to be the main strip, just a stone's throw from the ocean.

I didn't really want to spend money on a hotel, but it was very cold and morning was still a long way off so it seemed like the sensible thing to do.

The first few hotels that I passed were closed. Not just for the night, but seemingly for the whole winter. I reached a hotel with an illuminated sign, but the reception was closed for the night. The entire town was deserted.

I found Ocean City's famous boardwalk, which I could see in the dim moonlight stretching endlessly in either direction. I didn't know at the time that the boardwalk was famous. To be honest, I'm just going by what the Ocean City tourist board say on their website. It's extremely possible that nobody outside of Maryland has ever heard of its boardwalk before.

The boardwalk is particularly impressive, though, and I wandered up and down it aimlessly hoping it would pass the time. It did for about 20 minutes but it had not made much of a dent on the night and there was still an awful lot of it left.

I sat down on the beach by the sea wall and gazed up at the sky. Despite the cold, it was a beautifully clear night and the only sound was the lapping of the waves. Compared to Baltimore bus station, it was heaven.

I regretted leaving my sleeping bag in New York, but then I hadn't anticipated I would be sleeping on a beach. Instead, I put on all the clothes that I had with me and lay slumped against the wall on the beach. I spent the next few hours dozing in and out of sleep.

By 6.30am colour began to fill the sky and I walked down to the edge of the Atlantic Ocean. Half an hour later I got to witness one of the most beautiful sunrises I have ever seen. It was almost worth spending a cold, sleepless night on the beach for.

The icing on the cake – which sounds unbelievable when I repeat it – was a pod of about half a dozen dolphins swimming parallel to the shore through the dawn light. I was the only person on the entire beach to witness them. One of the dolphins leaped out of the water, looked at me, waved its little flipper, winked and then dived beneath the waves again.

I may have exaggerated the dolphin story very slightly.

I stared out to sea in the direction of home, and wondered what Rachel would be up to. I felt much more positive about the whole situation than I had the previous night in Baltimore. Daylight brought with it a sense of calm and perspective. Everything feels better once the sun rises.

I paced the boardwalk like I had done several times during the night. I saw one other person out walking their dog, but the rest of the town was still fast asleep. I read that the population of Ocean City swells to about 350,000 in the peak of summer. In October, it is closer to 35.

I found a hotel that said it was open, but it took several loud knocks to get someone to come and unlock the front door.

'Hi,' said the young man who opened the door. He stepped aside to let me in.

'Hi. I know it's early, but is there any chance I could book a room for tonight?'

'Well, we don't normally allow check in until 2pm.'

'I know, I understand. I spent the night on the beach last night and could really do with a shower and a couple of hours sleep.'

'You slept on the beach? In October? Are you crazy?'

'It wasn't really planned, and I didn't get a lot of sleep.'

'Well we set check in for 2pm to give cleaners a chance to get the rooms ready, but as there are only about two other guests in the entire hotel, I don't think it will be much of a problem. How many nights would you like to stay?'

'That's fantastic, thanks,' I said. 'Two nights please.'

I dumped my bag in the room, had a shower, ate an entire packet of biscuits that I had bought in Baltimore, collapsed on the bed and fell asleep instantly.

I woke at lunchtime and spent the afternoon strolling up and down the boardwalk. In the winter in Ocean City there is little else to do. I bought a six-pack of Budweiser and a selection of chips and dips from a nearby grocery store, and retired back to my hotel room to watch the World Series.

I felt like a proper American. I whooped and cheered as the New York Mets beat the Yankees in game 3 to end a 14-game Yankees winning streak in World Series play. This was apparently a pretty big deal and I was completely in love with baseball and America. The six beers had definitely contributed to this euphoria.

I had another whole day in Ocean City and as much as I loved that boardwalk, I felt that it was time for me to spread my wings.

Mike's Bikes was a bike rental place on the corner of Baltimore Avenue. It must have taken Mike a very long time to come up with the name for his bike rental shop. I'm slightly disappointed he didn't go with the more ambiguously titled Michael's Bike-ulls, though.

Michael was still opening up when I enquired about the possibility of hiring a bike-ull from him. For a bike rental shop, he stocked surprisingly few bikes. It was unlikely the rest were already rented, because apart from a handful of workers, I seemed to be the only person in the whole of Ocean City.

Michael reluctantly rented me a bicycle with big fat tyres and unnecessarily wide handlebars. It had one gear and no brakes and looked like a child's crap drawing of a Harley Davidson. I handed him my money, told him I would return the bike in 24 hours, and set off with a rucksack on my back and a huge piece of equipment between my legs. So to speak.

I couldn't resist another trip on the boardwalk, this time on the bike. The sound of the boards vibrating underneath my wheels was so therapeutic that once I reached the far end, I turned and rode the length of it back again. I then joined the main road and headed north.

During the summer months, I am sure that the coastal road that heads north from Ocean City gets heavily congested. In October, it was like my own private cycle track. Ocean City sits magnificently on a barrier spit surrounded on either side by the sea. The road was perfectly flat, immaculately surfaced and I had a view out to sea on both sides of me. I had no plans, no itinerary and no constraints. I was a free man in America and I could go wherever the hell I liked. I had never felt freer.

I discovered quickly that the bike did have brakes. They just functioned in a different way to which I was accustomed. After I had picked up a bit of speed and was cruising down my own two lane highway, I sat back in my saddle, raised my hands in the air Kate Winslet-style and shouted 'top of the worrrld'. I went to casually rotate the pedals backwards as I freewheeled and the back wheel locked tight. I lunged forward for the handlebars as the bike veered into the gravel at the side of the road and then spun out from under me. I grazed my knee slightly but was otherwise unhurt. Thankfully there was nobody there to witness my idiocy other than the decomposing body of a partially squashed raccoon on the tarmac. *Ok, so pedalling backwards activates the brakes. That's good to know.* It might have been helpful if Michael had mentioned this feature of the bike-ull when I rented it.

The road stretched up the coast and I crossed into the state of Delaware and through Bethany Beach and Rehoboth Beach – both pleasant seaside towns, both with non-existent winter populations – all the while with the sea on either side of me, and an endless blue sky.

It was there, miles from anywhere, on a rental bike in Delaware – a state famous only because Carl Perkins, the composer of Blue Suede Shoes once crashed his car there – that I realised why I needed to have this adventure and why I had definitely made the right decision to come to America. I was loving every minute of it.

I was particularly impressed by the roadkill. I don't mean that in a sadistic way. Back in Britain, we are accustomed to seeing dead rabbits on the road. Rabbits of all shapes and sizes, but still, just rabbits. Very, very occasionally you might see a badger or a fox, but that is all. On this stretch of highway, in the space of just a few miles, I saw a raccoon, a skunk, a large fox, a hare (or possibly just the biggest rabbit that had ever lived), something that I initially thought was a boa-constrictor but turned out to be a section of industrial tubing, a toad and a turtle. As horrible as it was to see any animal's life brought to a sudden end because of the intrusion of the motor car, it was such a strange feeling to see a squashed turtle on the road, where a rabbit should have been.

After a few miles, I cut inland and the sky began to darken. I assumed a storm was approaching. There was nowhere to take shelter, so I pressed on. It continued to darken yet there was no sign of imminent rain and the clouds didn't look particularly threatening. It then dawned on me. It was getting dark because the sun was setting. Like it does every frickin' day. In my excitement and naivety I had assumed that I had hours of daylight remaining. It had been a bright sunny day. I was in America – a country blessed with long hot days. Not in late October, of course. How could I have been so stupid? I had planned to be back in Ocean City before nightfall and imagined that this would be at about 9 or even 10pm. Not 5.30pm. I had no lights, no form of reflective clothing and I was a very long way from Ocean City.

I reached 'historic' Georgetown, which was historic for something that I never discovered. I had hoped to find a hotel, but it became apparent that Georgetown was not historically significant enough for anyone to want to spend longer than a day there. I had no option but to keep going and hope that I found somewhere to stay before dark.

A few miles beyond Georgetown my bike failed me spectacularly. Just at the point that I had started to feel quite anxious about my situation, my back tyre exploded for no apparent reason. I didn't notice driving over anything sharp, I'm not THAT heavy, and the road was impeccably surfaced. My tyre just decided that now was the time it was going to cease doing its job.

I climbed off my bike and began to push.

Up in the distance I saw a light. It was a bright shining beacon of hope. An illuminated symbol of salvation, and some other pretentious metaphors. It was the golden arches of McDonald's.

I had made a pact with myself before coming to America to try not to visit McDonald's during my time in the USA. This wasn't because of any anti-consumerist stance or anything. It was simply because McDonald's has come to symbolise America and its cuisine. I regularly frequent McDonald's back in the UK, and it seemed a shame to come to such a vast country and then eat the same food that I could eat back home.

When I arrived in New York a couple of days previously, I had been bursting for the toilet as I walked through Manhattan. As I reached the doors of McDonald's – the restroom visible just metres away and my bladder imminently about to explode – I somehow summoned the willpower to walk on by. I used the toilet in KFC next door instead, which is in no way the same thing.

But there I was, alone, scared and in a potentially life-threatening situation on a dark, busy road. It would have been foolish of me to avoid McDonald's out of principle.

As the giant yellow M got closer, I noticed a suspicious lack of any other lights. The sign was unmistakable as McDonald's, but there was no indication of any building nearby. I got closer still. My heart sank as I read the words beneath the sign:

McDonald's: 7 miles

It was at this point I decided to take refuge in the ditch, before eventually trying to thumb a lift. An hour later I was in a station wagon driven by two old, bearded men, as I lay spread-eagled on top of my bike in the back. America, fuck yeah!

4

'England, huh?' said the man in the passenger seat.

'That's right,' I replied, still sprawled awkwardly on top of my bike.

'Where you headed?'

'California.'

'On that bike?' blurted the driver.

'Oh no, sorry. I'm going to buy a car.'

'I meant where were you headed before you had a blow out?'

'I was hoping to get back to Ocean City tonight but I'd happily sleep anywhere. If you could drop me some place that might have a motel that would be amazing.'

'Well we live a few miles down this here road which is still a long way off Ocean City. You could either try to hitch another ride from there back to Ocean City, or there's a spare bed at ours which you can have for the night. Then we can drop you and your bike back at Ocean City in the morning.'

'Wow, that sounds fantastic, thank you. Are you sure you don't mind?'

'Not at all.'

Joe and Willie were brothers. Joe's wife passed away ten years previously and Willie, having never married, suggested that Joe move in with him. They had been living together ever since. They worked as farm labourers and handymen at a farm a few miles north. Their house was a simple wooden building surrounded by old pieces of farm machinery just off the main highway. They kindly offered me their spare room for the night.

Joe and Willie had already eaten before leaving work, but gave me a big bag of tortilla chips and a can of beer and we sat down to watch game 4 of the World Series together. This was turning into a nightly routine for me. The Yankees won the game convincingly with Derek Jeter scoring a homer from the first ball, for only the sixteenth time in World Series history, don't you know.

The following morning, despite it being many miles in the opposite direction, Joe and Willie dropped me and my bike back outside Mike's Bikes in Ocean City on their way to work. I had to wait an hour for Michael to open up and he was more than a little irritated with me for returning the bike-ull to him with a hole in the tyre.

I took one final stroll down the boardwalk and checked out of the hotel at which I hadn't even stayed that night. The guy at reception must have thought I was a very strange guest; checking in at 7am for two nights, sleeping all day and all night and then staying somewhere else for the second night.

I then boarded my bus back to Baltimore, which looked a lot more pleasant in the daylight – although, not pleasant enough for me to linger – and caught my connecting bus back to New York City.

I had spoken to Mark from a payphone in Ocean City before heading off on my bike ride and he told me that he had been unsuccessful with his visa appeal. This meant that he would only be allowed the standard 90 day tourist visa. This was extremely disappointing for him, and somewhat confusing for me, as I had planned to be in the USA for a lot longer. Still, 90 days was a long time and we would make damn sure we made the most of it.

Mark and I both arrived at Alexis's apartment within minutes of each other. After my brief mini-break in Maryland and Delaware, it was great to meet up with him, so that our proper adventure could begin.

'I'm glad you finally made it,' I said, giving him a hug. 'Shame about the visa.'

'Oh well,' he said. '90 days is better than nothing. The embassy got so fed up with my phone calls that at one point I thought they wouldn't let me into the country at all. So what have you been up to since you arrived?'

'Oh nothing much. Just walking around the mean streets of Baltimore in the dark, hanging out in a bus station, sleeping on a beach, hitchhiking on a freeway with a massive broken-down bike, sleeping at a stranger's house. Just a quiet couple of days really.'

'Sounds like I've been missing out.'

'Not at all. Now we get to have some proper fun.'

I had been best friends with Mark since primary school. My family moved house when I was eight, and my sister and I changed schools. Mark befriended me on my first day at the new school and we quickly became very close.

After only being at my new school for a couple of weeks, I was invited to dinner at Mark's house. I was nervous about meeting Mark's family and anxious to make a good first impression.

Midway through the meal, I leaned back and for some reason slipped my left elbow between two of the wooden slats in the back of the wooden chair. I think it was probably due to some subconscious nervous fidgeting. I then went to sit forward to continue my meal and realised that my elbow was stuck.

I tried pulling it a little harder but the elbow joint wouldn't budge. I didn't want to draw attention to the fact that I had managed to get stuck in a chair halfway through a meal, so I chatted away as if nothing was wrong. All the while, I was subtly trying to prise my arm from the chair.

'Everything ok?' asked Mark's mum, as I sat back in the chair, trying to make it look as casual as possible.

'Yes, fine thanks. The food is delicious. I'm just having a little break.'

When it was clear that everyone else was going to finish their meal long before me, I had no choice but to eat one handed. I used the fork in my right hand to shovel in the food quickly so as not to keep everyone waiting. I tried to make my strange seating position look as natural as I could. There were a few quizzical looks from Mark and his family about my unorthodox eating style, but I just about got away with it.

As our plates were cleared away, I sat back in my chair again and continued to try to free my elbow. It wouldn't shift.

Pudding was served. It was a delicious-looking chocolate tart with ice cream. I tried to cut it with my spoon, but the base was particularly crispy and I was worried I would send the entire bowl sailing across the room if I tried to eat it one handed.

I don't know why I didn't just own up about my predicament. I was worried I would be laughed at by Mark and his family. Mark's brother – who was a couple of years older and way cooler than us – would have enjoyed the moment immensely. Word would have soon spread through the children in the village that I was the new boy who had to be rescued from a chair during dinner. It wasn't worth the humiliation.

Instead, I casually picked up the bowl in my right hand and passed it to my left. I then ate the entire dessert holding the bowl with the hand of my trapped arm and the spoon in the hand of my free arm.

Mark's family looked on in astonishment. I disguised my unfortunate situation so well that they never suspected anything was amiss, other than my appalling table manners.

The table was cleared and Mark and his brother began to do the washing up. I just rudely sat there throughout, unable to offer any sort of help in my current mess. The table was wiped down and chores were carried out all around me. I stayed put.

I could tell Mark's mum and dad had both made a mental note to ensure that this rude new friend of Mark's was never invited to dinner again.

Eventually, when everyone's back was turned, I stood up – well, as far as my arm would allow me – and managed to straighten my arm down towards the floor very slightly. With the joint slightly relaxed, I was then somehow able to contort my elbow so that it squeezed painfully through the bars.

I breathed a huge sigh of relief and grabbed a tea-towel just in time to help with the last of the drying up. My behaviour was soon forgiven and I was invited to dinner the following week.

Dinner at Mark's house became a weekly event. I would go to his house every Monday and he would come to my house every Thursday. I kept my elbows well away from the backs of his chairs from then on.

Mark and I played for the same junior football team together, we went to the same secondary school, played in a band together, and went to universities just 30 miles apart so saw each other regularly throughout. It is fair to say that we knew each other very well. There was very little doubt that we would make ideal travelling companions.

We spent the next couple of days exploring Manhattan. We walked 130 blocks from Central Park downtown – stopping briefly for coffee and donuts – all the way to Battery Park at the southern tip, catching a ferry to Staten Island and back, before retracing our steps uptown.

We could have happily stayed in New York for several weeks but Mark's visa situation had added a greater sense of urgency to our trip. New York wasn't the America we had come to see. We wanted to hit the road and cover all those thousands of miles on America's back roads, visiting all those places in between, until we reached California on the west coast.

Alexis was a great host but he clearly wasn't used to having two dirty layabouts sleeping in his living room, and his constant sweeping of the floor around us was the visual clue we needed to signify that our time in Manhattan was up.

Mark had also been told to bring a smart pair of shoes with him because of the possibility of a trip to a posh steak restaurant. We made several subtle attempts to bring these into conversation and left our shiny shoes strategically placed around the apartment for Alexis to see.

'Why did you guys bring those shoes to backpack across America?' he asked.

'Well we just thought they might be useful if we ever went anywhere smart that required a dress code... such as a restaurant,' I said.

'Oh, fair enough. Seems a bit impractical, though,' he said, not taking the bait.

Those damn shoes stayed unworn in the bottom of our rucksacks for the entire time we were in America.

For some strange reason Mark and I decided that buying a car in Manhattan was a bad idea. It is a city full of taxis, buses and the subway, and we made the assumption that it would be easier and cheaper to buy a car elsewhere. We were also secretly irrationally adverse to the idea of haggling with a New York car salesman. We had visions of trying to negotiate with a character from *The Godfather* and ending up buying a car out of fear rather than desire.

We planned to seek the security of upstate New York instead, so packed a small rucksack each and boarded a bus to

Kingston, New York. We would return to Manhattan on our journey south (hopefully in our new car), to collect the rest of our belongings in a few days' time.

5

Kingston was the first capital of New York State back in 1777, until it was burned down by the British later that year (as several locals reminded us when they heard our accents). The capital then moved around for a few years before settling in Albany where it remains to this day.

We checked into a motel and went for a drink at a nearby bar. Whilst enjoying a few beers, we picked up a discarded copy of the local newspaper from an adjacent table and flicked to the classified adverts section. Scanning through the listings, one particular advert caught our eye:

1989 Dodge Caravan
Minivan
$1100

We didn't know what a Dodge Caravan was but after asking the barman, he confirmed that it was a car, rather than a caravan, and that it would probably be big enough for two people to sleep in.

I dialled the number from a payphone and a man named Daniel answered. He spoke in broken English and advised us that the car was still for sale and that he was happy for us to view it anytime.

Looking at a road map we had bought, we discovered that Daniel's house was located nearly 30 miles away in the middle of nowhere. We phoned Daniel back and told him we would be with him as soon as we could, but it would probably not be for a couple of days. We were going to walk there.

The journey to Daniel's house took us through the town of Woodstock, which lies about 10 miles up the road from

Kingston. But after many wrong turns – and because we stuck to the minor roads – our route was significantly longer. It was a beautiful sunny day, though, and we took our time meandering through the foothills of the Catskill Mountains, arriving in Woodstock late afternoon. We decided to stay for the night and complete our journey the following day.

Woodstock shares its name with the famous festival that took place in 1969 in Bethel, New York. Woodstock – the town – is 60 miles north-east of Bethel and has no direct connection to the festival, with the festival taking its name from 'Woodstock Ventures', the company that financed it. While many residents of Bethel disassociated themselves with the festival in the following years – even spreading manure onto the site to discourage fans from revisiting the area – the town of Woodstock embraced the association.

My dad states that his biggest regret in life is that he was in America in 1969 and didn't go to the Woodstock festival. Instead, he spent the summer working in an ice-cream van in Philadelphia, which sounds like a pretty cool alternative to me.

Having previously been a Mecca for artists and musicians, Woodstock has thrived as a hub for creativity ever since the festival, with many visitors to the area in 1969 having reportedly never left.

Woodstock is a wonderful little hippy town, with a very similar feel to the town of Glastonbury in England; lots of quaint little shops, vegetarian cafes, eccentrically dressed visitors and town residents in a seemingly permanent haze, enjoying a very slow pace of life.

We found a cheap hostel, drank a few organic beers, ate a bean burrito and went to sleep, excited – and slightly gassy – about the prospect of potentially buying our very own car.

It was another 15 mile walk the following day from Woodstock to Daniel's house in the backwoods of upstate

New York. Again, it was an extremely pleasant walk and we passed some fairly spectacular roadkill: two deer, a racoon and an unidentifiable creature that appeared to have the body of a squirrel and the head of a lizard. It was probably the last of an exceptionally rare species.

Walking for two days was a particularly daft, but extremely relaxing way to purchase a car. We tried not to think what would happen if we arrived at Daniel's only to discover it had already been sold. When we had raised this concern with him on the phone he seemed to think this was very unlikely, which was not a great indication of what he thought of the car.

I had phoned Rachel on my first morning in New York City, but hadn't spoken to her since. I called from a payphone midway through the morning to tell her about my time in Maryland and Delaware and update her on Mark's visa situation.

'So how long does that mean Mark is allowed to stay in America?' she asked.

'Just until the beginning of January.'

'What will you do then?'

'I don't know really. I haven't thought that far ahead yet.'

'Will you stay out there?'

'Yes, I think so. We are on our way to buy a car now, which I can keep for as long as I like. I don't think I should come home just because Mark does.'

Rachel didn't say anything. I could tell this wasn't the answer she was hoping for.

'So how's everything with you?' I asked. 'How's work?'

'Oh, you know, it's as brilliant as ever.'

'That good, huh? I miss you.'

'Hmph,' she said, which I hoped meant she missed me too.

We arrived at Daniel's address in the early afternoon. His house was located halfway up a wooded hillside, miles from any other buildings. We could see the car parked up outside the house and our first impressions were not good. It was a shit-brown coloured minivan with many ominous looking rust patches on the outside and plenty of suspicious looking stains inside. There was a large hole in the back windscreen, about an inch in diameter, which looked remarkably like it had been created by a bullet. The tyres were in a fairly poor condition, it had red velvety seats that were straight out of a 1970s porno (so I've been told) and the metalwork on the bonnet was discoloured so badly with white blotches that it appeared that the porno's big finale had taken place on it.

But there was something about the car that appealed to us. It was plenty big enough for the two of us to sleep in. It had two rows of seats in the back so we could have a row each and still have space for our bags and guitars. Yet it was small enough to still feel like a car. It wouldn't be a problem to drive, park or navigate America in.

'It's perfect,' I said.

'She's a beaut,' said Mark. 'I think I'm in love.'

'Me too.'

We were still lurking outside the house. Before knocking, we spent some time planning our bartering strategy. We had $1100 in cash, but didn't think the car looked to be worth anywhere near that. I handed Mark $400.

'You hide that somewhere, and then I'll pretend that we only have $700,' I said.

'Ok,' said Mark.

'Don't bring out the extra money under any circumstances unless I mention it. Ok?'

'Ok, gotcha.'

Daniel was from Brazil and the contents of his house were packed up into boxes. He seemed to be leaving the country in a hurry for reasons that he didn't divulge. We were in a difficult situation. It was clear that he was desperate to sell the car, but it was also brutally obvious that we were desperate to buy it based on the fact we had walked 30 miles to get there. There was no way that we had any intention of leaving without the car. And Daniel knew this.

'We've only got $700, I'm afraid. We would love to offer you more but that's all we have,' I said.

'The car is $1100. It's a very good car.'

'I'm sure it is, but we can't afford $1100. We have only budgeted $700.'

'Look what I just found in my pocket,' said Mark, holding up a wad of cash.

'Oh, that's great,' I said, raising my eyebrows at him and mouthing *'What the fuck are you doing?'*

'That's more like it. How much do you have?' said Daniel. 'I'm sure we can agree a price.'

'He's only got another $100. Haven't you, Mark?' I said, shooting him an evil glare.

'Err... no, I've got, well, err...'

'$100! That's all you have. Isn't it, Mark?'

'Oh yes, just another $100,' he said finally.

'It's worth more than $800,' said Daniel.

'It has a bullet hole in the back windscreen. What's with that?' I asked.

'Oh, nothing,' he said shiftily. 'Just the kids next door messing around with an air rifle.'

'It didn't look like you had any neighbours.'

'Well not next door, next door. Just kids in the nearby town. It's no big deal,' he said, looking extremely awkward.

'Considering we will have to get that replaced, I think $800 is a fair price.'

'Do you not have any more?' he asked.

'George, look what I just found in my pocket,' said Mark again, pulling out another wad of notes.

I put my face in my hands.

'Ok, $850 is our final offer. Deal?' I said.

Daniel paused. His eyes looked at Mark and then back to me.

'Deal!' he said eventually, shaking us both by the hands. 'I'll go and get the paperwork.'

As Daniel left the room, a beautiful looking Latino lady walked in.

'Hi. I'm Daniel's wife. Has he finally sold that car?'

'Yes, we just bought it,' I said, cringing at her use of the word 'finally.'

'What did you pay him for it?'

'$850.'

'Good for you. It's not worth a penny more than that. It's a big heap of shit,' she said, busying herself by assembling cardboard boxes. 'I mean, don't get me wrong, it's a decent enough car. I just don't think it was worth what he thought it was.'

Mark and I looked at each other. We were still holding the cash and hadn't signed any paperwork. At this point we should have walked out the front door and got as far away from that car as possible. Hindsight is a wonderful thing. At the time we felt like we had got ourselves a great deal. It was only $850. How big a heap of shit could it be?

Daniel handed us the keys and some paperwork and muttered something to us about licence plates and registrations and talked us through some quirks in the car that he had failed to mention before we agreed to buy it. Such as the fact that the ignition key had to be removed at a slightly different position to the normal OFF position in order to stop the battery draining completely within an hour. This was a fact that we forgot many times over the following months and had to rely on kind motorists to jump-start us.

'She's beautiful,' I said as we walked towards the car parked outside.

'My wife?' said Daniel.

'No, no, sorry. I was talking about the car. Not that your wife isn't beautiful, too.'

'Her name is Josephine,' he said.

'Your wife?' I asked.

'No, not my wife. This car. The car is called Josephine.'

Things were getting very confusing.

'That's a nice name. It suits her,' said Mark.

'Did you name her?' I asked.

'No. The person I buy it off tell me she is called Josephine. I bet she's got some stories to tell,' he said, laughing to himself and shaking his head.

I didn't want to think about what sort of stories he and Josephine shared. We were probably better off not knowing.

'Have a great trip,' he said, shaking our hands again, and disappearing quickly back inside his house.

I am almost certain he then went straight to the airport and got the first flight out of America.

'Right, do you want to drive first or shall I?' I said.

'You can do the first shift. I call shotgun!' said Mark.

'I don't think you have to call shotgun if there are only two of us. If you're not driving then I think it goes without saying that you'll probably be in the passenger seat.'

'I know. I just wanted to call Shotgun like they do in the films.'

'Good point. Should we climb in through the windows like they do in *The Dukes of Hazzard*, too?'

'No. Now you're taking it too far.'

'Ok.'

We hadn't taken Josephine for a test drive. We hadn't even started the engine. We couldn't even be sure that she had an engine. Yet we had just paid $850 for her. It was with a huge sense of relief that we turned the key and she purred into life. Well, I say purred, it was more of an angry growl. She spluttered and snarled like a dragon being woken from hibernation. Do dragons hibernate? Probably not. Anyway, Josephine did not sound healthy. I put my foot on the accelerator. I mean, I pumped the gas pedal, and the engine roared like we were in a 1980s American high-school movie. If we had got out to check, there would probably have been flames blasting from her exhaust pipe.

'Wow, listen to that,' said Mark.

'She sounds awesome!' I said, deciding to interpret the noise as a sign of Josephine's life, rather than her death. At least she was making a noise.

We had bought a car. In America. And we were ready to hit the road and start writing our own stories with Josephine.

I had very little experience of driving on the right hand side of the road. And by little experience, I mean no experience.

It had been completely impractical to spend three days travelling all the way to the middle of nowhere in upstate New York when we could have bought a car in Manhattan easily enough. I was very relieved, however, that my first experience of driving a left hand drive vehicle was on a nice deserted rural road, rather than down Fifth Avenue.

'Er, George, you're pretty close to the verge,' said Mark, peering out of his window.

'Alright!' I snapped. 'I'm just getting used to the car.'

'I was just saying.'

'Sorry, I didn't mean to shout. It's just shit scary driving this beast, let alone driving on the other side of the road.'

Our first priority was to get car insurance. If I was going to drive across America half on the road and half on the verge, then insurance was probably a good idea.

We passed an insurance broker in a small out-of-town mall and the staff were delighted by the sight of two strange Brits calling in for their custom.

Getting insurance proved more complicated than we thought. We needed an address in the United States and so had to make a visit to the Post Office and set up a PO Box (even though we would never return to check it) and then go back to the insurance broker to complete all the paperwork.

'How long will you want the insurance for?'

'Well, I'll need it for up to a year, I guess,' I said.

'Why not pay for the first three months now and then you can send us the money in three months, and then six months and nine months?' said the smiling lady.

'It might just be easier for me to pay it all up front. Then at least I will know I'm covered,' I said.

'Sure you'll be covered. Here's your documentation that proves you're covered for 12 months from today.'

'But we only need to pay for 3 months today?'

'Why would you want to pay for more? You can just send us other instalments later, but you've got your cover sorted for the year.'

She looked at us with an expression that said: *'look here, you simpletons, I am giving you your insurance for a quarter of the cost that you should pay. Don't question it.'*

'Ok then. Thanks, we'll just pay for the first three months now. And then we will pay the rest in instalments,' I said, adding a wink which I instantly regretted.

The lady then explained what we needed to do with regards registering the vehicle and gave us directions to the local Department of Motor Vehicles which we should be able to get to just before it closed.

Thankfully the vehicle testing requirements in America are – or at least were – extremely lax compared to the UK. There was no real equivalent to the UK's MOT test where a vehicle can be deemed unroadworthy for any number of relatively minor faults, including partially worn windscreen wipers, not having enough screenwash in the tank, a sticker on a window or mirror causing a visibility obstruction, or a poor choice of music on the car stereo. In the USA, a vehicle had to pass a smog test. That was about it. Josephine somehow had a valid smog test sticker, although judging by the volcanic clouds issuing from her exhaust pipe, I have no idea how.

The dream of getting into a car and hitting the open road becomes increasingly more distant when you are presented with the blockade of bureaucracy involved with registering a car. The whole procedure was ridiculously tiresome and involved an absurd amount of blue forms, pink forms and white forms. It would be tedious for a normal American citizen, but we had the added complication of having UK driving licences, which, before the current plastic ones were introduced, were basically just a scraggy piece of green paper that looked like they had been printed off on a home computer. We also only had a PO Box, rather than an actual address, and an assortment of foreign bank cards. At several points, Mark and I felt like the whole thing was too much and we almost abandoned Josephine there and then, opting to see America by public transport instead.

But we persisted, and the kind and patient – but painfully slow and thorough – DMV lady stayed well after closing to process our application. Eventually our perseverance was rewarded with our very own licence plates. We were the proud, legal owners (and legally insured for a few months at least) of a battered up 1989 Dodge Caravan named Josephine. We could not have been happier.

6

'We did it!' I shouted, as Mark took a turn at the wheel.

'Finally. I can't believe we own a car. How cool is that?'

'Er, Mark, you're getting a bit close to the verge on this side.'

'Alright!' he snapped. 'I'm just getting used to the car.'

'I was just saying.'

'Ok, you were right. Driving a left-hand drive takes a little getting used to.'

We joined Route 9W as the sun began to set and were treated to frequent views of the Hudson River through the trees on our left as we headed south towards New York City.

'What did we have for lunch?' asked Mark.

'I think we missed lunch. What time is it now?'

'6.30pm. What did we have for breakfast?'

'We shared that muffin at the hostel in Woodstock.'

'Was that really only this morning? That feels like days ago. Is that all we've eaten today?'

'Yes, I think so. No wonder I feel so crap.'

We turned off the road at the next exit and checked into a motel on the outskirts of Poughkeepsie.

Americans sure know how to celebrate Halloween. I had been in the USA for 12 days and from the moment I set foot off the aeroplane, the build up to Halloween was evident. Shops in the arrivals terminal sold Halloween merchandise, businesses in Manhattan had tailored their window displays accordingly; skeletons, cobwebs and bats filled every window. Even the deserted streets of Ocean City, Maryland were bedecked in Halloween paraphernalia. In the rural areas of upstate New York, there were piles of pumpkins for sale all along the highways, and people had built extensive Halloween exhibits in their front gardens.

In recent years Halloween has become more commercialised in Great Britain too. But we are still a very long way from the scale with which it is celebrated in America.

It was Halloween in Poughkeepsie and every front porch of every house on every street in the neighbourhood surrounding our motel was decked out like the set of *Thriller*.

I used to love trick-or-treating as a child. My costume would usually involve an old sheet over my head with a couple of eye holes cut through. It was simple but effective. The neighbours where we grew up were not used to getting many trick-or-treaters, so rarely had any treats prepared. There would be a look of surprise on their faces as they answered the door and they would then disappear into the kitchen for a few minutes before returning with a measly packet of raisins or a half-eaten granola bar.

One neighbour decided that it was too much effort to go and look for anything to give us so stood where she was and simply said 'trick'. We weren't expecting this response so stood there awkwardly.

My friend James bravely spoke up.

'Right... err... we are g-g-going to egg your car then. But first we've got to … er… nip home to get some eggs.'

'You'd better bloody not!' the lady said firmly.

Like the world's worst trick-or-treaters, we turned and ran from her driveway. We didn't return to her house that night or ever again in the subsequent years.

The area around our motel in Poughkeepsie was crawling with people kitted out in Halloween fancy dress. But not just young children as we had expected, but large groups of teenagers all wearing zombie costumes or the mask from the slasher film *Scream*. Our motel room was located on the relative safety of the first floor, but over the balcony we could look down on the different groups assembling, preparing to terrorise the neighbourhood (or ask politely for candy, if you're going to be pedantic). It was horrifying.

'What are we going to do for food? I'm starving,' I asked Mark.

'I don't know but I don't fancy going out with that lot about.'

'Let's order a takeaway. We can get it delivered and then we don't even have to leave the room.'

'Great idea.'

It turned out the rest of the town had also had the same great idea and the estimated delivery time was three hours. The Chinese restaurant was just across the street. You could even see it from our window. I needed to man up and run the gauntlet.

'Do you want me to come too?' said Mark.

'No, I think we'd draw too much attention if we both went. You stay here and cover me from the balcony. If I get attacked by any zombies, you cause a distraction.'

'Ok. I got your back, bro.'

I zipped my fleece all the way to the top – I don't know why, but it felt like the sort of thing I should do – and crept along the balcony to the stairwell. I stealthily slunk down the stairs and took cover behind some wheelie bins, as a group of giggling teens dressed as the Addams Family walked past. With the coast clear, I darted towards a parked car that was situated between me and the Chinese restaurant. Hiding behind the car, I looked up at Mark who was watching covertly from the balcony. He gave me the thumbs up and gesticulated that I should make a run for it. A passing car was driving up the street, forming a barrier between me and the cluster of youths on the opposite pavement. I took a deep breath and did a weird crouch/run alongside the car, shielding myself from view. I would have made a lousy cop.

I flung open the door to the Chinese restaurant and dived inside, landing at the feet of a group of five or six customers, all with equally terrified looks on their faces.

'It's like hell on Earth out there, isn't it?' said a middle-aged lady.

'I picked up my takeout ten minutes ago but I'm too scared to leave,' said another.

I ordered our food (Singapore noodles, kung po chicken, crispy chilli beef, egg fried rice and prawn crackers, if you are interested. Yes, it was very nice, thank you), and by the time it was ready 20 minutes later, most of the youths outside had dispersed. I assumed that meant my route was clear, but after crossing the road I found them swarming all over the motel. Surely motels are no-go zones for trick-or-treaters, and a safe-haven for guests? Apparently not. They were already banging on doors at random, and I saw a few terrified guests handing over their most treasured possessions – their Haribo.

But our room was on the first floor. Surely trick-or-treaters would not be audacious enough to knock on upstairs doors, would they?

When I reached the top of the stairs, I looked down the row of rooms to my right and a small group of four teenage girls were already knocking on a door. I crept along the balcony to my left, hoping that they hadn't spotted me, and just as I reached our room, one of them shouted:

'Look, there's someone! Oi, Mister!'

I pretended not to hear them, burst in through our door, locked and bolted it behind me and quickly shut the curtains.

'They're everywhere,' said Mark. 'I've already had three different groups knocking.'

'Really? What did you do?'

'The first time, I opened the door.'

'You opened the door? Why?'

'I thought it was you. I didn't know if you'd taken a key or not. I wasn't expecting them to come all the way up here.'

'What happened?'

'They said 'trick or treat?'.'

'Yeah, then what happened?'

'Well, I didn't have any sweets so I gave them some money.'

'Money? How much?'

'Just a dollar… each.'

'A dollar EACH? How many were there?'

'Five.'

'You spent five bucks on trick-or-treaters? Jesus, we could have got some spring rolls and an extra bag of prawn crackers for that.'

'I know. They seemed delighted. They were very polite and grateful.'

'I bet they were. They've probably gone to tell all their mates about the rich English guy handing out free money.'

There was another loud bang at the door.

'Triiiick or treeeat?' they called sinisterly.

'Oh shit. What shall we do?' Mark whispered.

I held my finger to my lips.

'Nothing. Don't say a word. The British didn't burn down Poughkeepsie too, did they?' I asked Mark as we crept to the other side of the room. 'Maybe they are seeking revenge.'

'No, I don't think so,' whispered Mark.

They knocked again. We didn't have any sweets, we couldn't afford to pay them, and we certainly weren't going to give away any of our Chinese takeaway, considering how hungry we both were and what I had been through to get it. Saying 'trick' was too risky. Who knows what response we would have got, and we would possibly have ended up as a news item in the local paper. Our only option was to stay quiet.

The revellers eventually departed. I switched off the light and Mark and I sat with our backs to the bed, eating our takeout in the darkness. A few more trick-or-treaters came and went, but we stayed put and after a couple of hours it fell silent. I stepped outside onto the balcony, breathing in the fresh air as though I had just been released from captivity. The street below was deserted and we had miraculously survived our first American Halloween.

7

There hadn't seemed any pressing need to get Josephine's back window fixed, as it had been dry and relatively mild. As we set off to drive back to New York City, the weather took a turn for the worse and water began to stream through the hole in the window. We planned to find a mechanic at the next town we passed through, but on a stretch of road in the middle of nowhere we came across a scrap yard. Mark had the ingenious idea of just getting an entire new back door fitted. He thought it would probably work out cheaper and quicker than having a brand spanking new window fitted.

The scrap yard was run by a large bearded man with a red baseball cap stained so black with car grease that the logo beneath was unidentifiable. He did have another Dodge Caravan in the yard that looked ok from the front, but the back door was crumpled like a crisp packet.

'Yeah, got rear-ended did that one,' he said.

'Oh well, it was worth a try. We'll just get a new window fitted at a garage instead,' I said.

'I've got a Plymouth Voyager that's in decent condition.'

'Thanks, but it's a Dodge Caravan that we need.'

'It's the same vehicle. Just a different name.'

'Really? So the back door would fit ok?'

'Sure.'

'And the lights? Will they all work too?' asked Mark.

'Of course. It will be exactly like the one you got, but there won't be no big-ass hole in the window, and it won't look as rusty. Oh, and it will be blue.'

'That sounds good to me,' I said. 'I like blue. How much?'

'Call it $30 all in.'

'Brilliant, thanks,' said Mark. 'Let's go for it.'

This was a fraction of the cost of a new window and the man had the old door detached and the new one installed in less than ten minutes. If we had known what problems a car with a different make and model on the back would cause later in the trip, we probably would have spent the extra on a new window instead. At the time, it felt like we had got the bargain of the century.

'Did you want to keep the old door?' he asked, after we had paid him the money.

Mark and I looked at each other and smiled, wondering what the hell we would do with a spare door.

'Nah, you can keep that thanks,' I said.

Driving into Manhattan was an unforgettable experience. Mark and I had been taking it in turns to drive, but I happened to be in the driver's seat as the quiet, rural highways of upstate New York became more and more congested as other freeways merged from either side, like ventricles to the heart. Suddenly I was being swept along on a five lane interstate, the road as straight as an arrow, undulating only slightly under my wheels. The surrounding buildings increased in height and density and that famous Manhattan skyline rose above us.

'Hooolllly shiiiiiiit,' I said, 'I'm driving in New York City!'

'Careful! There's a yellow taxi just coming up in the lane to the left,' said Mark.

'There's one to the right, too. They're everywhere.'

'What happens when we want to turn off this road?'

'I've no idea. I just want to keep driving in a straight line.'

Eventually we reached a street name that we recognised. We knew we needed to make a turn in three blocks' time. Switching the indicator on, and sticking my arm out of the window for good measure, I edged into the right hand lane. There was a loud blast of a horn, which I took to mean, 'there you go, buddy, I'm letting you out', rather than, 'hey asshole, learn to drive, you piece of shit.' I gave a cheery wave and then repeated the same thing again to the next lane and eventually turned off on the road on which Alexis's apartment was situated.

We parked up on the street outside and spent a couple of hours with Alexis, watching TV and eating peanut butter on toast. We made a few more subtle mentions about our smart shoes, but no invitation to a posh steak restaurant was forthcoming, so we packed up our bags, loaded them and our guitars into Josephine, and hit the road at 11.00pm. Destination: Washington DC.

This was what it was all about. Guitars in the back, potato chips in the front, and carefree smiles on our faces. The radio was blaring out Bruce Springsteen's *Born in the USA* (it wasn't), and we hit the New Jersey Turnpike with a wealth of choices and opportunities ahead of us. It was almost too good to be true.

And it was.

We had not travelled more than an hour out of New York City when there was an almighty bang from Josephine's engine. The power died completely and I was only just able to drift onto the hard-shoulder of the interstate before she came to a complete standstill. The New Jersey Turnpike is one of the busiest and most notoriously dangerous roads in the whole of America. We could not have picked a worse place to break down.

As it was after midnight, the traffic was fairly quiet (by New Jersey Turnpike standards), but we were extremely vulnerable parked on the hard-shoulder. Leaving the hazard lights on, we both walked a few hundred metres to an emergency telephone where we called for assistance.

A recovery truck arrived within the hour and we asked him to tow us to the nearest garage, which was situated on an industrial estate just outside Trenton, New Jersey.

Before I left England, I had been assured that my breakdown cover in the UK would entitle me to reciprocal cover in the US, but the recovery driver refused to acknowledge my battered AA membership card and we were forced to pay the $100 call out fee. He unloaded Josephine onto the forecourt of the garage and drove off into the night.

It was 2am. There were no motels in the vicinity, so we settled down for our first night in Josephine. It was one of the coldest nights I had ever experienced (little did I know I would suffer many more far colder ones later), and we both took it in turns to warm up in the toilet of a nearby gas station that had a fan blowing warm – and most probably toxic – air from a dodgy looking unit in the wall.

We drifted in and out of sleep and were awoken by a tapping on Josephine's window at 7.30am by a man in greasy overalls.

'You boys mind moving your car? It's blocking our garage,' he said, in a polite but direct manner.

'Sorry, we got towed here late last night. It won't move,' I said, rubbing my eyes. 'We were hoping you might be able to take a look at it for us.'

'Sure thing. You boys go and help yourself to coffee in the waiting area and I'll get one of my men to take a look as soon as possible.'

An hour or so later he approached us again, wiping his hands on a paper towel, with a look on his face like a Doctor in an emergency room about to break some terrible news.

'It's not good, I'm afraid,' he said. 'The transmission's had it. It's going to need an entire new one. It's an expensive fix and it'll take a few days.'

'A few days?' said Mark.

'I'm afraid so. We have to order in the parts and it's a big job.'

'How expensive is expensive?'

'We're talking about two and a half thousand bucks.'

'$2500?' I blurted, slopping hot coffee down my legs. 'We have only owned the car for a couple of days.'

'Well, I may be wrong but I would suggest that whoever sold you this car was pulling a fast one on you.'

'What do you mean?'

'Well, there are ways and means of sorta temporarily fixing a broken transmission so that it appears to be working fine.'

'So you think the transmission might have been broken before we bought it?'

'It's possible. Yes.'

'That fucking bastard,' I said.

'So, do you want us to go ahead and order the parts?'

'Well I guess so, we don't really have much choice,' said Mark.

'We could just buy another car,' I suggested. 'It would be significantly cheaper.'

We considered this for a while and then Mark and I both admitted that despite her obvious shitness, we were both already smitten by Josephine and we would pay anything to have her restored to her former glory. Which, admittedly, was not very glorious at all.

We had been on our way to visit a distant relative of Mark's who lived just outside Washington DC. Our intention was to call in, have a cup of tea, and then be on our way. We now had a week to kill.

Mark phoned Kathleen, his relative, and after some polite small talk, asked if there was any chance that our brief visit could be extended into a week's stay. Kathleen was absolutely delighted with the idea – or at least pretended to be – so we booked a taxi from the garage to Trenton train station.

Our driver was a lively man named Larry. He gave us his card and told us to call him when we got back to Trenton. We had debated hitch-hiking to DC, like proper backpackers, but with our large rucksacks and guitars, we were not the most appealing of hitchers so we settled on the train instead.

Because of America's vastness, the passenger rail network is rather sparse, with the majority of Americans relying on cars, taxis or buses. The train from Trenton to Washington DC made a welcome change, though, and it was extremely satisfying to watch the countryside whizz by without the fear of our transport self-destructing at any moment.

8

A smiling, well-dressed lady in her mid-fifties met us at the train station. Kathleen was the second cousin of Mark's mum's milkman's brother's nephew – or something tenuous like that. She worked as a civil servant in DC and lived in a large house with an immaculate front lawn, just like you see in the films, with a huge double size fridge and carpet so deep that you could lose your feet.

Kathleen was tremendously welcoming and seemed genuinely excited about having us to stay. She had kitted out her downstairs office with two day-beds for us to call home for the week.

We spent the following few days exploring Washington DC, which was a short bus ride from the suburb of Manassas where Kathleen lived. Our stay in Washington DC coincided with the presidential election, during which several recounts were made to establish the winner between George Bush Jnr and Al Gore. Being a civil servant, Kathleen had to work longer hours as a result, and there was a heightened feeling of excitement and anticipation in the air.

Mark studied American History for three years at university so Washington DC was pretty much his idea of heaven. He had a particular fascination with dead presidents and made sure we saw every single one of the memorials.

The Smithsonian Museums are dotted all over DC. They are all free, fantastic and – on a weekday in November – completely empty. We looked at the FBI building, visited the American History museum – which makes the most of America's relatively recent history – we looked at the capitol, and visited the Air and Space museum. We also visited the nearby Manassas Battlefield where two major American Civil

War battles were fought: the First Battle of Bull Run and the Second Battle of Bull Run.

We spent another day wandering the beautiful streets of Georgetown, which is an upmarket neighbourhood of DC on the banks of the Potomac River. It is also the location of the prestigious Georgetown University. With many art galleries, coffee shops, parks with people roller-blading and boutique restaurants, it was a far cry from the student areas in the UK that I was used to. Instead of art galleries, we had nightclubs with revolving dance floors that served beer at £1 a pint. The coffee shops were swapped for kebab houses, and the parks were filled with the regurgitated beer and kebabs from the students' stomachs. Ah, those were the days.

Mark and I were invited to a party in Georgetown at a house belonging to a friend of Kathleen's lodger, so we went along for a few hours. We stood in the corner making polite conversation with a group of nice students, drinking from red plastic cups – just like in the films. What is with those red cups and how did they get such a monopoly over the American party drinking vessel market?

This was not a fraternity type party, however, with people playing beer pong and swinging from the light-fittings. It was a sedate Georgetown party with sophisticated students having mature discussions about the current election. Mark and I stood awkwardly in the corner, wishing we could play beer pong.

On the fifth day, feeling like we had seen enough museums and memorials of dead presidents, we took a walk from Kathleen's house in Manassas. We set off on foot (because that's how walking works) and got hopelessly lost in the countryside. We stumbled upon a golf course and considered having a game, before realising that it was far too expensive for us beginners. The fact that we didn't have any golf clubs was also a slight hindrance.

Instead, we invented our own golf-related game on the long walk home with a couple of golf balls we found in the grass outside the club. The game was called Golfball and I am fairly certain it will be an Olympic sport one day. Golfball is a unique game in that it's one on one, but you also have to work with your opponent in order to score points. The idea is to bounce the golf ball in creative ways, on a variety of terrains, for your opponent to catch. Each throw would vary in its height, trajectory, speed and distance, and the opponent would have to catch the ball before it hit the ground for the second time, or after the second bounce but for fewer points. Bonus points were scored for throws between the legs or behind the back and were also awarded for spectacular catches.

To begin with we played on a quiet, smoothly surfaced country lane. We then tried Rural Extreme Golfball along a stretch of woodland track, where the rocky surface provided completely unpredictable bounce and the many trees and hidden roots caused additional challenges for the catcher.

The game then ended with a round of Urban Golfball. Urban Golfball introduced new obstacles such as curbs (or kerbs), drain covers, parked cars and the occasional moving car. The game came to an abrupt end when the first of our golf balls disappeared over a garden wall, and then our backup ball was squashed by a passing truck.

Kathleen held a party at her house one evening with the sole intention of showing off her English guests. She had invited every person whom she had ever met and they all congregated in the kitchen, taking it in turns to ask us questions about our trip and interrogate us about life in England. They were all extremely kind and excited that we had chosen to come and explore their beautiful country, and we had an enjoyable evening being the guests of honour.

Kathleen had already started asking us about our plans for Thanksgiving. It was November 9th and Thanksgiving was still two weeks away. As much as we enjoyed staying in Manassas, we hoped to be far from Washington DC before then. Right on cue, the garage in Trenton called to say that Josephine was all fixed up and ready to go. The time had come for us to leave.

We took the Greyhound back to New Jersey as it was cheaper than the train. On hearing our English accents, a girl on the bus asked us if we knew Prince William. I had heard that many Americans assume that all Brits are close friends with the Royal Family, but assumed it was an urban myth. It turns out some Americans do think that, and I was comforted by the thought of our small and intimate island back home. I was also disappointed that I didn't actually know Prince William. But I of course told the girl that I did.

The bus stopped briefly at Baltimore bus station on the way up the coast. I wanted to show Mark the chairs with the coin-operated televisions, but we were there for less than a minute. Even the Greyhound driver didn't want to hang around in Baltimore.

We spent half an hour in Philadelphia, which looked promising, but we didn't get to explore much further than the blocks surrounding the bus station. We did have time to make a mad dash to the Liberty Bell (the iconic symbol of American independence), tick it off our list, and rush back to the Greyhound.

Arriving in Trenton I called Larry, the lively cab driver who had driven us to the train station.

'Of course I'll pick you up,' he said. 'Where are you?'

'We're at the coach station,' I said.

'The coach station? Where the hell is the coach station?'

'The big building where all the coaches go.'

'I don't know of no coach station. I've lived in Trenton all my life and there ain't no damn coach station.'

'We just got off the Greyhound.'

'Oh, you mean the bus terminal?'

'Yeah, that's what I said. The coach station.'

'Look here. This country has everything. Apart from coach stations. Oh, and a president.'

'Ah, right. Sorry. Yes, we are at the bus terminal.'

'I'll be there in five. I'll meet you outside.'

'So you guys had fun in DC, did you?' asked Larry once we had loaded our bags into the trunk.

'Yeah, great thanks,' said Mark.

'And your minivan is all fixed?'

'Yes. Although it's cost us most of our money.'

'How much did they charge you?'

'$2500.'

'$2500?' he shouted. 'You gotta be kidding me. $2500 for a new tranny?'

'A new what?' said Mark, looking over at me in the back of the cab and mouthing the word 'tranny' with a smirk.

'A tranny. An automatic transmission. That's what you had replaced, right?'

'Right, yes. A new tranny,' I said.

'Well it sounds to me like they are greasing you up and screwing you. Let me call my buddy and see what he says.'

Mark and I looked at each other again.

'Rocko, Larry here. Listen, I've got two British guys with me. We're just on the way back to the repair shop. They've just had a new tranny fitted for their Dodge Caravan. What year, boys?' he said, looking back at Mark with the phone tucked under his chin.

‘’89,’ said Mark.

‘An ’89 Dodge Caravan. It’s costing them twenty five hundred bucks. Are they being greased up and screwed? Cos when they told me the cost it sounded to me like they are being greased up and screwed.’

There was a pause.

‘Yeah, that’s what I thought. Thanks Rocko. We’ll meet for that beer soon.’

He hung up the phone.

‘Rocko thinks you’re being greased up and screwed. Let me call my buddy Kurt as well. He’ll confirm it,’ he said, pressing a few more buttons on his phone. ‘Kurt, my main man. Larry here. Listen...’ and he repeated the details to Kurt, who, from the response we heard from Larry, seemed to concur that we were being greased up and screwed.

‘What’s the verdict then, Larry?’ I said, as he threw his phone onto the passenger seat. ‘Are we being greased up and screwed?’

‘It sounds to me like they are greasing you up and screwing you fucking big time. I know trannies are expensive but you’re paying well over what it should cost.’

‘What should we do? Try to haggle?’ asked Mark as we pulled onto the forecourt of the garage.

‘Damn right you should!’

‘But they told us the price before and we said ok,’ I said.

‘That don’t mean shit. At the end of the day, you don’t have to pay them a cent.’

‘But then we don’t get our car back.’

‘Well that’s true, but you need to go in there and you tell ‘em you ain’t going to be dicked around.’

‘Thanks, Larry,’ said Mark. ‘We really appreciate your help, but I don’t think we’d be much good at that. We know absolutely nothing about cars.’

‘Fuck it. I’m going in then. You boys wait here.’ He climbed out of the car, slammed the door and marched towards the garage’s office.

‘Should we go after him?’ asked Mark.

‘I guess we should wait here, like he said.’

‘Larry is the greatest taxi driver ever.’

‘He sure is. And all this talk of trannies, dicking around and being greased up and screwed is making me horny.’

‘You’re sick, do you know that?’

After five minutes, Larry returned with a big grin on his face.

‘There you go, boys. I’ve saved you a few bucks.’

We thanked Larry profusely and gave him a hefty tip which he refused to accept, reminding us that we still had a significant repair bill to pay. He wished us luck on our journey and we promised we would give him a call if we were ever in Trenton again.

‘For your sake, boys,’ he said, ‘I hope you never are.’

I have no idea what Larry said or did in that office but when we went to settle up, the bill had mysteriously been reduced by $500.

Josephine’s engine purred into life. She sounded far healthier than she did before the transmission exploded. The steering felt like it had a slight wobble to it but we naively assumed that this was something to do with the new transmission and hoped it would settle down in time.

We left New Jersey and drove through some charming villages and into Pennsylvania. We pulled into a rest area which would be our campsite for the night.

The American road networks are dotted with 'rest areas', which are glorified lay-bys. They usually have a designated slip road from the main highway. Most have proper toilet facilities, picnic benches and dog walking areas. Unlike motorway service stations in the UK, they don't tend to have shops, restaurants or petrol stations, so are almost always unmanned. We had planned to use these rest areas to park up in at night and sleep in Josephine.

We had read that rest areas were not the safest places to sleep, but seeing as there were two of us we decided to take our chances. Most states only allow people to stay in rest areas for a few hours, but we figured that it would not be very easy to prove a vehicle had been there for more than the designated time limit. We also decided that state troopers would hopefully use a bit of common sense and prefer drivers to sleep in their cars in a rest area, rather than at the wheel in the fast lane of the interstate.

Josephine had two rows of seats in the back and Mark and I took a row each, which would become our bunks for the rest of the trip. The back row was a full three seats so I offered this to Mark. The middle row was only two seats wide because it had a large foot well by the sliding side door. I have an excitable bladder and knew I would be far more likely than Mark to have to venture out in the night to the toilet, so I took the middle row with its easier access to the door. We piled our rucksacks in the foot well which then formed the end of my bed. Both guitars had to be moved through to the front seats each night to create enough space for us to sleep.

It wasn't the most comfortable of beds, but we both felt incredibly lucky. We had a car (a shitty car, but a car nonetheless) that we had spent almost all of our savings on. But it worked and we had the freedom to drive wherever we liked and park up and sleep in our own little rusty box for free.

9

The following morning we passed unknowingly into Amish territory. Many families, all dressed in their simple traditional clothes, travelled along the roadside either on foot or in horse-drawn carts, laden with farm produce. It was fascinating to witness a glimpse of history in the modern day.

It is difficult to strike the balance between curiosity and intrusion. Some Amish communities have embraced tourism and allow tours of their farms, whereas others hugely resent the interference into their lives. We chose to pass through without stopping and enjoyed our brief glimpse of their way of life from the car window.

We passed through Intercourse, Pennsylvania (grow up!) and across the north-western tip of Maryland towards West Virginia.

While Mark filled up Josephine at a gas station, I used a payphone to call Rachel.

Phone conversations with Rachel had become more and more difficult. I always had plenty to tell her about places we had been, things we had seen and people we had met. She made lots of positive noises, trying to show enthusiasm, but it was clear she was finding things very difficult. I thought about Rachel all the time, but I also had plenty of new things to keep my mind occupied and stop myself getting too down about our less than ideal relationship situation.

I asked Rachel lots about what she had been up to, but things had stayed pretty much the same for her. She went to work in an office job she hated, came home to her parents' house each night, went swimming a couple of times a week and met up with friends occasionally at the weekend. She had plenty of time to think about things and it's understandable that there was still a degree of underlying resentment towards me for packing up and disappearing to the other side of the world. I hoped the situation would improve over time, but if anything, it seemed to be getting worse.

Whilst on the phone, something caught my eye. Stuck to the window on the inside of the phone box was an advert.

GOLF BREAK
3 rounds of golf
2 nights
$50

Instinctively, I stuffed the flier into my pocket.

Darkness arrived sooner than we thought so we parked up in a gravel area by the roadside in some woods just before the West Virginia state border.

After spending way more money on car repairs than we had planned to, we needed to budget for food a bit better. We had begun a diet of bologna sandwiches and bananas. Bologna sandwiches were cheap and easy. American bread, we discovered, lasts forever. It's weird and spongy, with an almost cake-like texture. It tastes quite like cake too, but is apparently bread. Its seemingly unlimited shelf life makes it a backpacker's best friend.

It wasn't until we were tucked up in our sleeping bags that I studied our map and realised we were in Burkittsville, Maryland.

'Mark, I've heard of Burkittsville. What's it famous for?'

'I dunno,' said Mark. 'It does sound vaguely familiar though.'

'You're the historian. Did some famous battle take place here?'

'I don't think so. Not that I know of anyway.'

I lay there thinking about it for a while when it suddenly dawned on me.

'*The Blair Witch Project!*' I shouted.

'What about *The Blair Witch Project?*' groaned Mark. 'I was almost asleep.'

'Burkittsville! That's where it all happened.'

'You do know that it was a fictional film?'

'Yeah, of course. But it's still a bit scary to think it was based here.'

'If you say so,' he groaned, and rolled over to go to sleep.

Of all the woods, in all of America, we had chosen to park up in the one recently featured in a terrifying horror film. I hardly slept at all that night.

Having survived the night in the woods, we spent the following day visiting the wonderful Shenandoah National Park. The park sits in a large section of the Blue Ridge Mountains in Virginia. During the autumn months, visitor numbers increase as people flock to the park to witness the stunning display of colours. We were lucky enough to time our visit during the peak of the park's fall display.

A large section of the park was closed due to forest fires, but the parts that we could visit were spectacular. Our guide book boasted about the park's *'grand vistas at every bend'* and we could not dispute this. A steady stream of cars snaked their way up and down the 104 mile Skyline Drive so we parked up by a trail to Marshall Point – a recommended lookout – and once we had left the parking lot, we didn't see another human being there or back. The vast majority of visitors to Shenandoah enjoy these grand vistas from the comfort of their car seats.

We were so impressed with Shenandoah that we invested in a National Park annual pass so that we could take our pick from the 59 National Parks in the United States.

We didn't have any sort of route planned for our road trip. Armed with a Rand McNally road atlas and a couple of guide books, we decided to make it up as we went along. As winter was approaching, we planned to head south and then work our way gradually west towards California.

We headed down Interstate 81 and onto 64 through George Washington National Forest towards West Virginia. It was dark and Mark was at the wheel. He had just pulled off the interstate for us to look for a place to park up and sleep when there was a huge clunking sound from the front of Josephine. Mark pressed the accelerator again and the engine screamed but Josephine didn't move forwards any faster. He managed to guide her to the side of the road where she rolled to a stop.

'What the hell just happened?' I said.

'I think the transmission has gone again,' said Mark. 'There's no power.'

'The transmission that we just spent $2000 getting replaced?'

'Looks like it. Maybe something went wrong when they installed it, or maybe they fitted a dodgy one.'

'The bastards!' I shouted. 'They properly were greasing us up and screwing us, knowing full well that we would be miles away before anything happened.'

Yet again Josephine had decided to malfunction at the worst possible time. It was dark, raining, and not only were we far from any form of civilisation, we didn't even know which state we were in.

'I think I saw some lights up ahead, just as we came over that hill,' I said. 'I'll go and try and find a phone, find out where we are, and then call the breakdown people.'

'Is that the car breakdown people or the mental breakdown people?' said Mark.

'Both.'

'Good.'

I trudged up the unlit road towards a red glow in the distance that I hoped was a form of civilisation, or at least somewhere with a phone. Thankfully it was gas station, which was deserted of cars, but open.

'What pump?' said the young female attendant at the counter.

'I'm not buying any gas, thanks,' I said, gazing out onto the empty forecourt, slightly surprised that she hadn't noticed there were no cars to be seen.

'What can I get you then?' she sighed, in a way that made it clear she was counting down the seconds until her shift was over.

'We've broken down on the slip-road that way. Do you have a payphone please?'

'There's one at the back. Just next to the restroom,' she said, lazily pointing her finger to the other side of the store.

'Could you tell me where we are?'

'The gas station,' she said.

'Thanks. I mean what road is this?'

'Jeez, I don't know.'

'Oh. You don't know what road this is?'

'Why would I? I only live a couple miles away. I don't need to follow no signs to get here.'

'Well what town do you live in?'

'Covington.'

'And what state is that in?'

'What state?' she laughed. 'And you thought it was strange I didn't know what road this was? Why it's Covington, Virginia, of course.'

She looked at me as if I was the dumbest fuck in the world.

'Thanks. Just checking.'

I called the AAA, this time confirming before they came that we were eligible for cover. I told the representative the name of the garage I was calling from and the proximity of our car from that garage, hoping that was enough for them to locate us.

'Any luck?' said Mark once I had made it back to the car.

'I hope so. Even the lady at the garage doesn't know where we are.'

'Oh. Where are we?'

'Covington, Virginia apparently. At least, that's a town not far from here.'

'Did you ring the Triple A?'

'Yes. Hopefully they will be here within the hour. If they can find us.'

The brief excursion to the garage had taken my mind off the critical fact that we were once again the owners of a car that would presumably soon be lumped with another hefty repair bill.

'What a piece of shit fucking car,' I said, kicking Josephine's front tyre with all my might, and then trying to disguise the fact that I really hurt my toe in the process.

'We'll ring that garage in Trenton in the morning,' suggested Mark. 'If it's the transmission then surely it should be covered by some sort of warranty? We've only had it a few days.'

'Yes, but New Jersey is a long bloody way from here, so I doubt they are going to be able to do much about it.'

Another night on a garage forecourt didn't appeal, so when the recovery truck eventually arrived, we decided to forget about Josephine's mechanical problems and instead asked to be towed to the nearest motel. We made ourselves some bologna sandwiches and went to sleep, secretly hoping that Josephine would be miraculously cured by the morning.

Unsurprisingly she wasn't.

In fact, if anything, the night had been unkind to Josephine, and something in the engine gave an even more sinister growl when I optimistically tried to turn the ignition key. Although we had got a decent night's sleep, we were only marginally better off than we were the previous night. We still had a car that wouldn't work, and were several miles from the nearest garage.

'We could try ringing the Triple A again and pretend we broke down here,' I suggested.

'But they'll have it on their system that they towed us here last night.'

'They might not. Remember the guy last night said that our card number wasn't recognised on his system so he just made a note on a scrap of paper instead.'

'That's true. Let's give it a go.'

I called up the AAA and, sure enough, they seemed to have no record of our call last night and said they would send someone straight out.

I next phoned the New Jersey mechanics and had a long rant down the phone at them. They assured me that it would not be a transmission problem, but if it was they would be happy to repair or replace it, providing we could get Josephine the 400 miles back to Trenton.

The recovery truck arrived and we were relieved to see it was a different driver to the previous night. As he hooked up Josephine to the back of his truck, Mark nudged me with his elbow.

'Maybe we should just do this every day. We could just get towed the entire way across America.'

'That's actually a great idea,' I laughed. 'We wouldn't even have to pay for any fuel.'

'And we wouldn't have to cope with your driving.'

'What do you mean? What's wrong with my driving?'

'Well, it's sometimes a little bit on the erratic side.'

'You can talk. You're the one who broke the car last night.'

'That had nothing to do with me. Anyway, you were driving when it broke down in New Jersey so we're evens now.'

'Fine. We're evens.'

Josephine was unloaded outside Dressler Motors in downtown Covington. We were greeted by a smiley elderly man who said he would book Josephine in to be looked at. We followed him inside to fill in some paperwork.

'Great, that's all I need from you for now,' he said. 'If you give me the keys and then give us a call in… oooh… let's say… about ten days, we should have her ready for you.'

'TEN days?' I said.

'Is there no chance you could take a look at it today?' added Mark.

'I'm sorry but we're completely backed up at the moment. Are you not local?'

'No, we're from England,' I said.

'England? What you doing out here in Virginia?'

'We are on our way to California but we seem to be spending more time getting our car repaired than driving.'

Mark and I looked at each other, and looked outside to watch the recovery vehicle pulling out onto the main road. We should have checked how busy they were before being dropped off. From what we saw of Covington on the way through town there was little to occupy us for an afternoon, let alone ten days.

'Where are you boys staying?' he said.

'In the car mostly. We weren't planning on staying in Covington. No offence.'

'None taken. Listen, I think we can help you out. We'll take a quick look at your vehicle for you. I can't guarantee we'll be able to fix it quickly, but we'll at least take a look at it.'

The man's name was Bill. He was an astonishing 85 years old. 85 years old and still gallantly working as a mechanic. Not out of any obligation; just simply because he loved his job. His team of equally elderly mechanics set to work on Josephine straight away.

Bill had worked at the family business all his life. Within minutes of meeting him, he had told us all about his experiences in World War II when he served in the 1st Armoured Division in North Africa and Italy. He was severely wounded in 1944 and awarded the Purple Heart for his duties. He rolled up his trousers to reveal a hole in his leg.

'It was almost blown clean off,' he said proudly. 'I'm very lucky to still have both my legs.'

'And here you are, still running a car business at the age of 85. That's incredible.'

'Well, I gotta keep myself busy somehow.'

We were sitting drinking coffee in the waiting room, marvelling at Bill and his team, when Verne burst through the door completely out of breath. Verne was one of the main mechanics, and, like Bill, was well into his 80s.

'She's got a broken front axle,' he panted.

'So nothing to do with the transmission?' I said.

'Nope. Just bad luck I guess.'

I felt a pang of guilt about being so aggressive on the phone to the New Jersey garage. That soon passed when I realised how they had tried to grease us up and screw us.

'How long will it take to order the part and get it fitted?' I asked, expecting a wait of at least a couple of days.

'It's already ordered. It will be here within a couple hours and then we'll get it fitted for you right away,' said Verne.

'You're our saviours. Thank you,' said Mark. 'Perhaps we'll go and have a wander around Covington for a couple of hours then.'

'I doubt it will take you that long. There's not a lot to see,' said Bill.

Covington was a nice little town, but Bill was right, and we were sitting back in the waiting room half an hour later.

'Back already?' asked Verne. 'Come with me. There's something I want to show you.'

Verne and Bill took us through the repair shop where they opened a door in the far corner. We followed them up a dusty staircase that led to the floor above (as staircases tend to do). I had no idea what to expect when we got up there.

We reached another doorway and Verne opened it to reveal complete darkness. Bill flicked a switch on the wall and row upon row of fluorescent lights flickered on, revealing a vacuous upstairs storage area, where lined up in neat rows were at least a dozen vehicles covered in dust sheets.

'What is this?' I asked.

'This...' said Bill, '... is Dressler Motors' little secret. It's our own private car collection. These have never been shown in public, and very few people have ever been up here.'

Verne walked up to the first vehicle and, despite his age, managed to whip the dust sheet off in one quick movement like a magician with a tablecloth. Underneath sat a gleaming red sports car. I would love to be more descriptive at this point and mention some crucial bits of the car's anatomy, but I know very little (nothing) about cars and so it would all be fake. It was shiny and red and it looked really, really fast. How's that?

'It's a 1993 Dodge Viper,' said Verne proudly. 'It's never been driven.'

'Never been driven?' I said. 'Since 1993?'

'That's correct. I doubt you'll see a better version of this car anywhere in the world.'

'Amazing,' said Mark.

'Wow,' I said.

Verne and Bill led us around the room, whipping off a sheet every now and then and presenting another classic vehicle. Even for two ignorant Brits who knew nothing about cars, it was simply astonishing. Bill paused by a dust sheet in the far corner and waited for us to gather round.

'And this… is my personal favourite,' he said, as he pulled the dust sheet free, more slowly and carefully than he had with the others.

Mark and I let out a collective gasp.

'A 1969 Dodge Charger Daytona,' said Bill. 'It has never even been titled.'

'What does that mean?' asked Mark.

'It means,' said Bill, flashing a grin, 'that technically it doesn't even exist.'

'They only made 503 of these cars,' said Verne, 'and as far as we know, this is the only one never to be sold. It came straight from the production line to the showroom here at Dressler Motors. Been here ever since.'

'Unbelievable,' I said, reaching out a hand to touch it and looking to Verne for approval.

'Sure, you can touch it. Just don't put any dents in it.'

'How much would a car like this be worth?' asked Mark.

'Difficult to say, because it's so rare. There's nothing to compare it to,' said Bill. 'But, in the right auction, and with the right buyer, you'd probably be looking at upwards of half a million bucks.'

'Oh my god,' I said. 'So this car is basically your pension?'

'Ha, well you could say that. Although, as you can see, I'm long past retirement age.'

We felt truly honoured to have been given a private tour of their secret car collection, and felt weirdly blessed that Josephine had decided to break down when she had.

'You English folk are crazy,' said Verne, as he hobbled back down the stairs.

'Why do you think that?' I laughed.

'Well you all drive on the wrong side of the road. Doesn't that cause all sorts of problems?'

'No, because to us it's the correct side of the road,' I said. 'It's you lot who all drive on the wrong side.'

'Most of the world drive on the right like us. It's definitely yous that's wacko.'

'True, but people always used to travel on the left. I think it goes way back to Roman times and jousting. Riders would hold their lances in their right hand and pass other riders on the left to have their lance or sword as protection.'

'Well I'll be damned,' said Verne. 'Then why does the rest of the world drive on the right?'

It was Mark the historian's turn to shine.

'That was because of Napoleon,' he said. 'He started travelling on the right, partly just to be awkward and annoying for his enemy, but also because he was left handed.'

'Ah. What about America?'

'The French colonised parts of America early on,' said Mark, 'so they probably just travelled in the same way they had back home. Also, there was something to do with wagons and horses and it making more sense to travel on the right, but I can't quite remember why.'

'Well I think you English are all lunatics,' he said. 'I'm surprised there aren't way more crashes. And you all call the hood the bonnet, and the trunk the boot. That's the craziest thing I've ever heard in my whole life. Yous are all completely wacko.'

The axle had arrived by the time we got back downstairs and we noticed a spindly pair of legs protruding from underneath Josephine. The body that was attached to these legs emerged to reveal another man, much younger than Bill and Verne. He was only in his late 70s. He had a bandaged right hand so offered us his left as a greeting.

'I'm just having a few problems getting the axle into place,' he said. 'Got a fractured hand so it's not as easy as it should be. My name's Wilber.'

'Hi Wilber. I'm George and this is Mark. Can we help at all?'

'Sure, that would be great. A couple of strong boys like you and we'll have her fixed in no time.'

The whole situation would have made a brilliant sitcom. Three old men – one with a fractured hand, another with severe arthritis, and the third with a huge hole in his leg – all manning a car repair shop.

A few minutes later, Wilber had wedged a large crowbar deep into Josephine's engine and he and Verne were holding it in place.

'Right, boys,' said Wilber. 'I need you two to pull on this bar as hard as you possibly can, OK?'

'Ok.'

Mark and I both pulled hard on the crowbar. A creaking noise came from deep within Josephine's guts but there was no feeling of any movement.

'Hold up,' said Wilber sliding back under the car. 'Let me just adjust this slightly.'

He emerged a few seconds later and took his place again by the engine.

'Ok, pull!' he said.

Mark and I heaved on the bar as hard as we could, putting all our weight into it. There was a popping sound and the crowbar slipped free from the engine.

'You did it!' shouted Wilber. 'We did it!'

He gave us each a high-five with his good hand, and slapped us both on the backs, as though Josephine had just given birth.

'Yee-hah,' he said, dancing around Josephine like an excited toddler.

Mark and I couldn't help but be swept up in the excitement too, and we felt an extra sense of achievement at having helped bring Josephine back from the dead once again.

Bill had originally told us that it would be ten days before they could look at Josephine, but we were in and out of Dressler Motors in less than three hours. It was, bizarrely, three of the most enjoyable hours of our trip so far. We did not expect a garage in the small town of Covington, Virginia to provide such brilliant entertainment. You certainly don't get that kind of experience at Kwik Fit.

We said goodbye to Bill, Verne and Wilber, and thanked them for their amazing service and for being such an inspiration.

From Covington, we followed minor roads into West Virginia and parked up on the outskirts of a town called Beaver, purely because it made us smile. Despite yet another repair bill, we felt optimistic that Josephine's problems were now behind us.

As I pulled my trousers on in the back of the car the following morning, the flier that I had taken from the payphone in Intercourse, Pennsylvania fell onto the seat beside me.

'Mark, look at this. $50 for two nights' accommodation and three rounds of golf.'

'That sounds amazing. Where is it?'

‘At a course near Beckley,’ I said, looking at the map. ‘It’s about five miles from here.’

‘Are you tempted?’

‘I’m very tempted. What about you? It could be our treat after such a crap week with the car.’

‘Sounds good to me. Shall we go there today?’

‘Let’s do it. It’s almost cheaper than staying in motels.’

10

So our rough and ready trip across the USA suddenly took a slight change of direction with a civilised two night stay at a quaint golf and country club in the hills of West Virginia.

The idea of these golf breaks is to bring in golfers during the quiet winter months in the hope that they will eat and drink at the hotel too. We were, we soon discovered, the only people in the entire resort. During three rounds of golf and a two night stay, the only other people we saw were a small handful of staff.

We obviously didn't have golf clubs with us so had to hire some at a cost almost equal to our entire stay. They reluctantly agreed to let us share a set.

It was a beautiful course, nestled in a valley with thick woodland bordering many of the holes, and snow-capped hills looming above. Deer dotted the fairways and they became more of a hazard than the many bunkers and lakes.

One deer stood munching the grass in the middle of the seventh fairway, about 100 yards from us. We tried whooping and clapping but it was completely oblivious to our efforts to scare it. It was Mark's shot and the green was a good 200 yards away, so the deer should not have proved any obstacle for the average golfer. Mark and I were not average golfers.

Mark struck the ball with his 4-iron, but instead of hitting it cleanly, he caught it so that it flew just a couple of feet above the ground. It struck the deer at the top of its hind quarters without bouncing. The deer looked up with a startled look at if to say, 'what the fuck was that?' did a quick scan of the area, and then resumed its eating.

We were the worst kind of guests; taking advantage of the cheap deal, but not buying food and drinks in the restaurant.

We were miles from the nearest grocery store but we had a healthy supply of bologna in our cool box and some ever-lasting bread, so we ate bologna sandwiches in our room.

After two rounds we were all square, and the final round was tied heading up the 18th. Mark and I both miraculously made the green in two. We both then putted to within three feet. I holed mine, via a couple of laps of the hole, and then Mark had a short putt to force a play off. We hadn't decided on what format the play off would take, but it would have probably involved an arm wrestle or a bare fist fight. Mark's putt rolled up millimetres short and he was forced to clean out Josephine for his punishment.

We could have happily stayed another week at the golf club. But as idyllic as it had been, no great American road trips are set in country clubs. Besides, it was getting too cold in West Virginia. Winter was on its way.

It was time to head south to Tennessee.

Josephine had not had any mechanical faults for four days, which was the longest period so far without a problem. This was due to the fact that for three of those days she was parked up outside a country club. But still, we saw this as progress.

As we entered Tennessee it began to rain. I flicked the windscreen wipers on. They swished from one side to the other – as windscreen wipers tend to do – and then they stopped. I tried the lever again. Nothing.

'I can't see a bloody thing,' I said to Mark.

'You're going to have to pull over.'

'No shit,' I said, as the rain battered the windscreen.

I rolled the window down and stuck my head out. We were alongside a patch of gravel so I pulled over and turned the engine off and on again, hoping that it would fix the wipers. It didn't.

We sat around waiting for the rain to cease, but it showed no sign of relenting so we decided to have an early night.

We awoke in the early hours to blue flashing lights and a single blast of a police car's siren. Bleary eyed, I wound down the back window.

'Good evening, Officer,' I said, shielding my eyes from the torch that he pointed in my face. He then used it to scan the car, surveying Mark as he sat upright in his sleeping bag on the back seat.

'We received reports of a suspicious vehicle parked outside the fire station. I've come to check it out.'

'Fire station?' I said. 'I'm really sorry. We had no idea that's where we are parked. Our windscreen wipers failed last night. It was raining and dark so we pulled over.'

'Can I see some identification please?'

'Yes, of course,' I said, sitting up and fumbling in my rucksack for my passport and driving licence. Mark did the same and we handed him a pile of scraggy bits of paper.

'What is this?' he said, holding up my driver's licence which was ripped and frayed all around the edges.

'It's my driving licence. We're from the UK.'

'You're kidding me. This is what you use for licences back there?'

'Yes, I'm afraid so.'

'You boys wait here please.'

He walked back to his patrol car and returned a few minutes later.

'Please step outside the vehicle for me and put your hands where I can see them.'

'Yes, Officer. Is there a problem?' said Mark, as we climbed out of the car in our boxer shorts.

'The licence plate didn't check out. This isn't the vehicle it is registered to.'

'What?…' I began. And then it suddenly clicked. 'Ah, we had to get a new boot fitted.'

'A new boot?' he said. 'What's this got to do with boots?'

'Sorry, I mean tailgate. This vehicle is a Dodge Caravan but it's got a Plymouth Voyager tailgate.'

'I see. Why did you have to get it changed?'

'The other one had a bullet hole in it,' blurted Mark.

I glared at him.

'A bullet hole, eh? You boys get into some trouble in New York? Is that why you're out in Tennessee?'

'No sir,' I said. 'It had a hole in the window when we bought it.'

'Is that so? Stay where you are. I'll be back.'

He said *'I'll be back'* in a fairly normal voice, by the way. Although slightly intimidating, he wasn't in the least bit like The Terminator.

'Ok, that all checks out,' he said, handing back our passports and licences. 'If you wouldn't mind moving the vehicle somewhere other than the front of the fire station please, that would be appreciated.'

'Yes, of course,' said Mark. 'Thank you, Officer.'

'You boys have a safe trip now.'

It was 5am. There was little point in trying to get back to sleep, and after a fairly decent night's rest, we decided we might as well start the day.

We headed west on route number something towards nowhere in particular. After a hearty breakfast at a diner in Morristown, Tennessee we passed through Jefferson City and onto the impressive Norris Dam where we stopped for a short walk.

We crossed a timeline in Tennessee, which was the first time we had ever driven across one. It was a strange experience as it felt like we had gone back in time. Technically we had. Mark did a u-turn and we crossed over it again, just so we could go back to the future. We laughed at our immaturity, and then he swung the car around and we drove back to the past.

After another freezing cold night in a rest area, we decided to head towards Memphis. No road trip across America would be complete without a visit to Memphis. Interstate 40 was particularly uninspiring. So we turned off and followed the back roads, dotted with derelict buildings of businesses whose trade presumably vanished overnight once the interstate opened.

We stopped at Mousetail Landing State Park, which sits on the banks of the Tennessee River. We walked a couple of trails and sat beside the river imagining how nice it would be in summer. The river even had its own beach. Well, I say beach, it was a stony, clayey patch of ground, but it was still very pleasant and we had the entire park to ourselves.

Later that evening we checked into a horrendous motel outside Jackson, manned by a bearded lady who yelled at her children the entire time she served us. The room was disgusting and it had a heater of questionable safety, but it was so cold we decided carbon monoxide poisoning was preferable to hypothermia.

We ventured to buy beers from the Walmart across the street. By street, I mean a multi-lane freeway, and we high-fived after we successfully made it across.

It was our first ever visit to Walmart and that was an experience in itself. It sucks you in like a black hole. In Walmart, nobody can hear you scream. The first thing we noticed was the completely unnecessarily high ceiling –

perhaps to cover the eventuality that they start selling Boeing 747s on special offer.

There is absolutely no logic at all to Walmart's aisles. They have no order or continuity. Supermarkets in the UK seem to have some sense of logic to them. Aisles tend to at least run parallel to each other. Not in Walmart. No, Walmart says to hell with logic. Walmart just puts rows and aisles wherever the fuck it likes. We were in there for two hours. One of those hours was spent trying to locate the exit. We only went in to buy beer, and we came out fully laden with all sorts of crap we didn't need.

After successfully negotiating the highway again, we settled down for a night of beer, tuna mayo sandwiches (a welcome change from bologna) and carbon monoxide poisoning.

11

We arrived in Memphis just before lunch the following day. We checked into a cheap hotel on the edge of town and then took a walk along the waterfront. Memphis had been one of the places I had been most looking forward to visiting, but based on my first impressions I was incredibly underwhelmed. What was all the fuss about?

And then we reached Beale Street and I suddenly understood.

It was a Sunday in November and there were very few people about, but every single bar and restaurant on Beale Street was open and music was blaring out of their wide open doors.

We had a delicious bowl of Alligator Gumbo (yes, it tastes like chicken) at the Rum Boogie Cafe decorated with dozens of guitars hanging from the walls. It looked just like a bar in Memphis should look. We thought it only fair to see some of Beale Street's other bars so launched straight into a bar crawl that extended late into the night.

Bar 2 – The Flying Saucer.

This was a nice bar boasting over 200 beers from around the world, including a number of 'real ales' from England that were curiously served ice cold. We drank a couple of highly recommended local craft beers, while quietly bitching about how the Americans didn't understand proper beer, before eventually admitting that the American craft beer we were drinking tasted better than anything we had ever tasted in England. Damn Americans.

Bar 3 – Alfred's

Alfred's was a huge bar with a large stage on which a full band played rock 'n' roll to an almost empty room. There was a small group of lively college students who left after ten minutes, leaving us as the only drinkers. It was incredible to witness Memphis's dedication to music. It was the middle of the afternoon on a Sunday and a 7-piece band was playing for our ears only.

We felt guilty about leaving, but after an hour and a couple of beers, we doffed our imaginary caps to the band, put a few dollars in their tip box and left the bar.

Bar 4 – Irish pub – probably called Paddy O' Leprechaun's or something.

It had to be done. We had a pint of Guinness, just to see how it compared to the other side of the Atlantic. It tasted every bit as good.

Paddy O' Leprechaun's had a musician playing too, of course. This time it was a lone male pianist, playing *Fairytale of New York* on a continuous loop. Probably.

Bar 5 – this one didn't have a sign outside, which meant it was really cool. It was busier than the previous bars and a lively soul band played in the corner. We sat at the bar and ate catfish sandwiches and fries. Next to the band, a small boy, four years old at the most, mimed and played air guitar for their entire set. Nobody was watching the band. We were all transfixed by this potential star of the future.

'That kid's incredible,' I said to the barman, as we ordered a second beer.

'He's my son,' said the barman.

'No way! He's got a big future ahead of him.'

'He's in here every night, so he knows the band's set better than they do.'

I wish I had got his name as I'm sure he must now be working in the music industry in some form. I tried to give him a dollar tip, but he ran off, so we made a hasty retreat to the next bar.

Bar 6 – I don't remember an awful lot about this bar, other than the fact I kept asking the stylish jazz band if they knew any S Club 7. Mark made me leave.

Bar 7 – I realised halfway through my pint that I had drunk way too much and we should probably get back to the hotel while we still could. Mark agreed. I bloody loved Memphis, and I bloody love you.

Mark had been talking a lot about Mud Island since before we arrived in Memphis. It was high on his list of places he wanted to visit.

'What is there to see at Mud Island?' I said, as we walked through a park along the edge of the Mississippi the following morning.

'Absolutely loads.'

'Cool. Like what?'

'There's a museum. All about the Mississippi.'

'Riiight… anything else?'

'There's a model replica of the river.'

'A replica? But the real river is just there,' I said, pointing to the real river which was just there.

'I just think it sounds quite cool. I'd like to see it.'

'Fine by me. Let's go. It would be fun to go to an island anyway. Do we have to get a boat? That would be cool.'

'No. It's not actually a real island. We can just drive to it. There's a road.'

'Oh.'

So we drove to Mud Island.

It was closed.

We visited Graceland instead.

Mark and I were both fairly fond of Elvis before visiting Graceland. When we left, we felt like we were Elvis's biggest fans. Yes, Graceland is slightly tacky, very expensive and incredibly touristy, but Americans sure know how to run a visitor attraction. The whole thing was brilliantly done and immensely enjoyable. We couldn't stop talking about Elvis and his incredible house for several days. He had a television room with THREE televisions. What a guy!

We crossed the Mississippi away from Memphis with the intention of sleeping in Josephine, but we were both still suffering with our Beale Street hangovers, so treated ourselves to a meatball sub and a motel instead. It was our third consecutive night in a motel which felt so wrong, yet so good.

The following morning, Mark insisted that we try visiting Mud Island again. It was still closed. Some further enquiries told us that it was closed for the whole winter and would not reopen until April.

'Shall we wait?' I said to Mark. 'It's only six more months.'

'Don't be a dick,' he said. 'I wasn't that desperate to see it.'

'I'm sure you'll get to see your replica Mississippi one day. Until then, we'll have to settle for the real thing.'

We visited the fairly recently opened Rock 'n' Soul museum instead, which documented the fascinating story of how a group of musical pioneers defied socio-economic and racial problems to change the music world forever.

Having left Memphis the night before, we had unintentionally been sucked back into the heart of it, and we somehow found ourselves sitting outside a bar on Beale Street once again. There was, of course, live music playing in every bar. This time, however, our beverage of choice was coffee. We wrote some postcards to send back to friends and family in England, and then decided it was time to leave Memphis for real.

We crossed the bridge over the Mississippi again into Arkansas before realising we had made a huge mistake. A mistake with our navigating, that is. The short time we spent in Arkansas was perfectly pleasant, but we turned around and crossed back into Tennessee.

'We're not in Ar-Kansas any more,' said Mark.

'Er, I think you'll find it is pronounced Ar-kun-saw,' I said.

'Yes, I know. But we're not in Ar-Kansas anymore.'

'I know. We are in Tennessee again. And it was Ar-kun-saw, not Ar-Kansas. I thought you were supposed to be the American expert?'

'I said, we're not in Ar-Kansas anymore. Geddit?'

'No. Get what?'

'It's a line from *The Wizard of Oz*. Dorothy says to Toto, *'we're not in Kansas anymore'*, and I changed it to Ar-Kansas.'

'*The Wizard of Oz*? How old are you? Six?'

'Oh just forget about it. I don't know why I bother.'

12

We headed south-east on Route 78 through the towns of Olive Branch and Hickory Flat towards Tupelo, Mississippi. Tupelo is the birthplace of Elvis and, as we were now two of his biggest fans, the town would therefore form the second leg of our Elvis tour.

We went to the cinema at a mall on the outskirts of town and then slept in Josephine outside a Texaco garage that advertised 'hot showers', which we looked forward to for the morning.

The showers weren't hot. It was a cruel lie. They were $3 for five ice cold minutes, but we felt so invigorated afterwards that it almost made them worth the money.

Elvis's birthplace in Tupelo was closed, bringing an abrupt end to our Elvis tour. We got to have a good look at it from the outside, however, and had a pleasant wander around the neighbourhood. It didn't do anything to dampen our enthusiasm for the great man.

'Sean I'd say the best one came from Tupelo, Mississippi. I'll tell you now that grown men cry and Irish girls are pretty,' sang The Proclaimers in one of my favourite songs of all time. In the song – called simply *Sean* – singer Charlie Reid imparts some of his wisdom on to his son. I always knew the last two facts to be true, and after a few days in Tennessee, I was now convinced by the first one, too.

From Tupelo we joined the famous Natchez Trace Parkway, a 440-mile non-commercial stretch of road between Natchez and Nashville. The road commemorates the original route of the Old Natchez Trace which was a popular trail used throughout the centuries by Native Americans and later by American and European explorers.

The Natchez Trace Parkway weaved its way through beautiful woodland. As we headed gradually deeper into the southern United States, we seemed to be following the autumn season, chasing the leaves south as they changed colour.

The area is rich in history and so there are marked 'points of interest' every few miles. These amused Mark and me greatly, as it was clear that a huge amount of poetic licence had been used to determine which things were worthy of a mention.

We passed several signs directing us towards an ancient Indian Trading Post, so we eagerly pulled over, cameras at the ready.

After following a short trail, we reached a plaque that said something along the lines of:

'Nearby was an Indian Trading Post. The building no longer exists, but the memories still remain.'

There were many other such examples along this route, and very, very rarely was there anything physical to actually see. One sign led us to a small patch of mud that had apparently been there since the Ice Age.

It was with great anticipation that we stopped again at Pigeon Roost Creek. Finally, we would at least get to see something. Even if it was only in the form of some lowly pigeons. We parked up, and walked up expectantly to a big wooden information board:

'Pigeon Roost Creek, to your left, is a reminder of the millions of migrating passenger pigeons that once roosted in trees in this area. The species has been completely destroyed.'

What? You cannot be serious. Not even any pigeons? Why not erect a sign saying: *'dinosaurs may have once roamed here.'*

We stopped at French Camp and were relieved to find real buildings and real people. The small town has been there since 1810 when Frenchman, Louis Lefleur, set up a trading post and inn. The locals referred to it as Frenchman's Camp – later shortened to French Camp – and the name stuck.

At the Council House café, I ate an unbelievably good Cajun Roast Beef sandwich and Mark ate a Big Willie. It's the name of one of Council House's sandwiches. Made with 10 pieces of crispy bacon, the Big Willie BLT is topped with lettuce, tomato, and the one-and-only Council House spicy garlic mayonnaise. Writing about it now makes me want to go back and devour both sandwiches. I would even be prepared to stop and gawp at some non-existent pigeons on the way.

To give our journey some variety, we took a detour off the Natchez Trace Parkway to visit Yazoo City for no other reason than it sounded awesome. It wasn't. Yazoo City was quite pleasant looking, but we were slightly unnerved by a large threatening sign in the centre of town stating that *'The 10 commandments are NOT multiple choice.'*

We continued on through Vicksburg which might have been nice had the entire town not shut down in anticipation of Thanksgiving the following day. Our guidebook recommended several rib restaurants but we could only find one of them. It was closed. The 24 hour casino was pretty much the only place open. We considered going in for a flutter but pressed on instead.

It was early evening when we reached the town of Port Gibson, Mississippi. In 1863, during the American Civil War, a battle took place in Port Gibson and over 200 Union and Confederate soldiers lost their lives. Former president, Ulysses S. Grant – and, at the time, the Commanding General of the United States Army – reportedly claimed that Port Gibson was *'too beautiful to burn'*, so many of the town's buildings survived the Civil War.

We ate a fairly decent catfish sandwich at Grant's Place, which was presumably started by former president Ulysses S. Grant. I like to think that he arrived in Port Gibson, saved the town on account of its beauty, and then set up a small restaurant selling fairly decent catfish sandwiches.

We were the only customers in Grant's Place and the lady that served us wore a state-of-the-art headset microphone. What made this particularly strange was that she was the only member of staff. She took our order, went over to the kitchen, prepared the food and then brought it back to us. What part did the microphone play? I imagine she quietly placed orders to herself.

'Hey Shona, two catfish sandwiches, fries and two large cokes for table three please.'

'Coming right up, Shona,' she would reply in a slightly different voice.

'And table eight needs wiping down, Shona.'

'No problem. I'll get right on it, Shona.'

After we finished eating, we rejoined the Natchez Trace Parkway and found a campsite to park up for the night.

'Are you sleeping in a tent?' asked the man at reception.

'No, we'll be sleeping in the car,' I said.

'Then I should probably charge you for an RV pitch.'

'But it's not really an RV. It's just a regular sized car.'

'Well if you're sleeping in it then it sort of is a recreational vehicle.'

'But we'll be taking up less space than if we had brought a tent. We don't need electricity or a water hook-up.'

'Yes, I suppose that's true. Ok, I'm feeling generous. I'll let you just pay for a standard pitch.'

'Thanks, that's really kind of you,' I said, as Mark and I secretly rolled our eyes at each other.

We pitched camp, which involved pulling on the handbrake, and had a wander around the site. It was the night before Thanksgiving and the RV Park was full of families crammed into their vehicles. We gazed longingly through their windows as they sat in warmth and comfort, eating hot meals and playing cards or watching television. We crawled into our dark, cold Josephine, ate a tube of Pringles (other stackable snacks are available) and went to sleep.

It rained heavily all night. We were parked under a tree which meant that the swollen drops of rain that gathered on leaves fell onto Josephine's roof, the noise echoing around the inside like a biscuit tin being beaten with a spoon. This occurred a couple of times a second throughout the night and, needless to say, neither of us got a huge amount of sleep.

'Happy Thanksgiving,' muttered Mark, soon after sunrise.

'Huh? Oh, happy Thanksgiving to you too,' I said.

Up until a few days earlier, Thanksgiving had been an American celebration that I knew of, but didn't really understand. You see it regularly celebrated in films and TV shows, but it hadn't fully registered on my consciousness. Mark, the resident American historian, filled me in on the details.

Thanksgiving is basically the same as the British harvest festival. But, as with many aspects of life, the Americans know how to do it properly. In America, Thanksgiving involves big family parties, a day or two off work, and schools and colleges close for four or five days. In comparison, at a harvest festival in Britain, a primary school child might possibly donate an out-of-date can of baked beans to the local church. That is as far as our celebration goes.

We could already hear the early morning festivities and celebrations beginning in the surrounding RVs and it felt quite dispiriting to delve into our cool box and share half a bruised banana each for breakfast.

I realised during the cold night that I had stupidly left my one and only fleece at Grant's Place, where Shona had no doubt reported the discovery of it on her headset microphone… to herself. It wasn't too far to retrace our steps, so we headed back towards Port Gibson to retrieve it.

On the way there, we were distracted by a signpost to Rocky Springs ghost town.

The definition of a ghost town is, *'an abandoned village, town or city, usually one which contains substantial visible remains'*. Surely Rocky Springs wouldn't disappoint.

As we had come to expect from any 'point of interest' along the Natchez Trace Parkway, Rocky Springs didn't quite live up to this definition. In fact, it should probably be charged with fraud.

Rocky Springs ghost town is in fact so ghostly that it no longer exists at all. Ok, so there is a small church, but the rest of the 'town' consists of plaques about where different buildings once stood.

Not wanting to be dismissive of all of Mississippi's tourist attractions, we had one last hope. From Rocky Springs, we saw a signpost for a trail that lead to Owen's Creek Waterfall. It was a 2.5 mile walk, but it was Thanksgiving and we had nothing else to do. Most of the signposted buildings and structures along the Natchez Trace Parkway had left us disappointed. But this was a waterfall. There was no way that nature could possibly let us down.

It took us close to an hour to reach the waterfall. Or where the waterfall should have been. Instead, we were greeted with a sign that looked like it had been there for many years. It read:

'Owen's Creek Waterfall – The sounds of a busy woodland stream and the quiet murmur of a lazy waterfall have long been stilled here.'

WHAT? You have got to be fucking kidding me.

'Over the years the water table has dropped several feet, and the spring which feeds Owen's Creek has all but disappeared. Little remains of a scene once familiar to early residents of the Rocky Springs community.'

We stood there in silence, unable to believe what we were reading. How can a waterfall that is no longer there be considered a worthy tourist attraction? I understand that water levels change and that streams reroute, but don't make bloody signposts to them then. The PR Manager for Mississippi is one hell of a creative person. He or she certainly knows how to polish a turd.

This was the final straw. We couldn't take it any longer. It was time for us to leave the Natchez Trace Parkway.

Grant's Place was of course closed. It was Thanksgiving. This meant that I had to say goodbye to my fleece. I tried to look at it as a way of freeing myself from materialistic possessions, but then I realised I was frickin' freezing without it. I put on the rest of the clothes that I owned instead.

Despite the cold, it was a beautiful sunny day and we walked around the deserted streets of Port Gibson, grateful that Ulysses S. Grant had spared it. In the centre of town, there is a striking cream-coloured church, and sitting atop, where you would normally find a cross or weathervane, there is a giant gold hand with a finger pointing up towards the sky – presumably in a sort of *'he went that way,'* kind of way. The church was closed. It was Thanksgiving.

We headed towards the city of Natchez, looking for somewhere to have lunch but everywhere was closed. It was Thanksgiving, if you haven't got the message yet.

Thankfully Walmart was open. It was 2pm and our shared banana had been our only food of the day. We bought a huge bucket of fried chicken and a pot of BBQ beans and sat and ate it in the parking lot.

It wasn't until we clocked the sad and sympathetic expressions aimed at us by all of the American families that walked by, heavily laden with last minute additions to their Thanksgiving meals, that we suddenly felt incredibly lonely. If we had been back in England then we wouldn't have given Thanksgiving a second thought. But here, surrounded by happy American families, we suddenly felt extraordinarily homesick.

I called Rachel from a payphone outside Walmart, hoping it would cheer me up. She sounded so distant – both geographically and emotionally – that our brief conversation only compounded my misery. The sadness and homesickness I felt at watching the happy American families was something that Rachel was experiencing on a daily basis, as I continued my travels without her. What the hell had I done? I had walked away from the best thing that had ever happened to me.

Feeling sorry for ourselves, Mark and I decided to take the rest of the day off. We found a motel, bought a case of beer, got drunk and watched TV for the rest of the day. Happy Thanksgiving.

13

After an all-you-can-eat breakfast, we explored Natchez and it was nice to see our old friend the Mississippi again after a few days apart. We hadn't planned to spend the morning in Natchez but it was raining heavily and Josephine's windscreen wipers still didn't work. We replaced the fuse but this didn't solve the problem, which meant it was a more complicated and therefore more expensive problem. Windscreen wipers were a luxury we would have to live without. If it rained, we would simply stop driving.

It was late afternoon by the time we left Natchez, and we followed the river down into Louisiana to the town of St Francisville. St Francisville was a quaint little place full of many beautiful antebellum houses that had survived the Civil War. Built along a ridge above the Mississippi, St Francisville is referred to as, *'the town two miles long and two yards wide'*.

We had a fun evening eating delicious chilli burritos at the Magnolia Cafe, listening to a live band, drinking beers and smiling at the pretty waitress who seemed to have a thing for English accents. After a diet based predominantly on bruised bananas and bologna sandwiches (not together), these evenings out were always even more special.

It seems to be a rite of passage in the Deep South to go and lie down on the banks of the Mississippi and look at the stars. Actually, I don't know if anyone actually does that, but after a few beers Mark and I concluded that's what everyone did.

So that's what we did.

The waitress gave us directions and told us that it was only a couple of miles walk, so we staggered tipsily down there by the light of the moon. For a river as big as the Mississippi, it was eerily quiet. We could see the moonlight reflecting on the oil-like surface but it was stealth-like in its silence. It was a cold but perfectly clear night so we lay down on the muddy bank and gazed up at the mesmerizing sky.

'This must have been what that golden hand on the church in Port Gibson was pointing at,' I said.

'Yeah, it looks pretty awesome up there,' said Mark.

Just then we heard an ominous splash in the river next to us. We were on our feet and back up the bank before the ripples had receded.

'What the hell was that?' I said.

'I've no idea, but I didn't want to hang about to find out.'

'Do they have crocodiles or alligators here?'

'I thought they were usually in the swamp parts of the Mississippi delta, but now I'm not so sure.'

We staggered back towards the town, laughing at how our one quiet moment of reflection had ended so suddenly. We climbed into Josephine, which we had stupidly parked outside a local police station and jail, and fell fast asleep.

We were thankfully not disturbed by police or inmates during the night, which was a relief considering our drunken state. From St Francisville we boarded a ferry to the town of New Roads, Louisiana, on the opposite side of the river. There is something childishly exciting about driving a car onto a boat. And crossing the river helped give us some perspective of just how big the Mississippi is.

Following the levee of the Miss, we headed south from New Roads, all the way down to New Orleans – the road lined with spectacular houses all built close to the river, despite the obvious risk of flooding.

We stopped for gas late morning. We had long since stopped calling it petrol. Since being in America, the word 'petrol' felt ugly, dirty and industrial. So we stopped and filled our car up with gas. Just to clarify for any confused British readers, we didn't fill our car with gas – that would have been idiotic – we filled it with petrol.

The reason I mention this particular petrol/gas stop is that Louie's Quickstop offered a free hot dog and soda with every $5 purchase. Louie was one generous man, so seeing as we filled Josephine's tank, we both ate and drank for free.

We chatted to Mary, the lady behind the counter, and she was mightily impressed by the progress of our road trip.

'Gee, you boys really driven all the way from New York City?' she said.

'We sure have. But we're not even halfway to California yet.'

'The furthest I've ever been is Tennessee.'

She gazed out of the window with a mixture of sadness and wonder in her eyes. Mary was at least 50 years old and her life experiences were all based within a 200 mile radius of Louie's Quickstop. It did make us appreciate just how incredibly lucky we were to be able to have the opportunity to go on such an adventure.

But Mary was evidently extremely happy. And why wouldn't she be? She got to witness the excited faces of customers being offered free hot dogs and sodas all day.

We arrived in New Orleans via some of the most ambitious driving manoeuvres ever attempted. Mark was at the wheel, and how we made it to the hostel in one piece I will never know. He left a trail of startled and angry motorists in his wake.

India House was a bohemian style hostel on the edge of the city. It had a welcoming feel to it with the walls plastered with photos of other backpackers enjoying life at the hostel and, strangely, a parachute suspended from the ceiling.

I had another bad phone conversation with Rachel just after lunch.

My justification for going to America without Rachel had always been that it was something that I needed to do with Mark. We had already committed to it before Rachel and I got together and I didn't want to let him down. But as Mark's trip would be coming to an end in January, it seemed selfish of me to stubbornly stay in America when there was no real reason for me to remain there instead of being with her.

I didn't see any way that our relationship could survive many more months of these phone calls, and it seemed inevitable that sooner or later we would drift an irreversible distance apart.

I then thought about the possibility of Rachel coming to America. It had never crossed my mind before. It had always been my thing, and Rachel had never expressed any interest in coming. But I knew she liked the idea of travelling, and maybe the perfect solution – the only solution – would be if the two of us continued this adventure together once Mark had flown home.

And if Rachel didn't like the idea of travelling with me in America, maybe I could at least persuade her to come over for a brief holiday, just so that we could see each other for a little while and help give our relationship a fighting chance.

After leaving our bags at the hostel, Mark and I hit the town and started drinking at 3.30pm.

Our initial impression was that New Orleans was full of weirdos. Brilliant weirdos, but weirdos nonetheless. There were buskers, drag queens, beggars, decorated cars, tap-dancing children, gospel singers, drunks, preachers and some people creatively playing many of those roles at once. It was just a normal Saturday in November, but it felt like it was the middle of Mardi Gras.

New Orleans is one of only a few places in the United States where it is legal to drink alcohol in a public street. This helps give the city – and particularly the popular French Quarter – a real carnival feel. We took full advantage of this law and spent several hours drinking beers on the streets of the French Quarter – New Orleans' oldest neighbourhood – and soaking up the vibes from this crazy and incredible city. We staggered back to the hostel, assuming that it was way past midnight. It was 8.30pm.

We played a drunken game of Trivial Pursuit in the hostel lounge (do we know how to party or what?) and then called it a night.

Our sleep was disturbed many times by our sociable roommates. There was the Israeli guy who woke us up when he came to bed to tell us of his plan to hire a gorilla costume and jump out on people in New York City for fun. We humoured him and told him this was a really, really brilliant idea and he should definitely do it and what a great idea and please leave us the hell alone. Then there was the Australian couple that decided to make-out in their single bunk bed in a 12-bed dormitory, seemingly oblivious to those around them. There were also the two American college boys who talked incessantly and very loudly about their friend 'Pete from Detroit' for two hours. By the end of the conversation I felt like I wanted to meet Pete from Detroit and punch his fucking head in. All of this was set to a backdrop of the loudest snoring you have ever heard from the large Mexican chap in the corner who happily slept through all the activity around him. It made sleeping outside the jail seem relaxing.

The man running the hostel offered to provide a cooked breakfast for an additional charge. He told us that he liked to experiment with his ingredients, so we took this to mean that he was an accomplished chef. We could not have been more wrong.

He served us his 'India House Special', which was an omelette, served with strawberries, cream and some strong liquor poured all over it. It was absolutely revolting but we smiled and told him we thought he was definitely onto something with his ambitious flavour combinations.

We spent the next day exploring New Orleans's cultural side including the Lower Garden District and the Warehouse District. We returned to the hostel late afternoon with the intention of having a quick shower and then heading back out, but that plan didn't quite materialise.

Instead we started chatting to some of the other hostel residents. We met Amber from Australia, who was on her way to Nashville to try and begin a career as a professional singer. She reminded me a lot of Rachel – although Rachel is not Australian and is certainly not the most naturally gifted singer, having been thrown out of her primary school choir for being too flat. But there was something about her that got me thinking about Rachel even more. I decided I would definitely ask her to come out to America.

As well as Amber, we chatted to Americans, Canadians, Scots, Italians and a mad Bulgarian who took an instant liking to me because I had once been skiing in Bulgaria and happened to mention the town of Plovdiv, where one of the airports is located, and coincidentally where he happened to live.

'I can't believe you know Plovdiv,' he said, giving me a bear hug. 'In all my travels in all of the world, you are the only person who has heard of anywhere in Bulgaria that isn't the capital Sofia. And most people haven't even heard of Sofia.' He smiled at me for the rest of the night. I wished I had never mentioned Plovdiv.

We met the Mexican snorer who was much nicer (and quieter) awake than asleep. We played cards and many variations of different drinking games from around the world. We chatted to the owner about American politics for several hours and I realised I knew more than I thought I did. Although, that might have just been the beer talking. It was 5.30am when we eventually made it back to the dormitory. The Mexican ensured we didn't get any sleep.

The owner tried to encourage us to try another of his breakfast specialities the following morning but we made our excuses and checked out of the hostel. Mark drove the first shift as I dozed in the passenger seat, enjoying fleeting glances of the stunning Louisiana bayous as we continued west.

I had heard and read a lot about po' boys. They seemed to be the food of choice in the Deep South in American road movies and travelogues. The name carries with it an air of mystery and intrigue. It turns out a po' boy is a sandwich. A sandwich made using French-style baguettes, but still just a sandwich.

We ate a roast beef po' boy, which was delicious but hardly revolutionary, and drove into Texas.

Our plan was to be in California in time for Christmas, where we would stay at my aunt and uncle's ranch in Petaluma – north of San Francisco – for a few weeks, to look after the place while they were in the UK. Mark would then head home at the beginning of January.

Having taken the decision to do this trip independently from Rachel, I now very much wanted her to be a part of it. I hatched a plan to persuade her to come and join us at the ranch for Christmas, and then potentially persuade her to stay longer. We stopped for a coffee in Sour Lake, Texas and I excitedly called her from a payphone.

'Why don't you come over to Petaluma for Christmas?' I said.

'No, I can't. You'll be doing your own thing with Mark.'

'He won't mind. He'll be leaving California soon after Christmas anyway.'

'It's a long way to come just for Christmas. I can't afford it.'

'Come for longer then. You and I can continue the road trip together.'

'Very funny.'

'I'm not joking. Why not?'

'Because this is your thing. The whole point was that you wanted to go and have this trip with Mark.'

'But I've done my trip with Mark now. He'll be going home. It would be great to do the next leg of the journey with you.'

'Hmph.'

'What does hmph mean?'

'Hmph.'

'Why are you saying that?'

'I'm just thinking.'

'About what?'

'You don't want me out there with you.'

'Of course I do. I'd love you to come and be out here with me.'

'Hmph,' she said again.

'Please stop saying that. Will you at least think about it?'

'Ok,' she said. 'I'll think about it.'

14

I was behind the wheel when we reached Houston just after nightfall. The dramatic city skyline rose from nowhere against an ominous looking sky. We were approaching the city on a four lane interstate at the height of rush-hour.

We saw the rain approaching a few seconds before it hit us, as it pounded off the asphalt up ahead (see, I'm getting with the lingo. It was tarmac really). I intuitively went to switch on the wipers in preparation, forgetting that they didn't work. As the rain hit us the visibility was reduced to zero in a split second. It was like we had driven into a carwash. But without those big blue brushes. I was in the middle lane and it was too dangerous to stop suddenly, but it was even more dangerous to keep going.

I instinctively wound down the window and stuck my head out, squinting into the rain to try and keep my eyes on the road. It was surprisingly effective. My hangover and lack of sleep from the night before had been lingering, but I was instantly revitalised. The wind and rain attacked my face like an extreme form of acupuncture. It is no wonder dogs enjoy sticking their heads out car windows so much. It was incredibly invigorating. Combined with the excitement I felt about the possibility of Rachel coming to America, I had never felt more alive.

'Are you ok?' shouted Mark from the passenger seat.

'Yeah! This is awesome! Houston, baby!'

'Can you see the road?'

'Yes. Well, I can see this half. Why don't you stick your head out your window and check I'm ok that side?'

'Er, ok.'

So we drove the final few miles into Houston with our heads out each window, like a pair of excited dogs. I managed to steer across to the slow lane and we trundled along until we were off the interstate and able to pull over to wait for the rain to stop.

We were heading to the home of another of Mark's distant relatives. This was the sister-in-law of the wife of Mark's mum's hairdresser's second-cousin (twice removed). She was practically his next-of-kin.

Maya and her family lived in an upmarket suburb of Houston called Sugar Land. They had three teenage children and lived in a big house with a swimming pool, hot tub and a basketball hoop above the garage door.

After meeting the family and having a tour of the house, Maya asked us what we would like to do.

'Something to eat? A beer? Bed?' she said.

It was 10.30pm. Mark and I looked at each other and then at the swimming pool and the pouring rain outside.

'Would it be ok to have a quick swim?' asked Mark.

'Sure, why not?' said Maya, slightly taken aback.

Neither of us had stayed at a house with a swimming pool before and we were eager to make the most of it. The rain and the darkness only added to our excitement. It was a warm evening (considering it was November), and the three teenage children all joined us in the pool too.

We followed this with a quick late night game of basketball against the children. Mark and I gained some respect by somehow whooping their American asses in a hoop-off (I'm not sure if that's the correct terminology), despite not having picked up a basketball since school.

We spent the next four days in Sugar Land, trapped inside some bizarre American sitcom. We did our own thing during the daytime while the children were at school and the parents were at work, then we all met up again in the evenings to eat dinner, play computer games, swim in the pool and shoot hoops.

We spent a day at NASA's Space Center and, unsurprisingly, the Americans had done a brilliant job of creating an immensely fun and interesting tourist attraction. We both left feeling stupidly giddy about space.

On another day we visited the wonderful Brazos Bend State Park. The park is only a few miles from Sugar Land and is home to a rich variety of plants and animals set in a mixture of woodland and marshland. But Brazos Bend is most famous for its large population of alligators, with some reported to be in excess of 10ft long. The largest we saw was about 3 ft, but it was still a thrill to see those prehistoric eyes emerging from the swampy water.

Mark and I were both big fans of the country singer Glen Campbell. Sugar Land is only an hour from Galveston on the Gulf Coast of Texas, and Galveston is the city where Glen Campbell so beautifully sang about leaving his girl as he set off for war.

'Galveston, oh, Galveston
I still hear your seawinds blowing
I still see her dark eyes glowing
She was twenty one, when I left Galveston'

American place names always sound wonderful in songs. If you replace the word *Galveston* with *Southampton* – Great Britain's geographically equivalent port at the southern tip of the country – it doesn't quite have the same effect.

A couple of years previously, Glen Campbell came to our home town of Northampton (127 miles from SOUTHampton and far from any seawinds blowing) as part of his UK tour. He played at the town's theatre in the early evening and then a second show later that night – such was the demand for tickets.

Mark and I had seats for his earlier performance. We were the youngest in the audience by at least 40 years. It was in a theatre, rather than a music venue, because the majority of the audience were incapable of standing for any length of time.

We went to play snooker afterwards and, after a couple of beers, I decided I should have bought a programme for posterity. We returned to the theatre and the lady at the desk told us to pop into the auditorium where we could purchase a programme from an usher. We opened one of the doors on the upper tier and crept in. Glen was mid *Wichita Lineman* and there were a couple of empty seats in a box to our right. It would have been rude not to sit down and listen. Then no sooner had *Wichita Lineman* finished than he had launched into *Both Sides Now* so we felt a duty to sit and watch this too. We ended up watching the remainder of his set, which was a full 40 minutes. He played a few different songs to those he had played earlier and he was every bit as good, and we felt every bit as young. I did buy a programme on the way out.

We drove down to Galveston during our stay in Sugar Land. Glen Campbell was right; it sure was windy. He had neglected to mention the jellyfish and hypodermic needles scattered along the beach, though. After an enjoyable lunch at a cafe on The Strand, we headed back to Sugar Land for more swimming, hot-tubbing and basketball.

Just days before our visit, the family had sold their grand piano, and purchased a giant flat-screen television instead. But it was missing a games console. After several days of persuasion, Maya finally relented and allowed the children to buy the latest Nintendo machine. Mark and I squashed into the back of a top of the range Toyota Land Cruiser alongside the teenage son, with the two girls up front – the eldest, just 16, had only recently acquired her licence. We drove to Circuit City at ridiculous speeds, with a Limp Bizkit track blaring out of the speakers at full blast. This was the scene in the American high-school films that usually ends in disaster. I squashed my head against the window in the back and closed my eyes, genuinely feeling like this idyllic life was going to come to an abrupt end for all of us.

This was Sugar Land, though. They were the perfect American family and this trip was never going to end badly. Instead, we bought the Nintendo plus a few games, drove home and played *Blitz* on the giant TV until Maya told the kids it was time for bed. Then Mark and I muted the television and continued to play until it was light outside.

Mark and I were teased incessantly about our English accents during our time in Sugar Land. But we got our revenge by regularly beating the children at basketball and Nintendo. We laughed together about the curiosities of English and American phrases, and talked about pants and waistcoats and wife-beaters.

The time had come for us to leave. Our days as part of our American sitcom had been an absolute pleasure but we were beginning to feel way too comfortable. Life was too easy. We had forgotten what it was like to try and find somewhere to sleep at night, we had forgotten what it was like to wee in a bush, and we had forgotten what bologna sandwiches tasted like.

Maya packed us a hamper of goodies to take with us. This included a 2kg bag of raisins. We'd be shitting those out for a fortnight. We said our goodbyes and hit the road.

We were heading for Austin, the state's capital. We stopped briefly in Ellinger – population about 3. The main street consisted of a single block of shops. The butcher/convenience store had a hand-written sign in the window advertising:

Rabbits – live or dressed.

It struck me as strange that, depending on your mood or requirements, you could either buy a rabbit as dinner or to keep as a pet. I suppose in a one block town, the businesses needed to try to be versatile. Despite the shop's resourcefulness, it appeared to have been closed for many years. So we couldn't buy ourselves a pet. Or lunch.

Like Memphis, Austin is also famous for its music, and this was evident as we walked down Sixth Street, past bar upon bar with live bands performing in the middle of the afternoon. At this point we should have stepped inside the first establishment we came across and started another day long bar crawl. But we both felt ridiculously tired and not in the mood for another big drinking session. Staying up all night playing Nintendo had certainly not helped.

Instead of a bar crawl listening to awesome bands, we walked up to the capitol and watched a school Christmas carol concert instead. It was December 1st. The carol concert was mildly enjoyable, but they weren't the most tuneful of school choirs and just when we thought it was drawing to a close, out came the recorders. I hate recorders. There is only one thing in the world more painful to the ears than a badly played recorder, and that is many badly played recorders.

'Oh god, let's get out of here,' I whispered to Mark as the screeching began.

'Let's go,' said Mark. 'My ears are bleeding. Although, we must remember to be grateful for recorders. Remember the time that they saved our lives?'

'Of course I do. How could I forget?'

Mark's house was located about a mile away from our primary school. On Mondays when I went to play at his house we used to walk home, and, if the weather was nice, we would take a shortcut across the fields. It shaved a few precious minutes off walking the road way, allowing extra time to play football, Subbuteo, or *Kick Off* on the Commodore Amiga.

One evening, we were taking this shortcut and we reached the border between two fields. There was a fence with a stile over it, then a two metre width of grass and then another fence with a stile. We were just about to climb the second stile when we looked up to see that all the cows in the field had wandered over and were encircling the stile; their eyes all focused intently on us.

'Shoo!' I shouted, clapping my hands

The cows just wandered closer until they were right against the stile forcing us back into the gap between the two fences.

Accepting defeat, we turned to head back to the road and noticed that all of the cows in the field we had just walked through – the cows that had been happily grazing and oblivious to our presence only moments before – suddenly wanted to see what all the fuss was about and had closed ranks behind us.

We were stuck.

There was no way for us to get past the herd of cows in front of us, and no way to get through the herd behind. I should probably add at this point that we were nine years old. Just in case you are picturing in your head two teenage boys being scared by some curious cows. Admittedly, even nine year olds shouldn't necessarily be scared of cows, but there were a huge number of them and they were extremely lively and inquisitive.

We started shouting at them, but they didn't budge. We clapped our hands louder and tried to scare them away. They just stared at us blankly. I then remembered that Monday was recorder practice day. Mark and I were both armed with recorders in our school bags – one of the world's most dangerous weapons. We weren't going to hit the cows with them, you understand. We were going to play the recorders.

Badly. We hoped it would have the opposite effect of the Pied Piper of Hamelin and they would scarper, rather than follow us.

We blew those recorders like our lives depended on it. By this point we had been trapped in between those fences for almost half an hour. The cows just continued to stare. It was almost as though they were hypnotised by our playing. The screeching of the recorders did not have the desired effect that we were hoping for, but what we didn't realise was that the ear-piercing noise was unwittingly acting as a distress signal.

We soon heard the tinkle of a bell, followed by lots of shouting and we looked up to see Mark's mum cycling through the muddy field towards us on her bicycle. The bike was a dark blue, single speed granny bike, with a wicker basket on the front. It was not designed for anything but paved roads, but that didn't stop Mark's mum ploughing on through. The cows parted like the Red Sea as she blazed a trail towards us.

She had been concerned when we were so late back from school and had set out to look for us when she heard the stricken cries of our recorders.

It felt like we had been rescued from certain death on a remote island. When in fact we had been rescued from a half hour stand-off in a field by some cattle.

We always took the road route home after that, and I have maintained a modicum of respect for recorders ever since.

We topped up Josephine's parking meter and spent several more hours that afternoon in Austin, drinking coffee in a cafe on Sixth Street and listening to the merged sounds of several bands from the neighbouring bars. After our third cup, we decided that sleep and an early night would be impossible, so headed out of town and parked up outside a cinema.

We watched a Ben Affleck film called *Bounce*, simply because every single time we had turned on a television in a motel room, we had seen an advert for the film. We were so familiar with the trailer that we could recite it word for word. There was a particular line in the trailer when Ben Affleck is discussing his relationship with Gwyneth Paltrow's character. He says, *'I'm more worried that she's gonna get tired of me'.* This was Mark's favourite line. He had nailed his rendition of it. So much so, that when he repeated it several times a day in the front of Josephine, it felt like I was sitting alongside Ben Affleck.

So we sat in the cinema, eagerly awaiting that scene, just so I could look over at Mark and smile that Ben had said his line. Only Ben Affleck didn't say the bloody line. In fact, the entire scene that formed one of the central parts of the trailer was not even included in the film.

As we walked out of the cinema screening feeling disgusted with Ben Affleck for denying us our only reason for seeing the film, we realised that the person to whom you show your tickets was positioned at a barrier between the cinema screens and the ticket office. There was nothing to stop us just walking into another screening of a different film. We did feel slightly guilty, but the small fortune we had spent on popcorn and soda made us feel less so. Plus we felt like Ben Affleck had short-changed us in the last film, so in some ways we were entitled to watch another. We watched a film with Kevin Spacey (he was starring in the film, not sitting alongside us). It was pretty good, and having not seen any trailers for it, we didn't feel cheated.

The film finished at midnight, by which point we were one of the last remaining cars in the car park. Rather than driving off to find a rest area, we crawled into our sleeping bags in the back of Josephine.

As I was lying there in the darkness, I remembered another of Ben Affleck's lines from the trailer. This one did make the final edit. In the scene, Ben's character is feeling upset that he doesn't have a *'last call of the day'* – someone to phone in the evening before bed to say goodnight to. It made me desperately want a last call, too. Because of the time difference, calling Rachel before bed would be about 5am her time. She's never at her best when woken at 5am. I had continued to pursue the thought of her coming to America, and it seemed like she was warming to the idea. I was very hopeful that she was going to fly out to San Francisco at Christmas and that we could potentially even drive Josephine back to New York together. And if she was there in America with me, I wouldn't need that last call of the day.

We were woken in the night by an ominous tapping and a flashlight blazing through the window. I could see the familiar outline of a policeman's badge glinting through the partially steamed up window.

'Here we go again,' I muttered to Mark. 'I thought it was a bit optimistic that we'd get a full night's sleep here.'

I wound down the window.

'Can I ask what you boys are doing here?' he said, scanning the car with his flashlight.

'I'm sorry, Officer, I know we probably shouldn't be sleeping here. We're on a road trip and we went to the cinema last night and we were too tired to drive anywhere so thought we would get a few hours sleep here.'

'Very sensible. You don't want to be driving when you're tired.'

'No, definitely not,' I said, expecting him to follow this up with some snide remark that required us to drive someplace else.

'Ok, you sleep well then,' he said, and climbed back into his patrol car and drove off.

'Wow, I bloody love Texas,' said Mark from the back seat.

15

Early the next morning we drove to Fredericksburg, with its main street so ridiculously wide it spans three time zones. Probably. We tried to cross it but got exhausted halfway so turned back.

We didn't stay in town long because we had been lured by the sound of Enchanted Rock State Park a few miles up the road. After our frustration with the 'points of interest' on the Natchez Trace Parkway, we prepared ourselves to expect a massive disappointment. We assumed we would reach the park, only to be presented with a sign that said:

'The enchanted rock has long since eroded away, but the memories still remain.'

Not only did Enchanted Rock actually exist, it exceeded all of our expectations.

Enchanted Rock is basically a smaller version of Australia's Uluru (Ayers Rock). That's not to say it's any less impressive. If anything, I would say that Enchanted Rock is even better. Texas is famous for being flat. It's an amazingly diverse state, but the terrain, as a whole, is fairly featureless. In most parts of Texas you can turn 360 degrees and see a flat horizon in every direction. That is partly what makes Enchanted Rock so special.

It genuinely was one of the most beautiful things I had ever seen. We spent a few hours walking its perimeter and then climbed up onto its summit. The surroundings of the rock were an oasis of streams, trees and cacti, with an abundance of wildlife too. The park is said to contain over 500 species of plant. We also saw lizards, birds of prey, squirrels and deer. It sounds corny but it really was like a little piece of paradise in the middle of the Texan desert.

We drove on towards San Angelo, passing through a series of towns that had lazily just been named after random people: Brady, Vick, Rowena, Miles and Melvin. I can imagine the early settlers to these towns declaring:

'I hereby declare this town called Melvin.'

'But that's your name, Melvin,' said Brady.

'Damn right,' said Melvin.

'Fine, well I'm naming the area around my house Brady.'

'And the land up near my place is now called Rowena,' said Rowena.

We then saw a signpost to a town called Veribest. Whoever created this town was either too ashamed of their name, or they wanted something that would trump whatever names sprang up around it.

Shortly after passing through Rowena, we caused our first roadkill. I say 'caused' but there was nothing we could have done about it. We had avoided many encounters so far with rabbits, deer, foxes and cattle, but this was something we had not anticipated. We somehow killed a flying bird.

We were driving along a completely deserted stretch of road, straight as an arrow, with the horizon visible in every direction. This bird – let's call it a blackbird, I'm not very good at birds – appeared to dive-bomb Josephine from above and struck the front of her with huge force. Mark was driving, and despite this not being his fault, I decided to add it onto his tally. 2-2 in the Josephine Destruction World Series, after he claimed I was responsible for Josephine's windscreen wiper malfunction.

There was no sign of the bird on the carriageway behind us in the rear-view mirror, but when we pulled over on the empty highway and walked around to the front of the car, the back end of the bird was protruding out of the engine grill, and the rest of its body was well and truly stuck inside.

'That's disgusting,' I said.

'Poor bird. How the hell did it fly into us on this empty stretch of road?'

'Maybe we interrupted its usual flight path. It's not as if it is likely to encounter much traffic along this road.'

'Or perhaps it thought Josephine was prey?'

'I don't think birds are known as being a threat to rusty shitmobiles.'

'Well who is going to be the one to remove it then?'

'Not me. You're the one who drove into it.'

'I didn't drive into it. It flew into me.'

'Either way, it was nothing to do with me. You should be the one to pull it out.'

'I'm not touching it.'

'Fine. Let's leave it then.'

'Fine.'

'Don't they often have animal heads on the front of cars in the Wild West anyway?' I said, as we climbed back into Josephine.

'You mean like bullhorns?'

'Yeah.'

'You realise people actually attach those to their vehicles deliberately. They are not left over from when people accidentally crashed into a cow.'

'Yeah, I know that. I was just saying.'

'Right.'

'Well at least we're sort of fitting in with the locals,' I said.

'Er, right. Because the limp back-end of a bird sticking out of the grill is pretty much the same as a huge set of horns, is it?'

'Almost identical,' I laughed. 'We'll be the envy of all the locals.'

Llano was a pretty town on the banks of the Llano River. We thought we would treat ourselves to some proper Texan food. We had eaten well in Texas – as all Texans do – but it had mostly been delicious home-cooked food in Sugar Land (and predominantly raisins since), not proper Texan food. We needed barbeque.

We stopped at Lairds BBQ (which we soon renamed Lards) with high-hopes. There were no other customers but the owner seemed like a nice guy and we eagerly ordered two barbequed pork rolls and sat, lips salivating at the thought of proper barbequed food. A series of bizarre noises, coughs and grunts came from the kitchen and we were quickly presented with two of the most disgusting looking, and foul tasting, culinary creations we had ever tasted. There was no meat inside, just hot jellied fat. I assume that they had run out of meat, and rather than turn us away, heated up some fatty off-cuts for us instead. I think the noises from the kitchen were probably to disguise the sound of the microwave.

'Everything ok?' asked the server.

'Mmmm, delicious thank you,' we both said in our pathetically reserved British way.

We managed a quarter of our roll each before wrapping the remainder in a napkin and discreetly disposing of it in the bin.

'Thank you. You come again,' he called after us.

'Thanks. We sure will,' we said.

If civilisation was to end and Lards BBQ was the only place left in the world with any food, I still wouldn't visit there again.

By the time we reached the outskirts of San Angelo, the bird had thankfully detached itself from the front of Josephine. I don't mean to suggest that it had made a miraculous recovery and somehow escaped. It had dropped off somewhere along the road between Llano and San Angelo and Josephine was no longer able to proudly display her trophy.

Still ravenous after our failed lunch, we bought some bread and pâté from a grocery store and found a rest area on a quiet back road just outside Sterling City.

'This pâté looks a bit weird,' said Mark, spreading some onto a piece of bread.

'It does. It's a really weird texture,' I said, picking up the packet, which was one of those orange plastic sausage-shaped things.

'What type of pâté is it?' said Mark.

'Oh. Apparently it's not pâté. It's sausage meat.'

'Sausage meat?'

'Yes. It says, *'this product must be cooked thoroughly before consumption.'*'

'Oh bollocks.'

'We've not had the best luck with food today.'

'Looks like it's a bread sandwich for dinner then.'

'I think I'll join you,' I said, taking a slice of bread and sandwiching it between two other pieces of bread.

A few years ago, the Royal Society of Chemistry conducted a scientific study to try to find Britain's cheapest meal. Their results concluded that a toast sandwich claimed this honour.

The humble toast sandwich can even be traced back as far as 1861 when Isabella Beeton included a recipe in her *Book of Household Management.* Two pieces of bread are spread with butter, salt and pepper is added to taste, and then each slice is placed either side of a piece of toast.

I have had a toast sandwich before and it is surprisingly good. The crunch of the toast gives the sandwich a really nice texture and it feels like a lot more than the sum of its parts. As for being the cheapest meal... surely our bread sandwich is much cheaper? We didn't even require the use of a toaster, let alone salt, pepper and butter.

Anyway, we had a couple of bread sandwiches each followed by a massive handful of Maya's raisins – Michelin starred fare compared to the pork roll we had for lunch – and we had an early night in a freezing cold Texas rest area.

16

We woke in the morning to find a couple of inches of snow. In Texas. This seemed highly unusual. We fired up the engine and defrosted our hands on Josephine's heaters and headed off in search of breakfast.

The City Café in Sterling City was an absolute gem. It was just how I pictured a café in small town America would be. It wasn't even 7am, yet the place was open and fairly busy and there were several pairs of antlers mounted on the wall. The waitress had poured us both a coffee before we even sat down. The sign outside boasted the *'biggest pancakes in Texas'* so it would have been foolish to order anything different.

'Do you get snow in Sterling City often?' I asked the waitress when she had taken our order.

'First time I've seen any in about 10 years I'd say,' she said.

'Wow.'

'Did you hear that some guy died outside a burger bar just up the road last night?' she said.

'No way. How did that happen?'

'I think he musta got drunk or somethin' and then passed out in the snow. Some folks just found him laying there dead this morning.'

'That's awful.'

'You boys must just be lucky to pass through Texas during the snow.'

'Or unlucky,' said Mark. 'We were sleeping in our car last night.'

'No frickin way! Yous lucky you didn't die, too.'

'Yes, very. That's why we were here so early.'

'Well you came to the right place. Our pancakes will sort you out. That I promise.'

The pancakes didn't disappoint. They were beasts the size of manhole covers, spilling over the sides of the plates onto the table. If you could eat three of them they were free, and both Mark and I did consider attempting it but we knew it was a battle we couldn't win. Only a small handful of people had ever successfully completed the challenge, including a 90 year old lady who resolutely sat there and ate them for an entire day.

'Sterling City seems like a nice place to live,' I said, as the waitress cleared our plates away.

'It's alright, I suppose. I didn't plan on livin' here this long, but then I got married and here I am.'

'Have you been working at City Café long?'

'Since just after I got married. I figured if I was going to wait on one, I might as well wait on a whole bunch of people and at least get paid to do it.'

We finished our pancakes and coffee and by the time we returned to Josephine, most of the snow from the road had melted. Soon after leaving Sterling City, we joined Route 176 through the hamlets of Lenorah and Tarzan and into New Mexico.

We stopped for gas in Artesia, New Mexico and I phoned Rachel.

'I've got some news,' she said, after we had been chatting for a while.

'What is it?'

'I'm moving to Ireland.'

'You're what? What do you mean you're moving to Ireland?'

'I've decided to move to Ireland for a few months. I'm going to live with my cousin just outside Dublin.'

'What?... why?.... when did you decide that?'

'Just this week. I've been thinking about what to do. I can't just carry on as normal here in Northampton while you are in America. It's really getting me down so I've decided I need a change.'

'That's why you should come to America.'

'I did think about it a lot. But America is your thing. I would just feel I was holding you back.'

'You wouldn't be holding me back from anything. I want you to come.'

'I know. But it doesn't feel right to just gatecrash your adventure.'

'You wouldn't be gatecra…'

'…anyway, my flight is booked and I've got a job in Dublin starting next week.'

'A job? How did you sort that so quickly?'

'It's just an admin job that I got through an agency. I start on Monday.'

I didn't know what to say. I had felt sure I had almost convinced Rachel to come out to America with me, and now not only was that not going to happen, but she was moving to a different country.

'What does this mean for us?' I said.

'Nothing. I'm not moving away forever. You're in America. I'll be in Ireland. When you get back then I'll probably come back from Ireland too and then we can be together.'

I didn't like her use of the word 'probably.'

'So that's that then?' I said.

'Don't be like that,' she said. 'If it wasn't for the fact that Mark's visa application failed then you would be with him for much longer anyway.'

'Yes, but…'

'You can't just expect me to come over and fill Mark's place once he's gone.'

'It's not like that.'

'Well, that's what it feels like.'

'Will there be a phone at your cousin's house so I can at least still talk to you?'

'Of course. If you give me a call over the weekend I'll give you all the details. I love you.'

'I love you, too.'

Our visit to Roswell, New Mexico turned out to be one of the biggest disappointments of the entire trip. Roswell is the site in which a United States Air Force surveillance balloon crash landed in the desert in 1947, prompting claims that continue today that it was in fact an extraterrestrial spaceship. Roswell promised so much, although I think we both secretly knew it would be shit. The entire town is built on conspiracy theories about government cover-ups and people looking to make money out of creating tenuous links with UFOs. They even have a UFO shaped McDonald's.

To be honest, my phone conversation with Rachel had put me in the most horrendous mood and Roswell could have had ten UFOs with actual real-life aliens walking the streets and I would still have thought it was overrated.

We checked into a motel which, if we had been used to high-standards, would have been considered a public health risk. However, our standards were somewhat lower, and after a couple of nights in the cold of Josephine, the lumpy smelly motel bed felt like a night at The Ritz.

We went off in search of food and found a small restaurant where we ate a 'Mexican Combo', which was basically rank mince, served three ways. All three ways were pretty much identical, and all were revolting.

From Roswell we drove to Picacho, New Mexico, hoping it would be some strange surreal Pokémon world. But it was just a farm.

We continued onwards to the town of Lincoln where we spent a couple of hours exploring its beautifully preserved historic district, including the Old Lincoln County Courthouse and Jail where Billy the Kid was imprisoned and later escaped.

It had been almost an hour since we had seen any form of civilisation. The road stretched endlessly ahead with dusty desert as far as the horizon on both sides of us. According to our map, it would likely be at least another hour before we reached the next town. It was therefore a surprise to find, miles from anywhere, a small golf course. There was not a car in the car park and the clubhouse was closed up. When I say clubhouse, I mean a small wooden shed, and by car park I mean a patch of gravel along the side of the road. There was a small handwritten sign instructing golfers to post their green fee ($5) through the letterbox, and to take a rubber mat to play all their shots off.

'Why do we need to take a mat?' I asked.

'To protect the grass, I guess,' said Mark.

'Really? What sort of a golf course is so protective over its grass that you can't actually hit the ball off it?'

'This one?'

We had bought two golf clubs – a 9 iron and a sand wedge – at a thrift store in New Orleans. I'm not sure why, but we thought they might be fun to use at some point while travelling, and damn, it turned out we were right.

It quickly became apparent what the mats were for. Far from being used to protect the grass, they were to be used because there wasn't any grass. This was New Mexico. This was the desert. Of course there wouldn't be any grass, unless it was an extremely upmarket golf course with extensive sprinkler systems, and this was certainly not such a course.

The fairways were indistinguishable from the surrounding terrain; hard, compacted, cracked dirt, scattered with rocks and thorny shrubs. The course did have small putting greens which were watered sporadically by sprinklers. This resulted in a patch of ground made up of a kaleidoscope of different shades of green depending on how far away the grass grew from the sprinkler.

The rubber mat that we carried around was to place the ball on, to make it marginally easier than hitting the ball directly off the dirt. As we didn't have a putter, we couldn't use the greens anyway.

Strategically placed signs along the fairways asked players to *'please replace divots'*. As Americans are not known for their grasp of irony, we didn't know if this sign was serious or not. Does a cloud of dry dust, or a scattering of stones count as a divot?

We managed four of the nine holes, before admitting defeat. We stuck $5 through the letterbox (seeing as we played fewer than half the holes), and left the course admiring the ingenuity of the person who created a self-service golf course in the middle of the New Mexico desert.

Speaking of entrepreneurs in the New Mexico desert, they don't come much better than Clyde Norman. Clyde Norman was a WWI veteran from Texas who had high hopes of striking it rich with a gold mine in New Mexico. When this didn't work out to be as lucrative as he planned, he started making apple pies instead. His home was situated on US 60 – the first coast-to-coast road across the USA – which meant there was always plenty of passing traffic. Word quickly spread about his pies to the extent that the settlement soon became known as Pie Town.

Mr Norman eventually sold the business to a cowboy named Harmon L. Craig who realised the potential of the pies, and Pie Town continues to attract pie lovers from all over to this day. They even host an annual Pie Festival in September.

By the time we reached Pie Town, the store and café had sadly closed for the day and we were forced to leave Pie Town pieless.

We found a motel in Quemado, New Mexico (population 228), where the lady proudly told us we had bagged the very last room.

'No offence, but what are so many people doing in Quemado in December?' I asked.

'Huntin' season,' she said.

'What are they hunting?'

'All sorts. Elk mostly.'

The television had two and a half channels, none of which showed us anything worth watching so we bought a sandwich and a beer in the café full of hunters next door and had an early night.

West of Socorro, the New Mexico landscape had started to look greener and less arid. At Pie Town, we had crossed the Continental Divide and the terrain took on a more rugged form, with occasional copses of trees punctuating the area.

We stopped by one of these copses to have a wee. Mark went to the bush closest to the road and I ventured to a tree a little further into the scrub.

'Where are you off to?' said Mark. 'What's wrong with this bush?'

'I'm not taking any chances going for a wee next to you.'

'What do you mean?'

'Remember that under-10s football tournament we played in?'

'You're not still going on about that, are you?'

Mark and I played football together from the age of eight. Our team was taking part in a tournament in a nearby town. We arrived at the pitch a few minutes before our first match was scheduled and all of the team rushed over to the nearby hedge to have our customary pre-match wee before kickoff.

I had taken my place by the hedge next to Mark. While we were doing our business I asked him what he thought our chances were against Sunnyside United Under 10s.

'I reckon we're gonna stuff 'em,' he said.

As he spoke to me he turned to face me. He was still mid-stream at the time and proceeded to wee all over my shorts and legs as he was chatting. It was a couple of seconds before he realised what he was doing, by which point my shorts were completely sodden.

'WHAT HAVE YOU DONE?' I shouted.

'Oops. Sorry,' he said.

The referee had blown his whistle and called for the two teams to come onto the pitch. There was no way I could play a match in a pair of urine-soaked shorts. Thankfully, Mark's dad – our team manager – came to the rescue and let me borrow a pair of his shorts while we hung mine on the car aerial to dry. They were far too big for me and made me look like I was wearing a skirt, but thankfully we still stuffed Sunnyside United Under 10s 4-0.

I am not one for holding a grudge, but I now always keep my distance from Mark when going to the toilet.

17

The playlist for local radio stations in the USA is incredibly short. We listened to the same cycle of a dozen or so songs on a continuous loop for weeks on end. Such was the limited range of the radio masts for each station, that soon after leaving a town the radio would crackle and we would have to tune it to another local station. This would then be adequate for a few more miles before losing its signal again. Because of the vast number of local radio stations, there was always the likelihood that once we had tuned to a new station it would play a song that we had only recently heard on another station. One particular song that we heard several times a day was called *There Is No Arizona* by Jamie O'Neal.

We knew the lyrics off by heart and belted out the chorus each time we heard it. It was a proper country power-ballad, if such a song genre exists.

'There is no Arizona
No Painted Desert, no Sedona
If there was a Grand Canyon
She could fill it up with the lies he's told her
But they don't exist, those dreams he sold her
She'll wake up and find
There is no Arizona'

We heard the song so many times that we almost believed that there was no Arizona. As we crossed the state line from New Mexico I looked at the welcome sign and then to Mark.

'I knew it!' I said. 'The lying cow.'

From Springerville – where we ate two Big Macs each (I had long since broken my pact to not visit the golden arches) and used the world's slowest internet at the town library – we headed north on route 191 through St Johns and Sanders and into the Hopi Reservation. The Hopi Reservation forms a part of the surrounding Navajo Nation – the largest retained Native-American area in the United States.

We stopped at Canyon de Chelly (pronounced da Shay), which we viewed as a taster before Arizona's main event – the Grand Canyon.

I have always liked how Americans 'hike' places. They don't go for walks. They hike. Hiking sounds much better than walking. So Mark and I hiked down to the bottom of the Canyon de Chelly. Let's be honest, if I told you we went on a little walk down a nice path to the bottom it would not sound very impressive. But if I tell you that we hiked down to the bottom of a canyon, that's pretty damn cool, right? Right!

We followed the White House Ruins trail down to the canyon floor. The scenery was stunning and we saw ancient cliff dwellings plus pictographs and petroglyphs etched onto the canyon walls. Ryan also proudly announced to the world in 1998 that he loved Mandy 4EVA, and it was there in spray paint on the rock for us all to see. The dickhead.

Despite being December, the canyon seemed to soak up the heat from the sun and we sat in the shade of a cottonwood tree for a while before beginning our ascent. On the way up, we passed a large flock of sheep being precariously herded up the narrow and steep canyon path by a Navajo shepherd. It seemed an incredibly stressful journey – for both the shepherd and the sheep – but he smiled as we passed and made his work look so effortless.

After hiking back up to the canyon rim, we drove on through the Navajo settlement of Many Farms. *How many farms?* I hear you ask. Well, Mark and I decided to try and find out, by counting the homesteads that we could see out of the window on each side of Josephine. We lost count at 50, and most of those were houses, rather than farms, but we concluded that there were indeed many farms.

We continued north through Round Rock, Mexican Water and into the state of Utah where we parked up at about 6pm opposite a laundrette in the small town of Mexican Hat. Native Americans really are the masters at naming settlements.

We found a bar and spent the evening drinking beer and shooting pool. The bartender's name was Hawk, and he was undoubtedly the coolest barman, with the coolest name, that has ever lived. He wasn't too enamoured by us two drunken Brits but this only added to his character. We did manage to get a brief smile from him before we left. Actually, come to think of it, that's probably what made him smile.

Like Texas, it turns out that Utah also gets cold at night in December. Brutally cold. Despite the beers we'd consumed, neither of us slept much at all that night and we took it in turns to start up Josephine's engine and try to fill the car with hot air from the heaters. Only minutes after switching them off we would be able to see our breath again. I cursed myself for leaving my damn fleece in Port Gibson, and instead put on the rest of the clothes that I owned.

In the morning, the windows were coated with a thick layer of frost on both the inside and the outside. It was 6am and the gas station in Mexican Hat was not due to open until 8am. We decided to drive to Monument Valley for sunrise and try to find coffee on the way. It turns out there is nothing between Mexican Hat and Monument Valley.

Monument Valley must be one of the most recognisable sights in the world. It is the backdrop to scenes in many famous films, including: *The Searchers, Thelma and Louise, Forrest Gump, 2001: A Space Odyssey, Once Upon a Time in the West, Easy Rider,* and, of course, *National Lampoon's Vacation.*

We were the very first people to arrive. The car park was completely deserted and the wooden kiosks offering souvenirs and tours were still boarded up for the night. In the eerie pre-dawn light, Monument Valley was magical. As the sun slowly illuminated those perfectly formed buttes (grow up), it was hard to comprehend that we were the only people at one of the most famous sights in the world. It made our restless frozen night in Josephine seem a worthy sacrifice.

After an hour or so, workers gradually arrived and the kiosks began to open. We bought a coffee and a couple of shrink-wrapped burritos for breakfast.

We followed the 17-mile dirt road through the stone monoliths, stopping frequently at lay-bys to soak up the views. I imagine that in peak season, the road is probably a continuous snake of cars, but early on this cold morning in December, it was almost deserted.

We had been warned about the state of the 'road', with its crater-sized potholes, and rocks protruding all over the place. Josephine shook and rattled the entire way round, but she coped admirably.

We chatted to a French-Canadian couple at one of the lookouts. They were midway through a six-month road trip, and had also spent the night in their van nearby. They seemed like such a fun, loving couple and it made me think again of how much fun travelling with Rachel would have been. Spending a night in a freezing cold car would surely be more tolerable and warmer with her. But now that she was moving to Ireland, I needed to accept the fact that any travelling that Rachel and I would do together would likely be far off in the future.

By the time we made it back to the start, the car park was filling up with other tourists and a sort of Navajo flea market was in full swing. We had timed our exit to perfection.

From Monument Valley we drove back south into Arizona, stopping to hike some trails along the way. We arrived in Tuba City, where one of the town's high-schools had converted its old dorm rooms into a motel. We ordered pizza and ate it in our very own empty school, which was a surreal but enjoyable experience.

Again we had to scrape a thick layer of frost off Josephine in the morning. We turned the ignition key, she spluttered furiously, but wouldn't fire up. We tried again. No luck. And again. Each time she tormented us into thinking that she was going to burst into life, but each time she decided against it.

We thought that this was the end. We had made it all the way to Arizona and here Josephine would breathe her last breath. It would be difficult to justify spending any more money on getting her fixed, seeing as we were so close to California, where Mark had decided his trip would finish. From there, he planned to get a train back to New York via Chicago and Boston, to catch his flight home.

I had planned to spend some time at my uncle's house in Petaluma and then drive to Denver, Colorado where there was a possibility I could get some work. If Josephine needed more money spent on her then it didn't seem practical for me to keep her either. We could both just get a bus to Petaluma, and from there I could get a bus or hitch to Denver. It didn't fit the American road trip dream that I had envisaged, but my finances were in such an awful state that it didn't seem like I had much choice.

'What do you think we should do?' I said to Mark, as I sat with my head slumped on the steering wheel.

'Shall we go and get breakfast somewhere and have a think about it?'

'Yes, good plan. I always think better after breakfast.'

After a huge plate of waffles and bacon, we decided we would call the AAA and get Josephine towed one last time to a garage. If it was a simple fix, I would pay for it on a credit card, but if it turned out to be costly then we would have to wave goodbye to our beloved heap of junk and head to Petaluma by other means.

'We might as well give Josephine one more try before phoning the AAA,' said Mark, holding up the keys.

'Definitely. Although I'm not getting my hopes up.'

He climbed into the driving seat and turned the key. After a couple of seconds of stuttering, Josephine miraculously roared into life.

'GET IN!' he shouted.

'You absolute beauty,' I said, banging my hand on the bonnet and then climbing into the passenger seat. 'We are sorry for ever doubting you, Josephine.'

'Hopefully it was just the cold. She sounds good now,' said Mark, revving the engine and then slipping her into gear.

'Shall we get the oil changed?' I suggested.

'Why? Do you think that's what the problem was?'

'I haven't got a clue. Probably not. But it sounded like an intelligent suggestion in my head.'

'Is that expensive?'

'No. About $25 I think. Every garage we've driven past has offered *'oil changes'*. It seems to be something that people regularly do in America.'

'We can do. If you want. But it's not too far now to California.'

'Don't worry, this is my treat. I'm in this for the long haul. I want to give Josephine a fighting chance to make it back to the east coast.'

'The east coast? Really? Do you think you'll drive the whole way back?'

'Who knows? It would be nice to take her as far as I can. With an oil change I'm sure she'll be unstoppable.'

18

With Josephine's oil changed, we drove to the Grand Canyon – one of the world's most famous natural attractions. Five million visitors a year flock from all over the world to look at this hole in the Arizona desert. Surely a landmark as famous and recognisable as the Grand Canyon can't even remotely live up to the hype? Mark and I were both really excited about the prospect of seeing it, but expectant of the fact that we would most likely be disappointed. Visiting the Grand Canyon would surely always feel anti-climactic.

The north rim is closed during the winter months, so we entered the park via the south in mid afternoon. We could see a smog of tour buses parked up by what looked like the main visitor centre up ahead. So we pulled off the road before we reached it and decided to have a look at a quieter section of the canyon first.

It's a cliché to say it, but there are no words that can do justice to the Grand Canyon the first time you lay eyes on it. It is completely incomprehensible. It feels as though you are a part of some strange 3D IMAX experiment, designed to torment your senses. I was genuinely speechless.

It was the first natural wonder that I've looked at that has caused a weird butterfly sensation in my stomach, like going over a humpback bridge in the back of a car when you are a child. There is no way to gauge the size and scale of it either, as there are no visible buildings, cars or people to gain any sense of perspective from. It is just a vacuous hole, with a tiny little stream trickling along the canyon floor. Only it's not a tiny little stream. It's the bloody Colorado River. It's fast and it's wide and it's up to 110 feet deep in places. Yet from the canyon rim, it is barely even noticeable.

We spent the rest of the afternoon exploring the canyon's edge. We could hear the distant murmur of the tour groups at the main visitor centre, but there was not a single person in either direction in the area in which we sat. A large proportion of tourists to the Grand Canyon get out of their car or bus at Grand Canyon Village, wander to the main viewing area, take a few photos and then climb back into their bus. If you stroll a few hundred metres along the edge, it feels like the entire canyon is yours.

As the sun began to set, we inexplicably decided to get out our guitars and have an impromptu jam session on the edge of the canyon, like some god-awful cheesy '80s rock video. We had carried those bloody guitars with us the entire way across America, and we were going to make damn well sure we used them. Our guitar playing and singing was definitely a contributing factor to there being no other people in the vicinity.

Satisfied that we had made ourselves look as knobbish as possible, we loaded our guitars back into Josephine and left the Grand Canyon after dark and headed north towards Page. We parked up next to Lake Powell which we had heard great things about. The second largest man-made reservoir in the United States certainly looked spectacular in our guide book, but it was almost midnight when we arrived and we would have to wait until morning to see it properly.

A thick fog had descended in the night, and as we walked to the lookout point near to where we were parked, we could see even less of Lake Powell than we had at midnight. We left having only had the most fleeting of glimpses. Still, it looked spectacular in our guide book.

Zion National Park in the south-west corner of Utah was our next stop. There are several extremely popular walks, sorry, hikes, in Zion, but the name that kept cropping up when we spoke to other travellers was Angel's Landing.

'OMG you MUST hike Angel's Landing,' said the Australian singer from the hostel in New Orleans.

'The Angel's Landing walk has probably been the highlight of our entire trip so far,' said the French-Canadian couple we met at Monument Valley. 'But be warned, it's shit scary.'

It was a bright sunny day and although it was the middle of December, it felt warmer than it had done since the day I hired a bike in Ocean City. We picked up a map from the Visitor Centre and then drove to one of Zion's car parks near to the start of the Angel's Landing trail. The hike itself is only a five mile round trip, but it is the final section that has given it its fame and reputation as one of the best hikes in America.

The first couple of miles followed a smooth, wide path that meandered easily up the mountainside via a series of switchbacks.

'This is a piece of cake,' I said to Mark. 'I wonder what all the fuss is about.'

'I can't believe that couple at Monument Valley claimed this was scary. I mean, we're quite high up, but it's not exactly dangerous is it?'

As we neared the top, the edges of the path became more exposed and precipitous, and we started to appreciate just how high up we already were.

'Good luck up there,' said an older American couple coming the other way. 'We didn't make it all the way to the top. We bottled it.'

'Bottled it?' Mark whispered, once they were out of earshot. 'How hard can it be?'

A few minutes later we caught a glimpse of what was to come. A ridge, no more than about five feet wide in places, stretched out and then up to a rocky outcrop. There was a sheer drop of about 1000 feet on either side of this ridge, all the way to the valley floor below us. There was a chain anchored into the rock for most of this section, which was in someway reassuring, but was also confirmation of just how dangerous it was.

'Mark, you remember that peak with the vertical drop all around it that we could see from the car park?'

'You mean the one we joked about probably being Angel's Landing?'

'Yeah. It turns out it was Angel's Landing.'

'Ah! I'm starting to understand why people find this hike a little scary.'

But the fear we felt at this point was nothing compared to what was to come.

We passed another couple of men in their mid-forties who were also descending. They too had given up before the top.

'I think you two have got the whole mountain to yourself, boys,' said one of the men. 'I don't think there was anyone up ahead of us.'

'Er, great. I'm sure we'll be following you down very shortly once we wimp out,' I said.

'You'll be fine. A couple of young boys like you. Good luck.'

We edged out along the ridge, gripping the chain tightly in fear of our feet slipping out from underneath us on the slick rock. I am not scared of heights as such, but I have an extreme fear of plummeting to my death over a cliff edge. The middle section of the ridge dipped down slightly before the final ascent up to Angel's Landing. It was this final section that looked the most daunting. The path climbed steeply ahead of us, the rock no longer as smooth underfoot. The chain was still in place, but this part looked like it would require considerable effort to pull ourselves up, too. Could all that trust be put in some chains that had been anchored to the rock decades before?

'What do you reckon, Mark?' I said. 'If you don't fancy going up any further then I'm happy to call it a day here.'

Mark took off his glasses, gave them a rub on his t-shirt and put them back on before assessing the path ahead. I was hoping that he would take the bait and pull out here, allowing us both to head back to the valley floor. Via the path, I mean. Not the direct route.

'Well I'm happy to keep going,' he said. 'But if you want to wimp out then that's absolutely fine with me.'

'I'm not wimping out. I thought you might want to wimp out. And that's ok if you do.'

'Nope. It looks fine to me,' he said, with a slight croak to his voice that made it clear he thought it looked anything but.

But we were both too stubborn. Neither of us wanted to be the one to suggest we quit, even though we both probably wanted to more than anything. But sometimes fear can bring out the best in people and result in feelings that you could not otherwise experience. Providing we were careful, continuing to the top wasn't reckless. It was a recognised path that thousands of people had completed before us. There were signs warning people of the risks, and advising them to take care, and we had no intention of doing anything silly.

'Ok, let's go. After you,' I said.

'No, no, after you. I insist,' he said.

'Alright, fine,' I muttered as I grabbed the chain and slowly edged my way up.

Once we reached the top, the ridge opened up into a wider plateau, sloping gently towards the precipice. There was plenty of room to sit down and it was flat enough not to feel the need to cling onto the rock.

'That was incredible,' I said. 'It was way scarier than I thought it would be, but a hundred times better.'

'What a feeling!' said Mark. 'I'm so glad you decided not to wimp out.'

'Ha, yeah right. I pretty much had to coax you up here.'

'Whatever.'

The deep orange glow of the sandstone looked stunning in the afternoon sun. There was not a breath of wind and we lay back on the smooth rock and soaked up the moment. We celebrated our accomplishment with a satsuma each and the last of Maya's raisins.

We still had to do the whole thing again in reverse. I mean, retrace out steps, not walk down the mountain backwards. But the scary part had been done. Walking down should be easy.

'Was that thunder?' I said to Mark, as I gazed down the valley at the perfect blue sky ahead of us.

'It sounded like it. It must be far away though. The weather is perfect here.'

Out of curiosity, I turned around and looked up the valley behind us.

'Oh fuck!' I said. 'Look at that.'

Mark sat up and followed my gaze.

'Oh shit! Let's get off this ridge.'

The sky behind us looked like it had been badly photoshopped onto a postcard. It was a deep ominous black, with a swirling mist filling the valley. It was coming straight for us. There had been signs in the visitor centre about how the weather in Zion could change drastically in an instant. I had always assumed that to be a myth. It was a beautiful sunny day. How could the weather possibly turn bad? But it certainly had. And we were on a rocky outcrop with a 1000 foot drop all around us, and a narrow ridge to navigate back down to the main path.

As we started to descend the steep section from the top plateau, thinking that the weather couldn't possibly get any worse, it suddenly did. It started hailing. Ridiculously hard. Hailstones bounced off the rock all around us, and the already slick rock underfoot became even more treacherous.

I let out a huge cackle. I didn't know what else to do.

'What's so funny?' said Mark, looking back up at me as he clung on tightly to the chain.

'We are clinging onto a chain on top of a mountain, with vertical drops either side of us and we are now in a hailstorm.'

'Best day ever, isn't it?' laughed Mark.

'Hang on, Mark. Just hold it there while I take a quick photo of you.'

'Really?'

'Yes, really. We'll be talking about this moment for years to come and nobody will believe us.'

It was ludicrously scary making our descent from Angel's Landing, but the weather had made us increasingly aware of how dangerous our situation was, so we held on extra tightly to that chain, and demonstrated extra caution with our footing until we made it back to the relative safety of the main path.

'We survived!' I shouted, offering Mark a high-five which he readily accepted.

'It feels bloody great to still be alive.'

'I think that's probably the most amazing walk I've ever been on.'

'You mean a hike,' said Mark. 'That was definitely a hike.'

We hadn't seen a single person on our descent, and when we reached the car park at the bottom, Josephine was the only vehicle to be seen.

When we called into the visitor centre to use the toilets on our way out, we read that a man had fallen to his death from Angel's Landing a couple of months previously. Over the years there have been several deaths, including a particularly tragic one in more recent years when a 14 year old boy, taking part in a Boy Scout trip, fell to his death after accepting a $5 bet to etch his name into the rock at the edge of the cliff.

We left Zion cold and wet, but immeasurably proud, and found a cheap motel in nearby Springdale. We decided to treat ourselves to dinner at the neighbouring restaurant. After the waitress handed us the menus, we glanced at them and discovered that it was well out of our budget, so we made our excuses and left, getting a cheap sandwich at a nearby deli instead.

We returned to Zion the following day and spent most of the morning hiking the wonderful Hidden Canyon trail. There were a couple of short sections with a chain to hold, and some parts that required climbing over boulders, but it felt like a doddle compared to our escapades up Angel's Landing the previous day.

19

America is a nation of extreme contrasts. It has endless beauty and areas of complete wilderness, yet it also has some of the most modern and developed landscapes in the world. This disparity could not be better illustrated than on this day. Having spent the morning hiking in the remote Hidden Canyon of Zion National Park, almost devoid of any other humans or form of civilisation, we then arrived in early evening in Las Vegas, Nevada.

'Vegas Baby, Vegas!' we both shouted as we caught our first glimpses of Sin City from the freeway.

Neither of us knew what to expect from Las Vegas. It was a city we both felt like we had already visited. Its sights and sounds were so familiar to us, based on the countless films and TV shows set there. But until you actually experience it in person, there is no way to do Las Vegas justice.

We had no idea if we were just passing through, or whether we were going to stay for a week. We soon learned that it is not possible to just pass through Las Vegas. It's an electro-magnet that sucks you in and it is physically impossible to drive through without stopping.

We passed a hotel with a large *Free Parking* sign and despite my best efforts to keep driving, Josephine swerved from the main drag and down the ramp into the basement car park. The magnetic force found us a nice parking spot and pulled us in, before turning off the engine and placing the keys in my hand.

'Oh, how did that happen?' I said.

'Oh well. We're here now,' said Mark. 'We might as well have a quick look around.'

'I've got $15, so that's all I'm spending.'

We had heard that sleeping in your vehicle is illegal in the state of Nevada, but decided we would worry about that later. I think we secretly hoped that we might win some huge pot in Texas Hold'em and be offered complementary rooms by the casino staff, mistaking us for a couple of high-rollers. Starting with a budget of $15 made this prospect seem unlikely.

We spent the first couple of hours just walking circuits of each of the main casinos. I don't think I had been this awestruck by the inside of a building since visiting *It's a Small World* at Disneyland at the age of eight. The amount of money and work that goes into making the casinos eye-catching to punters was simply astonishing. There were cobbled streets, pyramids, wild animals, a replica Eiffel tower, mountains, rivers…. actual rivers… inside a casino. It was beyond belief.

We could have happily just wandered around the casinos all evening, soaking up the sights, but you can't get the full Vegas experience without gambling away some money. I wasn't brave enough to tackle the poker tables, so decided to start with Blackjack – a game so simple that even children can play.

I found a $5 minimum bet table and patiently waited my turn for a seat. Just as I sat down, the croupier flicked the sign over so that it read *$10 minimum bet.* I don't know whether this was a deliberate act to intimidate me, or just something that happened to this particular table at a certain point of the evening. I didn't let it faze me, and coolly sat down. A sweet old lady to my left held out her gloved hand for me to shake.

'Hi. I'm Patricia.'

'Hi, Patricia. I'm George.'

'Gosh, I love your accent. Where are you from?'

'England. What about you?'

'Vegas.'

'Wow, so you're a proper local. Do you come here often?' I said, wincing as I realised it sounded like I was trying to chat up a granny.

'About five or six nights a week,' she said. 'Occasionally I go to the one next door instead.'

It was bizarre to think that to many people, these casinos were a nightly ritual. Las Vegas is one of the fastest growing retirement spots for people in the United States, as seniors from all over the country come to live out their days in the city. And whether because of boredom, or loneliness, or because there's no avoiding it, a huge chunk of this retirement is often spent sat at casino tables.

Looking around the casinos, there were hundreds of other people like Patricia. Not all would be gambling addicts, but I'm sure a good proportion would be. I initially felt sorry for them, but then realised that there are far worse places to grow old. At least they were always surrounded by people, stimulation and entertainment. And if they wanted to spend their life savings on roulette and blackjack, then who was I to judge them?

The croupier dealt the cards. The two players to my right both twisted and then went bust. I had been dealt a ten and an eight and had chosen to stick. Patricia had a jack and a queen and was also sticking. I was quietly optimistic that my hand would be enough. The dealer's upcard was a ten. She flipped the other to reveal a nine. She gave me a sympathetic smile, took my chips, paid Patricia her winnings and then began to deal the next hand. My night in Vegas was as good as over.

'Oh well, it was very nice to meet you, Patricia,' I said, shaking her gloved hand again.

'Are you finished already? You've only played one hand,' she said.

'Yes, I only had $15.'

'Oh, that's a shame. There's plenty you can do for $5 in Vegas still. Go and play the slots instead. And take advantage of the free drinks,' she said, raising her glass of Scotch.

'Free drinks?'

'Of course. Why do you think we are all here? You see all of these waitresses walking around? Ask them for any drink you like and they'll bring it to you.'

'For free?'

'Yes. You're supposed to be playing the tables or slots so best to at least look like you are. And if you give them a small tip they'll keep on coming back to you.'

'Sounds brilliant. Thanks for the advice.'

It had been many years since I had played a fruit machine. A childhood incident with one had affected me very deeply.

There was a fruit machine in the beer garden of the village pub where I holidayed every year in Devon as a child. It was a 2p per spin machine and, instead of bells or dollar symbols, the top prize icon was a pig. Three pigs won the £2 jackpot, which, for an eleven year old, was a very big deal. The lady who ran the local shop refused to give change in 2ps because she knew they would be used at the fruit machine down the road. This was partly because she didn't want to encourage children to gamble. But mostly because she was a miserable cow who didn't have a single ounce of fun in her body.

So, one year, between holidays to Devon, I meticulously saved up all the 2ps that I found, or was given. By the time of our next holiday, I had amassed a decent quantity and filled a plastic coin bag with my precious 2ps.

The holiday had arrived, and on the very first morning I woke up and could feel the excitement and the lure of the fruit machine. I walked up to the pub later that morning, clutching that bag of 2ps like it was a million pounds. It promised to be one of the best mornings of my life. I had been looking forward to this moment since the end of the previous year's holiday. Unable to control my excitement, I began to twirl the plastic bag around my finger. I was singing a jolly song to myself, and I even broke into a light skip. The twirling of the bag became more and more vigorous the closer I got to the pub, as my anticipation escalated. Then, as I passed one of the last houses before the pub, my grip somehow slipped and the bag flew from my finger mid twirl. Time seemed to slow down as I watched my precious 2p collection, which I had worked so tirelessly to amass, arc gracefully through the air before landing in a hedge at the side of the road. The weight of the bag provided enough momentum for it to vanish deep inside the vegetation.

My shouts of despair echoed up the quiet village street as I dashed across the road to where the coins had disappeared from sight. I spent a good 15 minutes with my head inside that hedge, frantically scouring the depths for my beloved 2ps.

There was no sign of them.

I went back to our holiday house and persuaded some reluctant family members to aid my search. We eventually knocked on the door to the house whose garden the hedge bordered, and they allowed us in to search from the other side. After a further half an hour of rummaging, we still hadn't found the bag and the search was called off. That coin bag was never found. I was inconsolable. My holiday had been ruined on the first morning, and I hadn't played a fruit machine since.

But with the promise of free drinks, it was time for me to face my demons. So, for the next few hours, Mark and I sat on a couple of stools by the slots, pumping the occasional quarter in each time a waitress walked passed. We drank an endless stream of beers and cocktails, becoming more and more in love with Vegas as the night progressed. We occasionally moved casinos, just to vary our surroundings, but despite the pretence and the pyramids, tigers and rivers, all the casinos in Vegas are the same.

Mark started with a little more cash than me, but was determined not to lose it. We were both more than a little tipsy when he decided he might as well have a go at one of the poker tables. Unfortunately, not only had the alcohol diminished his senses, it had also increased his confidence. In the space of 15 minutes, Mark managed to lose $95 playing Texas Hold'em, when bloody Steve from Michigan trumped Mark's ace-high flush with his four nines. $95 was pennies compared to most of the other customers in the casino, but to us $95 was a huge amount. It was three nights in a motel. It was enough gas to cross several states.

Determined not to end the night on such a sour note, I then remembered hearing a theory about a roulette tactic that is supposedly foolproof. The idea is that you bet on either red or black, and if you win, you walk away. If you lose, you double your stake and bet again. If you win, you walk away, but if you lose, you double your stake again. You continue until you win at which point, you will have won more money than you have bet. It was completely foolproof. Providing you have the funds to be able to keep doubling your stake until you win. Mark still had $80 which meant at least four spins of the $5 roulette wheel. The odds were stacked in his favour that he would win on one of those spins, and recoup some of his Texas Hold'em losses.

'I'm going to stick with red. Red is my lucky colour,' he slurred.

'Great choice. Red is the best colour. Josephine is sort of red. And so are post boxes and phone boxes,' I nodded, as I swayed behind Mark who was now seated on a stool by the table.

The first spin hit black.

'That's ok, we don't want to win on the first spin,' I said, slapping him on the back. 'The longer it goes, the more you win.'

The second spin landed on black.

'That's ok. You'll get it next time,' I said confidently.

The next spin was black. And then the next. The wheel hit four blacks in a row. Mark was down another $75 and had only $5 remaining so was unable to double his stake. He bet the $5 anyway and finally hit red, leaving him with $10, but the damage was already done.

'Fucking Vegas!' said Mark as we walked back over to the fruit machines and ordered another beer.

'Well I've had a brilliant night anyway.'

'You didn't lose $170.'

'No, but I watched you lose it. It felt like my loss too.'

'Yeah right. I bet you loved it.'

'Of course I didn't,' I said, trying not to laugh. I didn't like seeing Mark lose money but the look on his face as that roulette wheel landed on black time after time was priceless.

I stuck another quarter into the fruit machine and pressed the big illuminated red button. The wheels stopped spinning on two bells. It gave a little beep and said I had 50 credits in the bank, which I assumed meant I had 50 free goes. This seemed a little strange, as two bells didn't seem particularly good, but I kept pressing the button and the wheels kept spinning.

After a while, I started getting bored of my credits and was about to walk off and leave the machine with 26 credits still remaining, when I noticed a blinking yellow button at the top of the machine that I hadn't seen before. It said *'collect'*. I pressed it expecting it to maybe cough out a couple of tokens in exchange for the credits. Instead it spat out 26 tokens, each one worth a dollar.

'Oops,' I said.

'So if you'd pressed that button half an hour ago you would have won $50?' asked Mark.

'Er, yeah. It looks like it.'

'You dick.'

'How can two bells win you $50? Back in the day, three pigs only won you £2.'

'I don't know, but you're a jammy bastard. You won $26 dollars by spending a couple of bucks on a fruit machine, and I lost about $170 in the space of 15 minutes.'

'Yeah, sorry about that. I'll buy you some dinner. How about that?'

We got a bite to eat at the casino restaurant and then sat and drank more free drinks by pretending to play the fruit machines. When we eventually walked out of the casino it was beginning to get light outside. There are no windows in the casinos in Vegas. You lose all sense of time and the fact that there even is a world outside.

We were both too drunk to go to another casino, we obviously couldn't drive, and we had no intention of paying for a room for the night as the night was almost over. Instead we decided to take our chances and get a few hours sleep in Josephine.

When we awoke a couple of hours later I felt like death would have been preferable. My head was pounding and my mouth felt like a large animal had defecated in it. Mark looked annoyingly sprightly.

We made our way to the nearest casino, tempted in there by a poster we had seen advertising an eat-as-much-as-you-like buffet breakfast for $8.99. I always read eat-as-much-as-you-like as eat-as-much-as-you-CAN and see it as an eating contest. I will only ever leave a buffet when I feel sick and genuinely couldn't eat another mouthful. Unfortunately, on this morning in Vegas, I felt sicker than I ever had before, and that was before even starting the buffet.

Still, I was certain that my hangover was nothing that some greasy breakfast couldn't sort out. We piled our plates high with bacon, sausages, beans, fried potatoes, eggs and pancakes. Mark tucked straight into his. I just stared at my plate.

I sat there for an hour, hoping the nausea would pass, but if anything, being inside the casino again just made it worse. During the course of our breakfast I managed to eat three baked beans, and even that proved a struggle. At $3 per bean, they must surely work out to be the most expensive baked beans ever eaten. Mark demolished the contents of his plate and proudly announced that he felt heaps better.

'Good for you,' I said. 'At least I didn't lose $170 last night.'

'I was hoping that was just a really bad dream.'

'No, I'm afraid not. It was very real.'

'Let's never talk about it again. So, what do you fancy doing today? Shall we see what else Vegas has to offer?'

'I'm happy to have a quick wander around but I think I'm done with Vegas. It's beaten me.'

'Really?'

'Yes, I admit defeat. One night was plenty. Let's have a walk up and down the Strip and then get out of here.'

'Sounds good to me. I can't afford to lose any more money.'

We left Vegas by mid-afternoon. Mark drove and I sat curled up on the passenger seat trying not to vomit. We were heading for Death Valley, and the irony of how I felt was certainly not lost on me.

We reached the small town of Beatty a few miles west of Death Valley at about 5pm and decided to call it a day. Mark's hangover had slowly caught up with him and he was starting to feel the effects of the previous night. We didn't even switch on the television and just crashed onto the beds and slept for 14 hours straight.

20

Beatty is a few miles from the ghost town of Rhyolite, Nevada. It was far more impressive than the previous ghost town of Rocky Springs that we had visited on the Natchez Trace Parkway, in that it actually had buildings to look at.

Rhyolite sprang up in 1905 when a mine opened after the discovery of gold in the nearby hills. Over the following few years, the town thrived with up to 5000 people calling it home. As the ore deposits became exhausted, production fell and investors pulled out. The mine closed in 1911 and by 1920 there was almost nobody left in Rhyolite.

The derelict remains of the town were very interesting to look around, but I didn't get that eerie feeling I had hoped I would feel while visiting a ghost town. It's impossible to feel in the slightest bit spooked when it's nearly 30C at 10am in the morning.

We crossed the California state line and into Death Valley National Park.

Death Valley is the largest national park in the lower 48 states (the top four are all in Alaska) and holds many other records for being the hottest, driest and lowest place in America.

We drove up to take in the spectacular vistas from Dante's View, walked the Mesquite Flat Sand Dunes, stared in bewilderment at the salt flats of the Badwater Basin, marvelled at the lunar landscape of Devil's Golf Course, and even hit a few golf balls at a real driving range in Furnace Creek. The extreme variety of landscapes within one national park really was astonishing. It was no surprise to discover that many scenes from *Star Wars* were filmed in Death Valley.

Our enjoyment of the day was spoiled slightly by the attitude of one lone park ranger. On a perfectly straight section of road, Mark and I were minding our own business, when I spotted a blue flashing light in the rear-view mirror.

'Oh bollocks. What have I done now?' I said.

'Were you speeding?' asked Mark.

'I don't think so. I was doing about 40mph, but it's a big road.'

'Yeah, but we are in a National Park.'

I pulled over into a lay-by and the 'cop', who I then realised was a park ranger, swaggered slowly from his car towards ours.

'What's the deal with park rangers?' I asked Mark. 'Do they have the same powers as the police?'

'No idea. I guess we'll find out soon.'

I wound down the window.

The miserable looking park ranger – a man in his early 50s with dark hair and a face like a scrotum – placed his hand on the door frame and peered inside.

'Do you know what speed you were doing just then?' he said as he chewed vigorously on a piece of gum.

'Er, no sir. I don't think it was more than 40mph. Was I going too quickly?'

'You were doing 35mph. Thirty… five… miles… per hour.'

'I'm sorry. Is the speed limit 30mph? It's a big road, I honestly didn't realise.'

'The speed limit is 65mph.'

I looked at Mark and he bit down on his bottom lip to try and keep himself from laughing.

'Oh. Is there a problem?' I said.

'The speed limit is 65. You were doing 35. Licence and registration.'

By now we had made sure our licence and registration were easily accessible in the glove box. Mark flicked it open and went to reach inside.

'STOP RIGHT THERE!' shouted the ranger, placing his hand on a gun that I had only just noticed strapped to his belt. 'PUT BOTH HANDS WHERE I CAN SEE THEM!' he yelled. 'Right, now I want you to slowly reach in and pass me your licence and registration, ok? Nice and slowly.'

Mark and I looked at each other. We didn't need to say anything but we were both clearly thinking exactly the same thing: *'What is this asshole's problem?'*

He took off his sunglasses and studied our licence and registration slowly, presumably disappointed that it was all in order.

'Is there a problem, Sir?' I asked.

'Why were you driving so slowly?'

'Because we were looking at the scenery.'

'The speed limit is 65mph.'

'It's a National Park!' I said, getting slightly irritated for the first time.

'You think I don't know that?' he asked.

Of course I knew he knew that. Well, I hoped he knew that. He worked for the National Park Service after all. The bellend.

'No, no, I didn't mean that,' I said. 'I meant that I was driving slowly because we are here to look at the scenery. We're not just passing through.'

'So you're visiting for the day are you?' he said. 'And have you paid your entrance fees?'

He gave us a sly smile sensing he had finally caught us out. Unlike the majority of U.S. national parks, most roads into Death Valley don't have booths that require you to stop and pay the entrance fee. Some roads pass straight through Death Valley, but if you visit any of the park's attractions you are expected to pay at any of the automatic booths or the visitor centres. The ranger had decided that we must have been trying to get away without paying.

'No,' I said, 'but...'

'Thought not,' he interrupted. 'If you boys follow me to that visitor centre...'

'We've got one of these,' I said, handing him our National Park Annual Pass. 'I think that should cover us.'

He studied the pass, and I expected steam to start spurting from his ears. He didn't want to apologise or say anything remotely friendly.

Instead, he looked up the road to where another car had pulled over and the driver – a little old lady – had just let her dog run off into the undergrowth to do its business.

'HEY YOU!' he shouted. 'GET THAT DAMN DOG ON A LEASH!'

He thrust the pass back to me and turned and ran up the road to harass the old lady instead.

We sat for a brief moment watching the old lady receive a barrage of abuse from the ranger, before we pulled back onto the road, accelerating to a respectable 60mph and getting the hell out of Death Valley as quickly as possible.

'What the hell just happened there?' I asked.

'You got pulled over for driving too slowly.'

'Have you ever met such a prick?'

'No. He was certainly one of a kind. A failed cop, I'm thinking.'

'That was exactly what I was thinking. Couldn't make the grade in the police force, so decided to exert his authority over potential criminals in national parks instead.'

We exited Death Valley on the Nevada side and joined Route 95 to then loop around the northern edge of the park. Josephine was almost out of gas but the filling station that we passed just outside Death Valley was the most expensive we had seen in weeks. When you spend several hours a day driving, fuel prices become incredibly important. I took the decision to press on. We would soon be in California, where surely there would be a gas station every mile or so.

The road began to climb up and up, the needle dipping further and further into the red.

'I don't think we're going to make it,' I said.

'I told you we should have just filled up at that last gas station.'

'But it was really expensive.'

'Well at least it wouldn't have meant we would run out of petrol halfway up this hill.'

'Well, if we make it to the top of this hill then we should just be able to freewheel down the other side.'

'This looks like more than just a hill,' said Mark, taking a closer look at our road map.

'Why? Can you see where we are?'

'Yes,' he said, looking over the top of his glasses at me. I knew I wasn't going to like what he was about to say. 'This 'hill' we are driving up is the Piper Mountain Wilderness area in the White Mountains.'

'Oh. Is that bad?'

'Bad? Well, it's only part of a bloody long mountain range that has ridiculously high mountain passes.'

'Ah.'

'Perhaps it would have been sensible to pay the extra for the fuel. Even if we had only bought $10's worth.'

'Ok, it's easy for you to say now. Wow, look at all those snowy peaks. We are high up, aren't we?'

'Yes.'

'Is this the place where those people got stuck for the winter and had to eat each other?'

'You mean the Donner Pass? No, that's a little further up in the Sierra Nevada, but it's not too far from here.'

'Well if we do run out of petrol and get stranded here then I'm going to eat you first.'

'No chance. You won't even see me coming.'

Josephine continued to chug upwards as darkness fell, and the road twisted and turned with no sign of us reaching the top. I don't know if it was all in my head but it felt as if the accelerator was juddering slightly. Were we really going to run out of fuel simply because I was too tight to buy some over-priced gas?

Eventually we reached the summit at Westguard Pass (elevation 7271 ft).

'Get in! I told you we would make it,' I said.

'We made it to the top of the mountain, but we are still almost out of gas and we might still be miles away from a filling station. And even if we do find one, it'll probably be closed,' said Mark.

'Stop being so negative. We'll be fine,' I said, with false confidence.

I freewheeled almost all of the 14.7 miles down the side of the White Mountains, fearing that if I pressed the accelerator even the slightest bit it would burn away the last whiff of Josephine's fuel.

We rolled into the town of Big Pine, California just before 10pm. The gas was 4c a gallon cheaper than the station outside Death Valley.

'Never in doubt,' I said, pulling up alongside a pump.

'You were very lucky. And well done for saving, what's that, about 80c, if you fill her up?'

'Yes, probably. Still, 80c is 80c.'

Despite the 80c I'd saved, we didn't have enough money for both dinner and a motel, so we had a choice of one or the other. We opted for dinner and a night in Josephine. As it was already late, we wouldn't be getting our money's worth from a motel, so we bought a huge sandwich each from the nearby town of Bishop and parked up on a back street for the night.

21

I woke with a start in the morning. My chest felt tight and constricted, and my face was icy to the touch. The air was so cold that it stung when we breathed it. It was 6am. I stacked both guitars in the passenger seat and crawled through into the driver's seat, still in my sleeping bag. I started up Josephine and put the heaters on full.

'Oh my god, it's so cold,' said Mark from the back seat. 'What time is it?'

'6am.'

'I'm surprised we survived the night in this ice box.'

'Me too,' I said, turning on the radio and tuning it to the closest station I could find.

'*…there is no… Arizoooona…*' sang the voice.

'Oh shut up, Jamie O'Neal. We know you're lying!' I shouted.

'You are listening to Bob Jacobs on Radio KIBS from Bishop, California on this cold Tuesday morning,' said the DJ after the song had ended.

'Did he just say Radio KIBS?' said Mark.

'I think so, why?'

'Look out the window.'

We had parked up late the previous night on the side of a road in a small industrial estate on the edge of town. Across from where we were parked, there was a single light on in a ground floor office building. Through the window, we could see a man sitting at a desk wearing headphones with a microphone in front of him. Above the window was a small sign that said: *Radio KIBS*. The man sitting there was DJ Bob.

'Oh, wow! That's Bob!' I said. 'This is amazing. We are actually watching live radio.'

As the next song came to an end, we watched Bob lean in to the microphone, say a few words, press a few buttons and then sit back and take a sip from his coffee cup.

It was a very surreal experience. I can't imagine Bob had a huge audience at 6am on a Tuesday in December. In fact, it wouldn't surprise me if we were his only listeners. There he was, sitting across the street from us, giving us our own private radio show.

At this point, the story would be much better if Mark or I then hopped across the street in our sleeping bag, banged on the window, and asked Bob to play some Glen Campbell for us. But that didn't happen. We did strongly consider it, but it was just too damn cold. Josephine had filled nicely with hot air and the thought of even opening the door, let alone stepping outside into the dark morning, was far too unpleasant.

Instead, we sat there for half an hour and watched Bob play his hits, before driving off in search of coffee and breakfast.

Once the sun had risen, and we had fuelled ourselves with coffee and donuts, we were ready to face the day. Yosemite National Park was our destination. Unfortunately the east entrance was closed because of snow. If only DJ Bob had warned us about that.

'Is the whole National Park closed?' we asked the ranger who was stationed at the entrance.

'No, sir. A lot of the park is still open. You can still get in via the western entrance near Mariposa.'

'Ok, how do we get there?'

'Well you can drive around the north of the park, but snow chains are required because of the recent bad weather up there. And looking at the state of your vehicle, I would advise taking the southern route.'

'That's sounds good. How far is that then?' I asked, expecting him to tell us it was a diversion of a couple of miles.

'Well, it's a little over 400 miles by the time you get round to Mariposa.'

'I'm sorry,' I coughed. 'Did you just say four HUNDRED miles?'

'Yes sir. That's correct. Probably a little bit more.'

'I had no idea Yosemite was that big.'

'It's not. It's the Sierra Nevada mountain range. You've got to drive all the way down and round the bottom. There are no suitable mountain passes open at the moment, and the southern entrance to Yosemite is also closed.'

'Oh. Shit.'

We sat staring in disbelief at our road map. It seemed inconceivable that we were faced with a 400 mile detour to get to the other side of a national park that we were currently parked outside. It further illustrated the size and scale of America. In Britain, you could drive 400 miles from London and be fairly deep into Scotland. In America, people drive 400 miles as a diversion.

'Do we really want to see Yosemite that much?' I said to Mark.

'No, probably not, but whether we go to Yosemite or not, we've still got to get to the other side of the Sierra Nevada.'

'That's true.'

'Ok, let's do this,' said Mark, shifting Josephine into Drive mode. 'Mariposa, baby!'

It took us almost the entire day to reach Mariposa, our longest drive of the trip by far. We found a motel in the town and the man kindly offered us his 'special winter rate' which translated as 'thank-you-so-much-you-are-the-only-people-to-stop-here-in-a-very-long-time rate'.

We woke the following morning to a bright crisp day. The sky was blue but there was still an icy chill in the air. We approached the western entrance to Yosemite and were flagged down by a park ranger.

'Howdy, boys,' he said, peering in through the window.

'Good morning officer... er... Sir... er... Ranger... er... Mister... er... man,' I stuttered.

'Good morning, Man?' sniggered Mark quietly.

'You boys carrying a set of snow chains for this vehicle?' he asked.

'Snow chains?' I asked.

'That's right. Snow chains. Chains to go over your tyres in case of snow.'

'No, we're not.'

'Well I'm afraid only vehicles with snow chains can enter the park.'

'We've driven 400 miles around from the eastern entrance because that was closed due to the snow.'

'That's correct. This entrance is open, but you still need snow chains to enter the park.'

'But there's no snow on the road.'

'Not now, but it's just a precaution. If you don't have chains with you and it snows then you might never get out again.'

'Ok, well I guess we'd better go and buy some snow chains. Where's the nearest town where we can buy some?'

I expected him to send us 400 miles around another mountain range.

'Why that general store just back there,' he said, pointing to a general store that was just back there.

'Thank you. We'll be back in a bit.'

'We'd like to buy some snow chains,' I said to the young man behind the counter.

'Sure, they are all along that back wall there. We've got them to fit most tyre sizes. What size do you need?'

'George?' said Mark. 'What size tyres does Josephine have?'

'I don't know. About this big,' I said, holding up my hands a wheel size apart.

The man rolled his eyes.

'Go and take a look at the tyre rim,' he said. 'Remember the numbers that you see and then come back in and I'll get you the correct set.'

'Ok, thanks.'

We retreated outside. I went to the front tyre closest to us and Mark, seemingly thinking I was incapable of remembering a set of numbers, went to check one of the rear tyres.

'So, what size do you need?' asked the man at the counter when we were back inside.

'It's a 205/60R16,' I said.

'Er.. no, George. It's a 195/75R14,' said Mark.

'It's not, Mark. Trust me it's 205/60R16.'

'I knew you wouldn't remember it properly, that's why I checked. It's definitely 195/75R14.'

'I swear to you it is 205,' I said. 'I think I am capable of remembering a few numbers, thank you very much.'

'Well I can too, and I know I'm right.'

'I think you boys need to go back out there and take a look again,' said the man. 'Here, take this pen and paper and write it down this time, then you'll know you've got it correct.'

We stomped outside, both pissed off with each other for being so incompetent, and both safe in the knowledge that we were correct and that we could soon utter a smug 'I told you so', once the other had rechecked.

'Ha, I told you so!' I said. '205/60R16.'

'What do you mean? Look, it says here 195/75R14. You're obviously reading the wrong bit.'

'YOU must be reading the wrong bit,' I said, storming aggressively over to his tyre. 'Let me see,' I said, crouching down by his tyre. 'Oh, yours does say 195. Come and look at my one.'

'Do you know what?' said Mark 'I think one of Josephine's wheels is smaller than the other three.'

We stepped back and looked at it. It was obvious now that one of the tyres was significantly smaller than the others.

'Oh my god,' I said. 'So we've driven from New York to California with one tyre not much bigger than a temporary tyre. That can't be very safe.'

'To be honest, I did always think there looked to be something odd about Josephine, but I couldn't put my finger on it.'

'And that would explain why she pulls so much to the right when she's moving.'

'What do we do now?'

'Well I doubt there is anywhere nearby to get new tyres, so we'll buy some snow chains that fit three of the wheels, and then get a new tyre sorted once we've left Yosemite.'

'But what about the snow chains man?' said Mark. 'Do we tell him that we have one small wheel? He might report us.'

'Good point. You stay here and I'll go in and tell him that you're an idiot and got the size wrong.'

'Ok, that's fine by me.'

I returned to the shop and bought a set of chains that would fit three of Josephine's tyres. The shop assistant and I laughed at Mark's incompetence, and then I climbed into Josephine and we drove into Yosemite National Park.

Mark was not fazed by the discovery that we were driving with one miniature wheel, and navigated the winding road down to the valley floor on recently gritted roads like he was in NASCAR.

Yosemite was every bit as beautiful as we imagined, and well worth the ridiculous 400 mile detour. Because of the snow, only parts of the park were open, but we still had a fabulous day exploring the Yosemite Valley and walking the snow-covered, rocky trail up the switchbacks to views of Vernal Falls, where we could see lunatics swimming in the icy pools below.

Later that evening we checked back into the same motel, where the man offered us an even cheaper nightly rate. We ate at the nearby Happy Burger Diner in Mariposa, which proudly claims to have the *'largest menu in the Sierra'*.

The waitress took our order of two Club Sandwiches, and then after about 40 minutes she returned to our table and asked us if we would like anything else.

'No, thanks. Just the Club Sandwiches please,' I said.

'Ah, jeez, did I not bring you those yet?'

'No. Don't worry, there's no rush.'

'They're coming right up.'

'She must be rushed off her feet,' said Mark, as we gazed around at no more than eight other customers in the entire place.

The Club Sandwich was worth the wait and we returned to the Happy Burger Diner the following morning for breakfast, to tick another couple of items off its unnecessarily long menu.

From Mariposa, we headed north past Bear Valley, through Chinese Camp and then east on Highway 4 through to the imaginatively named Copperopolis – which you will be shocked to hear was a mining town, based not on gold like much of California, but copper.

22

During my first year of university, I became good friends with an American student named Todd. Todd was studying in England for a year as part of his degree at a university in California. We got on really well and he came to stay with my family during a couple of the school holidays so that he didn't have to fly back to California for each break.

Todd is the most deadpan person I have ever met. His expression never changes. Whatever his mood, whatever the circumstances, his facial expression remains exactly the same. He has a wicked sense of humour and would often acknowledge a joke with a brief snort from his nostrils, but his mouth or eyes would never move.

One weekend, a group of us took a day trip to the theme park Alton Towers. We all went on the Oblivion rollercoaster together, which, at the time, was the world's first 'dive coaster' with a 90-degree vertical drop. During this drop section, where the roller-coaster plummets at an obscene speed towards the ground, a camera takes a photo of those on the ride and then, if you so wish, you can take out a bank loan to be able to afford one of these photos in the form of a fridge magnet or mouse mat. We waited at the photo booth to view our photos on the screens. In our carriage there was Todd, me and two other friends. In the photograph, three of us had our mouths wide open, eyes bulging and were visibly in mid-terrified scream, our faces taut and features flared. Todd looked exactly the same as Todd always did.

Todd returned to California at the end of the school year to continue his studies and I stayed in Leeds for the final two years of my degree. We kept in touch via email, letter and the occasional phone call, but then lost touch. By the time I travelled to America it had been six months since I had last heard from him.

I had a copy of his address scribbled into the back of my notebook and I promised myself that if I ever made it to California I would pay Todd a visit. He had no knowledge that I was even planning a trip to America, let alone coming to visit him.

We arrived in the suburbs of Stockton in mid-afternoon and drove aimlessly around asking various people for help in finding the address I had for Todd. After many failed attempts, we eventually pulled up outside his house.

'What do you think he'll say when he sees you?' asked Mark.

'I've no idea. I hope he's surprised. I've never seen Todd look surprised, though.'

We walked nervously up the driveway. It was just after 4pm and there was a very strong likelihood that he wasn't back from work, or college, or whatever he was doing these days.

I rang the doorbell.

A Latino lady holding a baby answered the door. *Wow, Todd has worked quickly*, I thought. *Last I heard he was single and definitely child-free. Now he appears to have a partner and a young baby.*

The lady said 'hello', but she said it as a question rather than a greeting. She looked at me with her eyebrows raised. Poor Todd. His partner was one scary psycho.

'Hello, sorry to bother you. Does Todd live here please?'

'Todd?' she shouted. 'Todd?'

'Yes, Todd. Does he live here?'

'Todd?' she shouted. 'Todd?'

'Yes… Todd,' I repeated.

'Todd? Todd?'

'Er… yes… Todd. Does he live here?'

'I don't think she knows who Todd is,' whispered Mark.

'Yeah, thanks. I sort of worked that out. Did a man called Todd used to live here?'

'I not understand,' she said, and I was slightly relieved that she didn't shout Todd at me again.

Instead she shouted 'JIMMY!' and a large man soon appeared alongside her.

'Hello?' he asked too.

'Hi there. We were wondering if Todd still lives here?'

'Todd?' he said. 'Todd?'

'George,' said Mark, 'Let's not go through this again. We've obviously got the wrong address. They don't know Todd.'

'How long have you lived here?' I asked.

'About four five months,' said the man in broken English.

'Do you have an address of the people who lived here before you?'

'I don't understand.'

'Do you know who lived here before you? Where did they move to?'

'I don't know. Sorry.'

'George, let's go. You tried your best.'

'Ok, thanks anyway,' I said, waving goodbye and heading back to Josephine.

They had shut the front door almost before we had turned our backs.

'Oh well, at least you tried,' said Mark, as we climbed into the car. 'Not much you can do about it if it's the wrong address or if he's moved house.'

'I suppose. It just seems a shame to come all this way and then not see Todd.'

'Yeah, it would have been nice to see him. But you'll see him again.'

I sat there with my fingers on the ignition key, reluctant to start the engine. *Would I see him again? If I was in California, in*

Todd's home town, and I couldn't see him, then what chance did I have for any other time in the future? No, this might be the only chance I would have to see him again.

'Wait there. I've got an idea,' I said, climbing out of the car and walking back up towards the front door.

I rang the doorbell.

This time Jimmy answered.

'Look. Tom not live here,' he shouted.

'It's not Tom, it's Todd,' I said.

'Todd?' he said. 'Todd?'

'Look, forget about Todd. I won't mention him again. I'm sorry to bother you but do you have the name or address of the estate agent you bought your house off?'

He looked at me blankly, without a glimmer of recognition that he understood what I was saying.

'Is this YOUR house?'

'No,' he said. 'We rent.'

'Ok. Could I possibly have the telephone number or address of your landlord? The person you pay your rent to?'

'Si, si, si,' he said, and closed the door.

I stood there for a moment, wondering whether to press the doorbell again or admit defeat. I was just in the process of reaching for the doorbell when the door opened again. The man stood there and he handed me a piece of paper with a telephone number written on it.

'Here,' he said. 'Good luck.'

'Thank you. Thank you very much.'

'What have you got there?' asked Mark.

'A phone number.'

'Whose number is it? Todd's?'

'I'm not really sure. There's only one way to find out.'

We located a payphone at a nearby gas station and I dialled the number.

'Hello,' answered a gruff voice. It wasn't Todd.

'Hello. Sorry to disturb you, but I've been give your number and told that you are the landlord for 246 Hammerton Drive.'

'That's correct. Is there some problem?'

'No, no problem. I was hoping you could help me out. Were you the tenant of the house before you rented it?'

'No, I'm just the landlord. I own a few properties. What's this about?'

'I'm sorry. I'm trying to track down one of the previous occupants. He was a friend of mine. I don't suppose you have a forwarding address?'

'No, I don't. Sorry, I can't help you.'

'Did you buy the house through a private sale or an agent?'

'Through a realtor.'

'Could you possibly tell me the name of the realtor you used?'

'Yeah, I think it was Madison and Thomas, they're based over at the mall on Midsummer Boulevard.'

'Fantastic, thank you,' I said, frantically writing details onto the back on my hand.

'Any luck?' asked Mark.

'I've got an address.'

'For Todd?'

'No. Hopefully for the estate agent who sold their house. But we're getting closer.'

'Ok, which way do we go?' said Mark, shifting Josephine into gear.

'I don't know. I've got no idea where this place is.'

It took us half an hour to find the office of Madison and Thomas which was located in a mall on the other side of town. It was 5.30pm and we didn't hold out much hope of the place even being open, let alone them being able to help us.

We parked up Josephine and I dashed over to the office where a *'closed'* sign hanging on the door made my heart sink. I squashed my face against the window to see if there were any members of staff still inside. The small building was empty.

'Can I help you?' called a voice from behind me.

I turned around to see a man in a white sedan with his window down.

'Hi,' I said. 'Do you work here?'

'Yes, but we're closed for the day. We open at 9am tomorrow morning.'

'We won't be here tomorrow,' I said, walking towards his car with a needy expression on my face.

'Are you looking for a place to buy or rent?'

'Neither. We are trying to track down the previous owners of 246 Hammerton Drive. It's a property you sold a few months back.'

'Yeah, I know the place. I can't just give people's contact details out like that.'

'I know, and I wouldn't normally ask. Their son, Todd, was a very good friend of mine at university in England and we've come to surprise him.'

'You came all the way from England to surprise your friend and you don't know his address?'

'No sorry, I didn't mean that. We're over here in America doing a road trip for a few months, and as we were passing nearby to Stockton, I thought I would call in to surprise him. But he's moved house since I was last in contact with him.'

'That's a nice idea, but I still can't just give you an address like that. There are all sorts of data protection and client confidentiality rules.'

'If you have a phone number then you could phone him to ask if you can pass on the address? I promise that we're genuine.'

'Ah man, I was just heading home.'

'I'm really sorry.'

'Ok,' he said, turning off his car engine and undoing his seatbelt. 'You boys wait there. It might take me a few minutes.'

The man returned a few minutes later and handed me a piece of paper with an address written on it.

'There you go. I hope that helps,' he said.

'Thank you so much. I really appreciate it.'

'You're welcome. I hope you find your friend.'

'I hope so too. At least he still lives in Stockton,' I said glancing at the address. 'Is this place far?'

'No, it's just a couple of blocks that way.'

I couldn't wait to see Todd's reaction. We had flown across the Atlantic, driven thousands of miles from the east coast of America to the west coast, and spent most of an afternoon tracking down his new house, and we had finally ended up on his doorstep.

I rang the doorbell.

Todd answered.

'Hey, I was just thinking about you,' he said with that completely expressionless look I knew so well.

I stood there open-mouthed. I wanted to shake him, tell him how cool it was that I'd turned up on his doorstep, and why couldn't he show some visible sign of excitement for once. But this was Todd.

'Todd!' I said, giving him a slightly awkward hug. 'You were just thinking about me?'

'Yeah, about five minutes ago. And now here you are. On my doorstep. Come on in.'

Todd and Mark also knew each other as Mark had come to stay with me several times at university. Behind Todd's deadpan exterior, there was a definite feeling of excitement radiating from him. Although, to the untrained eye, it would have been impossible to detect.

'I didn't know you had my new address,' he said, as we went inside.

'I didn't. It only took us most of the day to track you down.'

Todd introduced us to his mum and dad and they were both extremely welcoming.

'You are staying for dinner, aren't you?' said Todd's mum.

'That's very kind of you, but we've got plenty of food in the car. We are already intruding enough as it is,' I said.

'Nonsense, we insist. It's wonderful to finally meet you. Todd has told us so much about you.'

'Where are you boys staying tonight?' asked Todd's dad.

'In a motel or probably in the car, depending on how far we drive tonight,' said Mark.

'You're both staying here tonight,' said Todd's mum resolutely.

'Honestly, that's very kind, but we…'

'I'm not going to argue. You can both sleep here. We can't have you sleeping in the car.'

I looked to Todd for reassurance.

'Just do as she says,' he said.

'Thank you,' said Mark. 'We would love to stay.'

We spent the evening being given a tour of Stockton by Todd in his car. He drove us around the beautiful college campus where he had studied either side of his year in England, the trees and buildings all immaculately decked out in Christmas lights.
Todd then randomly told us about his recent obsession with

Polish sausages (no, that's not a euphemism), and how we desperately needed to get some to cook for breakfast the following morning. We drove to three different supermarkets before we found some that Todd was happy with. We didn't have the heart to tell Todd that Polish sausages were readily available in the UK.

We returned back to Todd's house, where we drank a couple of beers and chatted late into the night, before going to sleep on a couple of airbeds in the front room.

After a breakfast of eggs and Polish sausages, it was time for us hit the road. Not that we actually had anywhere to go, but we didn't want to impose on Todd's family any longer.

'What are you guys doing for Christmas?' asked Todd.

'We're house-sitting at my uncle's ranch in Petaluma. Want to come?'

'Sure. How long will you be there for?'

'I don't know really. Two or three weeks, I guess.'

'We've got family over here for Christmas Day, but I've got no plans after that. Maybe I could come over?'

'Definitely. I'm not telling you the address, though. You'll have to find us.'

23

It was late afternoon by the time we arrived at my aunt and uncle's ranch in the hills outside the town of Petaluma, California. It was ten days before Christmas and we had been offered the chance to house-sit for a few weeks while my aunt, uncle and cousins all visited the UK.

They lived in a simple but stunning wooden house in the middle of a few hundred hilly acres of rambling ranch land. Their flight to London wasn't for a couple of days, so we had some time to get familiar with the place and spend time with my younger cousins. My uncle briefed us on a list of jobs that he had assigned for us while they were gone, for which he would pay us a modest hourly wage.

A few days later we waved them goodbye as they headed off to San Francisco airport. There was still a little over a week before Christmas and we wanted to get as many of our jobs done beforehand as possible.

The work was tough but fun and varied and made us feel manly. We shovelled gravel, dug holes, cut down trees, planted other trees, moved concrete slabs and stacked wood. We felt like proper ranchers parking up outside the builders' merchant downtown in a pickup truck and ordering half a tonne of gravel. But despite the pickup truck, the left arm tan, the baseball caps and the *'I LOVE AMERICA'* t-shirts (we didn't really wear those), we still couldn't get away with pretending to be locals. Our accents were a slight giveaway. The man inside the builders' merchant even guessed me to be related to my uncle, simply because his was the only other English accent the man knew.

There were at least 20 chickens on the ranch and they were all prolific layers. It was our responsibility to feed them each day, let them out each morning and lock them up each evening, making sure Fluffy was kept well away while they were out. Fluffy was my uncle's huge pet/guard dog Rottweiler, named after the three-headed dog in Harry Potter. Not that this Fluffy had three heads of course. Despite being very well trained and the most docile of dogs, Fluffy still liked to play with the chickens if he ever got the chance… with his teeth.

On the days we had overlapped with my aunt, uncle and three cousins, there had been enough eggs for us all to have them for breakfast each morning. Now there was only Mark and me, the only way for us to stay on top of the vast quantity of eggs was to eat them for three meals a day. They were good eggs, though, and as we had almost no money left, three free meals a day suited us perfectly. Mark was given the role of head egg chef as he was better at cooking scrambled eggs than me. I was his young apprentice.

Some of the work required a bit more manpower – for example, resurfacing the entire half mile long driveway – and we had been told by my uncle to go and hire some additional help for the day. This involved a journey in the pickup truck to a downtown 7-Eleven in the morning. We were advised to get there as early as possible to make sure we got the best workers. My uncle had briefed us on what to expect, but it still didn't prepare us for what happened.

Pulling into the 7-Eleven's parking lot, the truck quickly became surrounded by at least thirty people – mostly Mexican, and almost all men, ranging in age from about 15 to 60. They were all shouting to us and proudly displaying their muscles to prove how strong they were. We had been told to point to two of the strongest looking men, which we quickly did, and they speedily climbed into the back of the pickup truck. The rest of the assembled masses gave a brief sigh but accepted our decision graciously and walked off to wait for the next rancher.

The two men – Eduardo and José – worked tirelessly all day. We fed them lunch (scrambled eggs, of course) and gave them plenty of water. At the end of the day we paid them their money and dropped them back to the 7-Eleven.

I had not expected this sort of system to still operate in modern-day America. But it worked brilliantly. The workers were paid a decent wage for a day's work, and the ranchers were guaranteed reliable help if and when they needed it.

This would be our first Christmas Day spent away from our families. Because of our situation, we didn't feel in the least bit Christmassy and therefore didn't have much cause to celebrate it. It was warm and sunny and we were in California. There was no Christmas tree up at the ranch and no decorations, as my aunt and uncle knew they were going to be away for the holidays.

'What should we cook for Christmas dinner?' asked Mark.

'Scrambled eggs like we have for every other meal?' I said. 'Or we could experiment and try poached eggs instead?'

'I think we should do a proper Christmas dinner. The full works.'

'Just for the two of us?'

'Yeah, why not? We should at least try and make it feel a little bit like Christmas.'

'You're right. Let's do it.'

We made a trip to the supermarket on Christmas Eve to buy all the provisions for our meal. We bought Brussels sprouts, potatoes, packet stuffing, carrots, cranberry sauce and a turkey that was way too big for us. Above the fridge containing the turkeys was a sign saying, *Buy One Get One Free.*

'We might as well get two then,' I said to Mark.

'I suppose so, but it seems a bit silly getting two turkeys for the two of us.'

'They're probably doing the offer to make sure they get rid of them all before Christmas. They will only go to waste.'

So we piled another turkey into the trolley, and enough beer and wine to last us several days.

'Isn't this the wine of your uncle's that we drank last night?' asked Mark holding up a different bottle.

We had been drinking beer most nights and keeping my uncle's supply fully replenished, but we decided the previous night that our scrambled eggs on toast would taste better accompanied by a bottle of pinot noir. We were right. They certainly did.

'Yeah, it looks like it. Why?'

'It's $40 a bottle.'

'Oh shit. Really?'

'Yes. Well, actually it's usually $50. It's on sale for $40.'

'Oh dear. Perhaps we should have drunk it with something other than scrambled eggs.'

'I was thinking maybe we shouldn't have drunk it at all.'

'Oh yes. It was damn good though. Remember I spilled a glass of it on the carpet, didn't I? That would have been about $8 worth.'

'Are we going to have to buy a replacement bottle?'

'No way!' I said. 'We'll just destroy the empty bottle and deny everything.'

I think we got away with it because my uncle never mentioned the wine. And it's unlikely he'll ever read this book.

It wasn't until we got home that I looked at the till receipt and realised we had spent close to $200 on the two of us for Christmas dinner.

'You didn't put that expensive wine in the trolley did you?' I asked Mark.

'No, of course not. Let me have a look at that,' he said, snatching the receipt from me.

'We paid for two turkeys!' he said.

'But they were buy one get one free.'

'Well not according to this. There is no discount applied at the end, and the turkeys both have different descriptions.'

We checked the labels and realised that, in our excitement – and stupidity – we had picked up two completely different brands of turkey. Both had similar labels, but were different products so obviously not eligible for the offer.

'Great. So there are two of us for Christmas dinner and we've gone and bought two massive turkeys,' laughed Mark.

'We are not really cut out for this shit are we?'

Rather than cooking a turkey each – which we did strongly consider – we put one in my aunt and uncle's freezer as a gift for them to find at a later date. We considered it part-compensation for drinking their expensive bottle of wine.

I had a nice long phone call with Rachel on Christmas morning. She had returned to Northampton from Ireland for a few days. Our conversations had improved considerably since she had settled into life in Ireland. She didn't particularly enjoy her new job, but her new surroundings, new work colleagues and new accommodation gave us more to talk about, and it became more of a two-way conversation once again. I still hadn't completely given up on the idea of her coming out to America, and although she still stated categorically that she wouldn't come, there was something about her tone of voice that gave me a slight hope that maybe one of these days she would perhaps change her mind.

Our Christmas meal was very enjoyable and we both surprised ourselves with our culinary skills. It certainly made a change from scrambled eggs on toast three times a day.

With an absence of any gifts from friends or family in the UK to open on Christmas Day, Mark and I had set ourselves a $20 limit to buy each other a present in Petaluma a couple of days before Christmas. Mark bought me a really nice big photography book full of black and white photos of small-town America.

'I realised after I bought it that it's a completely impractical gift to give to someone who is going to be living out of a backpack for another six months,' he said.

'It's brilliant. Thanks very much,' I said. 'I'm sure I can squeeze it into my guitar case. If you think that book is impractical, wait until you see what I've got you.'

Mark tore the wrapping paper off his gift to reveal a large vintage carousel of poker chips.

'Awesome, thank you. Yes, you're right, they are completely impractical but it will be worth the effort to get these home.'

'I thought they could remind you of Vegas, too.'

'We said we would never mention Vegas again.'

I also bought Mark a San Diego Padres t-shirt that I found in a thrift store for $0.99. On the back, where the player's name is printed, it said *'ALBERT'S MOM'*. It was an intriguing t-shirt. Who was Albert? And was this really his Mom's t-shirt? Or was *Albert's Mom* printed as a dig at the player wearing it? Either way, Mark was delighted with it and wore it regularly for many years.

While the turkey was cooking, we took the quad bike, a pitch fork and our two golf clubs, and made our own golf course on the hills above the ranch. We took it in turns to drive the quad bike up and over various ridges, and plant the pitch fork into the grass to act as the flag. We hit a golf ball each and played out the hole before repeating it again and again over different parts of the ranch. It was a brilliant way to spend Christmas afternoon, and proved to be a welcome distraction from us being so far away from our loved ones. The evening was spent drinking Sierra Nevada Pale Ale and avoiding the temptation to raid my uncle's wine rack again.

Mark and I had worked tirelessly up until Christmas, taken a day off for Christmas Day, and then worked solidly for a couple more days. Todd was due to come and stay for a few days but we still had one last tedious job that needed to be crossed off our list.

There was a huge pile of paving slabs stacked next to the chicken coop. Each of these old paving slabs was about a metre square and caked with cement from wherever they had been dug up from. Each one required considerable effort for the two of us to move. This entire stack had to be moved and restacked at a location about 20 metres away. My uncle didn't have any current plan to use these slabs, but they were getting in the way where they were so needed to be relocated. He told us that if we found that any of the slabs were broken we should just load the pieces into the pickup truck and take them to the landfill.

For the first few hours we diligently heaved the slabs up onto the flatbed of the pickup truck one by one, and drove a small pile at a time across to the new site, where we had the more challenging task of lowering each slab onto the new stack. When we discovered a broken slab, we would throw the pieces into a pile at the far end of the truck, ready to be disposed of later. On one occasion, we loaded the slab with a little too much haste and it broke into several pieces as we lowered it onto the pickup.

'Oh well,' I said. 'That's one less one to unload.'

At this point, Mark pushed the top slab from the pile and it slid gracefully to the ground before breaking into pieces.

'Oops,' he said, slinging the manageable bits into the truck.

I picked up a sledgehammer that we had used to install some fence posts with.

'Oops,' I said, wielding it over my head and crashing it down on to the pile, breaking the top three slabs.

We continued to move the slabs, but as the hours went by, more and more of them succumbed to unfortunate accidents making them destined for the landfill instead, and easing our workload considerably.

With a few hours before Todd's arrival, we tidied up the area and drove to a nearby landfill to dispose of our broken slabs. On the way in, we drove over a weigh station which we assumed was checking the weight of the vehicle to make sure it wasn't over a certain limit. We were ushered onwards, where we smugly disposed of the broken slabs. It wasn't until we were reweighed on the way out that we realised they were calculating the weight of the stuff we were getting rid of. We were charged $63 for over half a tonne of paving slabs we had 'accidentally' broken.

It brought our list of jobs to a disappointing end, but we were now free to make the most of the last few days before Mark left California to begin his journey back to England.

24

Todd arrived early in the evening on December 27th. The night was surprisingly mild, and we sat on the large porch of the ranch house, drinking beer and listening to music.

It was great to get to spend time with Todd. After a year of knowing him as a tourist in Britain, it was nice to see a more confident side to him now that I was the tourist.

On Todd's second night at the ranch, we drove into Petaluma to do a small bar crawl.

First up was Andreson's. Stepping through its front doors was like walking into a John Wayne film. The walls were covered from floor to ceiling in stuffed animals. Of the taxidermy variety, that is, not cuddly toys. Animals of all shapes and sizes were mounted as trophies everywhere we looked, with many guns proudly hanging on the walls, too.

In true wild-west fashion, the occupants of the bar all stopped their conversations and turned to face us as we entered. Thankfully there were only four other customers, plus the barmaid. If the jukebox had been playing, it too would have stopped mid-track, as us three out-of-towners walked in.

We sat at bar stools along the bar in Andreson's and drank beer while the barmaid continually washed and dried beer glasses for the duration. The bar was almost empty so I'm sure she just did this out of habit rather than necessity.

One particular item on the wall got my attention more than most. It was a large deer head but it had a bobcat sprawled lavishly across its antlers, as though it was just having a bit of chill-out time. I sat at the bar staring at it, wondering who dreamed up that crazy idea of a wall display.

'Maybe the bobcat was just lazing on the deer like that when it got shot,' suggested Mark.

'You mean this is how they were in the wild when they were killed?'

'Maybe,' he said.

'I like that idea a lot. It does look very natural.'

Next up was a bar called Gale's – a fairly small bar set around an empty dance floor that took up half of the room. We were in the process of ordering our drinks when a man at the bar leaned over to us.

'Where you boys from?' he said.

'England,' said Mark.

'No frickin' way! What you doing all the way out here in Petaluma?'

'Road trip.'

'Let me get you boys a beer.'

'That's very kind, but you really don't…'

'I know I don't, but I wanna.'

'Thank you. That's very generous of you.'

'Janie, darling, get these boys a beer. Are you all from England?'

I looked over to Todd, expecting him to announce that he was actually from California, but instead he just said 'yes indeedy' in a really awful English accent. He was obviously worried the free beer would not have applied to him unless he was English.

The man's name was Ray. He was a rancher and Gale's was his local.

'How local is your local?' I asked.

'10 miles,' he said. 'Only used to take me a few minutes in the truck. Darn cops took away my licence.'

'Why?' asked Mark.

'DUI. I'd been driving that darn road for years at the end of a night here. Never had no problems ever.'

'How did you get caught?'

'Swerved off the road into a ditch.'

He clocked our looks of confusion.

'That sounds like a little bit of a problem,' I suggested.

'But that weren't cos of no drinking. It was just cos I was darn tired after a busy week at work.'

'How do you get here now? You're not still driving are you?'

'Hell no. Well, I did keep driving for a while but I got caught again. Drove into another ditch. Got let off with a final warning. If they catch me again I'll be going to prison.'

'So how do you get to the bar now?'

'By bike,' he said, pointing to an old mountain bike propped against the end of the bar. 'It's ain't no fun riding home at the end of the night, so I try and put it off for as long as possible.'

He downed the remainder of his beer and ordered another.

I was both mightily impressed and slightly concerned with Ray's commitment to his local bar. Judging by the state he was already in, I couldn't help feeling that he would not be any safer on a bicycle than he would be in a car. But at least other road users would be.

We were joined at the bar by another rancher by the name of Drew. Drew had spent a few of his school years in Tunbridge Wells in England.

'What did you think about growing up in the UK?' asked Mark.

'It was alright, I suppose. The only thing I learned in the UK was how to use my cutlery properly.'

We all laughed.

'He's right,' said Ray. 'He sure does use his cutlery real well.'

A little further down the street we played some pool and drank another beer at a lively little bar called Hide-away. The barman asked us for some ID, which was fairly standard in America, but when we presented him with our British passports he studied them for sometime and then asked, 'You got any ID to back these up?'

All I had with me was a school bus pass that had expired four years previously. I showed him this and he seemed satisfied. Mark didn't have anything to back his passport up, but the barman waved his hand as a sign of acceptance. He had probably realised that if we were going to go to the trouble to forge IDs to buy alcohol, we would probably have opted for something a little simpler than a passport.

After Hide-away, we moved on to Kodiac Jacks. Kodiac Jacks was dominated by a mechanical bucking rodeo bull at the front of the bar. It was a fun novelty idea and it certainly caused passers-by to stop and gawp through the window as drunken men and women were tossed around the room by a bull. We stood and watched others thrashing around for a few minutes, but even the thought of riding it was making me feel queasy. So we left.

We finished our drinks and stumbled to another bar called The Bottom Line, which seemed like a fitting name for a pub to end our night in. I don't remember much about the bar except that it served Boddingtons and Newcastle Brown, which seemed like the funniest thing in the world at the time.

We made our way slowly to a taxi rank, and had to walk past Josephine on the way, where we had left her parked on a quiet side street. There were at least a dozen people congregated on the corner waiting for taxis, and it was evident that it was going to take some time to get home.

'Maybe we should just drive,' suggested Todd.

'Yeah right,' I said. 'I think we've had a little too much to drink.'

'So? There's no houses between here and the ranch. We'd be fine.'

'Well I don't want to drive,' I said.

'I'll drive,' said Todd.

'No you won't. I'd rather drive than be driven by you.'

'Fine, you drive then.'

'No. I've never driven drunk before.'

'Never?'

'No, not once.'

'You do-gooder. Mark? Do you want to drive?' said Todd.

Mark stood there swaying.

'No, I don't think I should drive. Drink driving is verrry baaaad,' he said, wagging his finger at me and smiling.

'What if we get stopped? We'd lose our licence,' I said.

'We won't get stopped,' said Todd.

'But what if we do?'

'You wouldn't lose your UK licence. You probably wouldn't be able to drive in the States again, but that doesn't matter.'

'Well it kinda does. Driving a car is quite an important part of a road trip.'

'I thought your coast-to-coast was over?' he said.

'It is, for Mark. But I'm planning on driving Josephine back to New York.'

'So Mark should drive then,' said Todd categorically. 'It won't matter if he loses his licence.'

Mark held up his hands in indifference.

'No, that's not fair on Mark. Losing a licence is not really the point. It's dangerous and irresponsible.'

Todd stared at me, and for the first time since I had known him, I saw his facial expression change slightly. His stony emotionless eyes and his impassive smile slowly burst into life. It was a face that said he knew it was dangerous, he knew it was irresponsible, he knew it was reckless, but why should that stop us?

I stared back at him for several seconds.

'Ok, fine,' I said. 'Let's draw straws.'

'Old skool. I like it,' said Todd, and he picked up a small twig from the floor and snapped it into three.

We each pulled a piece of the stick from Todd's grip. I drew the short straw.

'Maybe we should just queue for the taxi,' said Mark sensibly.

We all looked over to the gathering of people on the corner and it appeared to have doubled in size since we last looked. There was still no sign of any actual taxis.

'It's going to be ok,' I said. 'I'll make sure we get home safely.'

We climbed into Josephine with Mark riding shotgun and Todd in the back. I turned the key and edged Josephine slowly down the street.

As we reached the end of the block, I turned the corner and the first thing we saw was a police car parked up at the side of the road. Three police officers were standing on the pavement, sorry, sidewalk, deep in conversation.

'Shit. This was a really stupid idea,' I said, my heart pounding outrageously quickly.

'Just stay calm,' said Todd. 'They've got no reason to pull us over.'

The police officers didn't even look up as we passed them. After another block we had reached the edge of town and it was just a few miles of countryside between us and home.

I have never driven so slowly or carefully in all my life. I don't think I went faster than 10mph for the duration of the journey. If that park ranger from Death Valley had seen me, he would have had a mental breakdown at my slowness.

Mark had a huge smirk on his face.

'This is like a proper road trip,' he shouted. 'It feels like we are characters in *On the Road* or something.'

'Ha, yeah right,' shouted Todd from the back seat. 'I don't remember Jack Kerouac driving at 8mph because he'd had a few beers.'

'You're like a 21st century Kerouac, George!' yelled Mark out of the open window as we crawled along at little more than walking pace.

Thankfully, we made it back to the ranch without incident and I have never driven under the influence since.

We took a drive into San Francisco for New Year's Eve with Todd, ate a Chinese meal and watched the fireworks over the bay. It was a pretty spectacular end to the year. Mark's adventure was almost over, but mine would soon be entering its next phase.

On New Year's Day we said goodbye to Todd and he drove back to Stockton. My aunt and uncle returned from their trip to the UK later that evening, relieved to find the house still standing, albeit a little dirtier than when they left.

On January 2nd it was time to say goodbye to Mark. This adventure of ours was always supposed to be the two of us until the very end, but it hadn't worked out that way. Mark's return flight was booked from New York, so he would take the train and spend a few days in Chicago and Boston on the way back east. I drove him to the station in San Francisco so he could begin the homeward stage of his journey.

'Thanks for everything,' I said, giving him a hug.

'It's been brilliant,' said Mark. 'I definitely feel like we've done my 90 days justice.'

'We sure have. It won't be the same without you.'

'You'll have an amazing time, wherever you end up next' he said. 'I hope you manage to persuade Rachel to come out here at some point.'

'I hope so too. Although I'm not getting my hopes up.'

'I'm going to miss you, too,' Mark said, turning to look at Josephine. 'You've been a bit heap of shit, but I still love you. Take care of her, George.'

Mark banged Josephine affectionately on the bonnet.

'Hey, be careful,' I said. 'You know what she's like. The engine will probably drop out if you do that too hard.'

We shook hands at the entrance to the train station. He walked towards the doors with his rucksack on his back, his guitar in one hand, and a carrier bag containing a carousel of poker chips in the other. He turned one last time and waved back, and then walked through the doors. I was left standing alone in America.

It was going to be very hard to get used to life without Mark. The prospect of driving across America without him sitting next to me suddenly felt daunting. But it was also an incredibly exciting prospect. Other than my brief excursion to Maryland and Delaware at the beginning of this trip, I had never travelled alone before. In the past I had always had to make decisions with other people about where to go, what to do, when to eat and where to sleep. I now had many months ahead of me and the freedom to shape my own adventure.

25

I spent another two weeks in Petaluma with my aunt, uncle and cousins. I earned some more money digging holes and planting an entire orchard of fruit trees behind the house. I played a lot of football with my young cousins and it was great to get a chance to spend time with them all. I enjoyed working on the ranch and feeling like a man, but again, life had become too comfortable. Mark and I had driven through most of the Southern states, but there was still an awful lot of America left to see, and I felt that my time in Petaluma was drawing to an end.

Despite more than her fair share of problems, and the huge expense she had caused, Josephine had done us well. She had successfully transported us several thousand miles from the east to the west coast of America. Mark's time with Josephine was over, but for me, we were still in the early stages of our relationship. We potentially had a very long way to go still.

I decided to treat Josephine to four new tyres. As we had embarrassingly discovered at Yosemite, one of her wheels was significantly smaller than the others. Due to this imbalance, it had put uneven wear on all four tyres, and the inside rims had run completely bald. Looking back, it was no wonder the axle had broken when it did.

The tyre fitting at the garage in Petaluma included wheel balance and alignment.

'I did the alignment as best I could,' said the mechanic, handing me the keys.

'What do you mean? Is there still a problem?'

'Well, not exactly. I mean she'll run much straighter than she did, but I think the whole car is kinda warped so it ain't possible to get them balanced totally right.'

'The whole car is warped?'

'Yeah, the chassis is completely outta whack. I'm surprised she's lasted this long.'

'Thanks for the vote of confidence.'

'You're welcome. Safe driving.'

Sleeping in Josephine at night had worked surprisingly well. Yes, there had been many sleepless nights due to the cold, disturbances from the police, fear of our surroundings, or just general discomfort. But despite all this, we had found it mostly a pleasurable experience. Most importantly, apart from a couple of nights in campsites, our nights in Josephine had not cost us a cent. If I was going to make it all the way back to the east coast with my meagre savings, I would need to spend many more nights in her.

Lying across the back seat had not been the most luxurious or comfortable of sleeping positions. Now that there was just me to accommodate, there was no reason that I shouldn't try and utilise the size of Josephine a bit better. Both sets of back seats could be easily unscrewed and disposed of, turning Josephine into a van (with windows), and creating a space almost the size of a double bed in the back. I certainly didn't need seven seats now there was only one of me.

I made another visit to the landfill, contemplating how I could get out of paying to get rid of the seats. As I was in a car, rather than a truck, I wasn't required to drive over the weigh station. Instead, a man in a high-vis vest flagged me down.

'What you got?' he asked.

'Er… I'm just chucking out some trash,' I said.

'What sort of trash?' he asked, peering into the back of Josephine, which was free from any trash.

'Err… just this crisp packet and this empty bottle,' I said.

'You came all the way out here to dispose of those? You know you could have just put those in any old trash can?'

'I know. I was just passing so I thought I'd get rid of them here.'

'Ok then,' he said in a way which meant, *'stupid Englishman.'*

I reversed up to the edge of the landfill, unclipped the seats, and pushed them into oblivion in the time it takes to dispose of a crisp packet and an empty bottle. The man in the high-vis vest, unaware of my deceit, gave me a cheery wave as I left. After the $63 we spent disposing of the broken slabs, I felt that the waste disposal site and I were now even.

On seeing my vast new sleeping quarters, my aunt offered me an old futon to use as a mattress.

'It's down in the shed by the chickens,' she said. 'It might be a bit damp, but it should still be very comfortable.'

I opened the shed door and found the folded futon mattress at the back behind the lawnmower. It was covered in dirt but looked like it would do the job perfectly. I dragged it outside and as I unfolded it, three or four mice ran in every direction, including across my bare feet. I shrieked, threw down the mattress, and ran several paces up the garden. I'm not usually scared of mice, but I'm not a fan of them running up my leg either.

Closer inspection revealed that the mice hadn't just been hanging out underneath the folded mattress; they had set up home inside it. A neat little hole in the blue cover led to a nice warm den in the lining. I gave the mattress a couple of whacks with a broom and two more mice made a run for it from the innards.

At this point, any sensible person would have walked away from it and left the futon to the mice. But after the scare I had given them, I realised the mice would be looking for premises elsewhere. So I might as well make use of it. Despite its recent occupants, the mattress did have a certain appeal. I had measured its width and it would fit snugly into the back of Josephine forming a soft wall-to-wall bed.

Using a sharp knife I cut away at the mattress cover. The mice's home was fairly extensive but it only penetrated through half the depth of the dense cotton wool-like filling. I was able to peel away and dispose of several layers that were contaminated with mouse shit. The part that remained was exactly the same length and width as it had been, but about half the depth, and it would still provide significantly greater comfort than the solid car floor. It looked fairly clean but smelled a bit musty. After leaving it out on the decking in the warm Californian sun for a couple of days, however, it smelled a little less offensive.

My aunt donated an old fitted sheet and a pillow and my luxury campervan was almost complete. Josephine was a minivan with windows down the length of each side, and sleeping in it didn't provide any degree of privacy whatsoever. Being so visible at night hadn't been a concern when I had Mark for protection, but I did feel more apprehensive about sleeping in this goldfish bowl on my own. Using a roll of old material and a length of washing line, I fashioned some curtains that I hung down both sides of Josephine, across the back window, and behind the backseats. These could be easily detached during the daytime, and then re-hung each night.

I didn't have any plan or timescale for the next phase of my journey. My open-ended return flight was booked from New York, so I had no constraints other than the fact I was heading vaguely east. In the meantime, Colorado seemed like a good place to aim for. A friend of my uncle ran a bar in Denver and there was a good chance I could get some work collecting glasses for a few weeks on my way through.

26

I left Petaluma late morning in bright sunshine, passed through the beautiful vineyards of the Napa Valley, and skirted around the city of Sacramento. But by the time I crossed the Sierra Nevada later that day, the weather conditions had deteriorated considerably. The Californian sunshine had fooled me. The Sierra Nevada mountain range is depicted on the map as a lush green, with sprightly trees dotted everywhere and the bright blue depiction of Lake Tahoe giving the area the impression of yearlong summer. I had forgotten the fact that it was mid-January and I was driving across a mountain range.

Heavy snow soon piled up on the windscreen and, because I hadn't experienced rain for several weeks, I had also forgotten that Josephine's windscreen wipers didn't work.

Interstate 80 was completely devoid of any other traffic, so I was able to stop the car every few hundred metres to get out and wipe the snow away with my arm. It was beginning to get thicker on the road too. Despite the new tyres, I could feel Josephine sliding about on the road surface. Thankfully I had an unused set of snow chains in the back. We had gone to all that trouble to buy them at Yosemite, and now they were going to come in very handy indeed.

I pulled over in a lay-by and set to work trying to attach the chains. Wrapping one around the front tyre it came up about an inch short. I tried again, but there was no way I could get the length of chain to reach the whole way around the tyre. Surely after that massive ordeal we hadn't bought the wrong chains? I checked the sizing on the box and then looked at the writing on the tyre.

With a sinking feeling I suddenly remembered the man in the tyre shop in Petaluma persuading me to upgrade to slightly 'sportier' – and, of course more expensive – tyres. I was feeling lavish at the time having been working at my uncle's for a few weeks and naively thought that buying Josephine expensive tyres would somehow make her a little less crap, and therefore less likely to suffer any more mechanical failures. Little did I know that 'sportier' also meant bigger and chunkier, and that they would make my set of brand new snow chains completely redundant.

I threw the snow chains into the back and started up Josephine again, feeling for the first time since leaving Petaluma that I was actually in a bit of a precarious situation. It was very dark now, and Josephine's pathetic headlights barely illuminated the road ahead.

The headlights flickered for a few seconds, and I had a brief panic that the electrics were going to fail completely because of the cold. The engine gave an ominous growl, Josephine juddered, and the wheels spun erratically on the road.

'DAMMIT! NOT TONIGHT, JOSEPHINE!' I shouted, banging my fist on the steering wheel and giving the horn a loud blast that nobody would hear but me.

'Please, Josephine…' I said, more calmly this time, '…not tonight.'

A mile or so later, a signpost bearing two words took my fear to a whole different level. Two words that Mark and I had joked about only a month before. Two words that you really don't want to see when you are alone on a deserted snow-covered highway on the top of a mountain:

Donner Summit.

The Donner Summit was the mountain pass on which the Donner party – a group of pioneers on their way to California – got their wagons stranded when they found the road impassable because of snow. They were forced to spend the winter on the mountain. Of the 81 people that set off, only 45 survived, some of them resorting to cannibalism to stay alive.

Mark and I had joked about being stranded on a mountain pass when we nearly ran out of petrol after leaving Death Valley. But the road at the time had been clear of snow, and I knew that I could always eat Mark if things got really desperate.

I inched slowly down the mountain, stopping frequently to scrape the front window, and cursing my stupidity for trying to cross the Sierra Nevada on my own at night in the middle of a snowstorm.

As I descended the mountain, I could see the lights of a city below me, and the road gradually became clearer as the snow turned to rain.

The city was Reno, Nevada. A name I was familiar with only from the Tony Christie song *Don't Go Down to Reno*. Well, I can assure you that Tony Christie never had to drive alone over the Donner Summit in a snowstorm in a car with no windscreen wipers. Because if he had, he would have known that driving into Reno is pretty much the greatest feeling in the world, and he would damn well have told everyone he knew they should Definitely Go Down to Reno.

Reno is a smaller, crapper version of Las Vegas, but it had cheap motels and dirty food, which was all I needed that night. I bought a pizza and a bottle of wine, avoided all the casinos, checked into a motel, and felt a huge sense of relief that I had somehow survived my first day driving on my own.

I left Reno early the following morning. Josephine was parked directly outside my room door – as is common with many motels – and as I loaded my bag into the back of the car, I bundled in the king-size blanket from the motel bed, and one of the sheets, too. This wasn't a spontaneous criminal act. It was a cleverly orchestrated crime that I had masterminded during my descent of the Sierra Nevada the night before when I realised that sleeping in Josephine in January was going to be much colder than I had anticipated. I even checked into the motel under a false name and address, just to help cover my tracks. I am such a badass.

From Reno, I followed the road south to the state capital, Carson City, where I joined Route 50 and headed east. In 1986, Life Magazine declared Route 50 *'the loneliest road in America'*. At the time, this was intended to be derogatory. But Nevadans thought otherwise and have embraced the name, proudly displaying it on many of the highway's official signs.

From the town of Fallon, about 20 miles east of Carson City, Route 50 goes from two lanes to one. I stopped for lunch and gas in Austin, a quaint ex-mining town in the foothills of the Toiyabe Mountains. I was tempted to book a motel for the night, but I then spotted the town of Eureka, Nevada on the map. With a name like that it was too tempting an opportunity to let pass.

Continuing onwards was a decision I came to regret almost immediately. The snow began to fall more heavily than the previous night, and although the road didn't climb quite as high as it had done, conditions were even more treacherous, and even in the late afternoon the visibility was down to virtually nothing.

Somehow, I eventually reached the town of Eureka well after dark and decided to have an early night. I parked up by a building site and lay down in the back of Josephine, the temperature already well below freezing. Despite wearing all my clothes and being in a sleeping bag with the extra blanket stolen from the motel, my teeth would not stop chattering and the cold was making it difficult for me to breathe. I couldn't stop shivering and the night was only going to get colder. I decided to do the sensible thing and check into a motel.

The bell on the door of the reception startled the elderly red-haired lady behind the counter as I entered. She looked at me in surprise as though I was the first person to walk through that door in many months. It's possible I was. I counted at least eight cats in the small office behind her, either curled up asleep on counters, or walking along the desk.

'Welcome,' she said, spreading her arms out wide.

She seemed delighted to see me, and also possibly very drunk.

'Good evening. Do you have a room for the night?'

'I have many rooms,' she said, gesturing to the rack of keys behind her. None of which were missing.

'That's brilliant, thank you. How much for a single?'

'For you, my darling, $40.'

This was a little more than I hoped, but the thought of anywhere warm was worth it.

'That's right,' she continued. '$35. Rooms are $35.'

'$35? I thought you said… Oh ok.'

Things were getting even better.

'I'll take it,' I said. 'Thanks.'

'Ok, fantastic. That'll be $45 dollars then please.'

'$45? I thought you said it was $35?'

'Yes, that's right. $30 please,' she said, and I realised she had rested her hand on mine and was gazing longingly into my eyes.

'Here you go,' I said, handing her $30.

She was like a human stock market with the price fluctuating rapidly. I thought I had got the room when prices had plummeted to their lowest, but she then opened the till and handed me $5 change.

'That's ok,' I said. 'You said the rooms were $30.'

'Did I? No, they are only $25 for a single.'

'Oh, ok then. Thank you.'

'Good night, my darling,' she said. 'Sweet dreams.'

She waved gently at me as I left the reception. I dumped my bag on the bed in the room and headed out to check out downtown Eureka.

The only place that showed any sign of life was the Owl Club on North Main Street. I hadn't seen any wildlife since entering Nevada. I had assumed this was because of the cold. But after stepping inside the Owl Club, it was apparent that the state's entire wildlife population was on display on its walls. I pulled up a stool at the bar and ordered a beer.

'Not from these parts by the sound of it?' said the barmaid.

'No, just passing through. I'm from England.'

'Well you can't pass through Eureka without trying some of the Owl Club's world famous food.'

'World famous? Is that right?'

'Damn right. The best food for miles around is served right here.'

'Wow, I had no idea,' I said, not wanting to point out that it also seemed to be the only place that served food for miles around. Maybe that was her little joke.

The bar area had several slot machines lined up against the far wall, and each one had a lone man sat by it pumping in quarters hoping that tonight was going to be his lucky night. I wanted to go and tap them on the shoulder and warn them to look out for the *'collect'* button illuminating, even if they only spun two bells, but I guessed they already knew that.

The restaurant was at the far end of the bar and was surprisingly busy for a weeknight in January. The diners were all middle-aged men, eating alone, presumably also just passing through Eureka. I had planned to just get some crisps from the gas station and eat them back in the motel, but the smell of the hot food was incredibly appealing. And I knew I was unlikely to be back at the Owl Club anytime soon.

'The special today is lamb stew and mashed potato,' said the waitress, handing me a menu.

'What are those guys eating? It looks good.'

'Today's special. It's the best lamb and mashed potato for miles around.'

'I'll have the lamb and mashed potato then please.'

'Sure thing.'

The lamb stew and mash was delicious and I can honestly say that, at the time, I had never tasted better food in Eureka, Nevada, and possibly even within a 50 mile radius of the Owl Club.

I ventured back to the motel via the gas station where I bought some beers and chocolate for me and a bottle of anti-freeze for Josephine.

The heater in the room didn't work, but I didn't have any desire to face my red-headed admirer again, so I brought in my sleeping bag and blanket from the car and settled down for a cold night in the motel.

I woke the following morning in a wonderful mood. The crisp air and endless blue sky made Eureka feel like the best place on Earth. I took out my camera to take a photo of the town, but as I clicked the shutter, the film wouldn't wind forward. It was so cold that the mechanism had seized completely. I opened a carrier bag in which I had put some bananas the day before but the entire bunch had turned black from the cold.

It made the $25 I paid for the motel seem like a very wise investment. I honestly think if I had gone to sleep in Josephine in Eureka, there is a very good chance I would never have woken up again.

I returned my key to the lady in reception, and she was still smiling away as though she had been sat at the desk with her cats all night. She insisted on opening the dividing hatch and coming round to my side of the desk and giving me an almighty hug. I didn't think she would ever let go.

With no bananas to eat, I treated myself to breakfast at the Pony Express Deli and ordered a three-egg chorizo burrito and a coffee. My morning had just got even better, and the Owl Club's 'world-famous' cuisine had just been knocked into second place by a deli just down the road. Bizarrely, the lady who served me breakfast was the same waitress who had worked in the Owl Club the night before. She asked me lots of questions about my trip and found it hysterical that I didn't even know where I was driving to next, let alone in a few weeks' time.

A man at the table next to me wore a battered *Eureka, Nevada* baseball cap. American place names always look particularly cool on clothing, just like they sound cool in songs. I can't imagine any shops doing a roaring trade with *Northampton, East Midlands* baseball caps.

Eureka, Nevada had promised great things with its name, and it certainly didn't disappoint. For such a small town, it had more than its fair share of characters. As I headed out of town, I passed the welcome sign on the edge of the highway for people entering from the opposite direction:

'Eureka, Nevada – the loneliest town in America.'

This seemed unfair. Although geographically Eureka is pretty damn lonely (the next nearest towns along Route 50 are Austin – 70 miles to the west, and Ely – 77 miles to the east), Eureka, Nevada felt anything but lonely. The town has since changed its welcome signs. They now read:

'You are entering the friendliest town on the loneliest road in America.'

This suits Eureka much better.

Route 50 had been a terrifying road to drive on in the snow at night. In the sunshine, however, it was fabulous. I had nobody else to share the road with and was able to regularly stop the car in the middle of the road to take photographs and marvel at the view; the road stretching endlessly off towards the foothills of the snow-capped mountains sitting serenely along the horizon.

I stopped in Ely to use the internet at the town library. The librarian was so surprised to hear an English accent that she dusted off a visitor's book and insisted that I sign my name. The previous entry was from a Londoner several months before.

I had an email from Rachel.

'Can you call me please.'

I called her straightaway from a nearby payphone.

'Is everything ok?' I said.

'Yes fine. I've just been thinking a lot about what you said the other day.'

'About you coming to America?'

'Yes.'

'And? Are you going to?'

'No, I'm really sorry. I can't.'

'Why not? You don't like your job much. You've saved up a bit of money. Come out here and we can have an adventure together.'

'I… no… it's not that simple.'

'Yes it is. You just book a plane ticket, get on the plane, and then you're here. We can be together. Isn't that what we both want?'

'It's just…'

'Just what? That's all there is to it.'

'I think I'm going to go to Australia,' she said.

'Wh… ? Australia?'

'Yes.'

'Australia? As in… Australia, Australia?'

'Yes.'

'How? Why?'

'I don't know. I thought coming to Ireland would make things easier, but it hasn't. I need to go on an adventure too.'

'That's why I keep telling you to come to America.'

'But that's your adventure. I need my own. I've always wanted to go to Australia, so I think I'll have saved up enough money to go some time in April.'

'Ok. Well I'd better go. My credit is about to run out,' I said, hanging up the phone and instantly regretting ending the conversation so badly.

When Rachel had told me she was moving to Ireland, I had found the concept very difficult to process. Now she was planning to go to Australia I felt physically sick. At least Ireland had been a little bit closer to America than Northampton. Now she was planning to move to the other side of the world.

Not once had she ever mentioned wanting to go to Australia. Perhaps she was doing it deliberately to get revenge? I knew I couldn't argue with her. I was the one who had disappeared halfway around the world, and now I had to deal with the consequences of whatever she chose to do with her life.

27

I had been driving for many miles with tears in my eyes, unable to comprehend what Rachel had told me. A few miles east of Ely, in the wide expanse of nothingness that occupies much of Nevada, I passed a sign:

PRISON AREA
HITCHIKING PROHIBITED

I smiled a tiny smile as I wiped away my tears and imagined passing a man dressed in bright orange, or black and white striped overalls (and possibly a bag with *SWAG* written on it), standing at the side of the road with his thumb out on a stretch of road miles from anywhere. I think even without the warning sign they would have looked a little out of place. I stopped to take a quick photo and then climbed back into Josephine much quicker than I normally would have. Just in case.

I stopped for a break at the Border Café on the Utah state border. Surrounded by desert, it was the last gambling threshold before the gambling-free state of Utah and many people were taking full advantage of this fact.

I called home to speak to my mum.

'You sound like wherever you are calling from is being raided,' she said, as the bells and sirens of the fruit machines around me kept blaring away.

'No, I'm in a casino,' I said.

'A casino? What time is it with you?'

'About 11am.'

'Why are you in a casino? Is that what you've been doing since leaving Petaluma?'

'No, I'm not doing anything in the casino. It's the only civilisation I've passed for miles. I'm in the middle of the desert and I stopped to use the toilet and phone you.'

'I can't hear you very well,' she said as the fruit machine next to me simulated a jackpot win by playing an immensely annoying tune. I reached behind the machine and switched it off at the plug.

'Is that better?'

'Yes, much.'

'Rachel's moving to Australia,' I said.

'Australia? What do you mean?'

'I spoke to her on the phone earlier. She's going to Australia.'

'For good?'

'No. Well, at least, I hope not. Just to do some travelling I think.'

'How long for?'

'I don't know. I don't think she knows. I don't know what to do.'

'What can you do? I guess you'll have to just try and support her with whatever she decides to do.'

'I'm thinking about coming home.'

'Don't do that. What's that going to achieve?'

'It might stop her going to Australia.'

'But if it does, Rachel will then just feel guilty for cutting your trip short.'

'But at least we'd be together.'

'You will be together. But if Rachel feels that she needs to go to Australia, then you'll have to just let her go. She let you go to America.'

'I know. But I'm starting to wish she hadn't.'

I continued east on Route 50. Driving for so long on *'the loneliest road in America'* probably didn't do much to help my emotional state, but I had quickly grown to love that road with its simplicity and solitude.

After spending so long laboriously converting Josephine into a luxurious campervan, I was yet to spend the night in her. Despite being in the desert, the nights were bitterly cold, and the truth was I was still a little apprehensive about sleeping in the car alone. After being paid for a few weeks' work by my uncle, I had money in my pocket and the temptation to spend it on motels and hot food was too much. I gave in and rented a room at a cheap motel in Salina, a small town in the middle of the Utah desert.

I ate a huge meal of chicken strips, fries and a milkshake from Calico Kitchen Drive In and then went to bed still angry at Rachel, but mostly at myself, and hoping everything would feel better in the morning.

By morning, my anger had been replaced by a crushing feeling of sadness. Even when Rachel had moved to Ireland, I was hopeful that it was only temporary and there would still be time for her to come and join me in America. But now with a trip to Australia on the cards, this seemed impossible.

I seriously considered cutting my trip short and booking a flight home immediately. Maybe if I was back in England, Rachel wouldn't feel the need to go to Australia. But my mum had been right. Although that would potentially solve the problem, it would no doubt lead to others. Rachel would feel as though she was partly responsible for my shortened trip, and I would have selfishly denied her the chance of her own adventure.

Fortunately there are no flights to the UK from the middle of the Utah desert, so flying home wasn't an option. I would press on for a few more days and see how I felt once I got to Denver.

I checked out of the motel and treated myself to another breakfast out. A good breakfast, I knew, could solve most problems. I ordered eggs, sausage, hash browns and coffee at Mom's Café on Main Street. I once read a book called *Blue Highways* by William Least Heat Moon. In it, the author travels the back roads of America. He has an obsession with the number of calendars displayed on the walls of cafés. His theory is that the higher the number of calendars on the wall, the better the quality of the food and service. The humble calendar has declined in modern years, with pocket diaries and electronic calendars taking over. So despite my searching, it was quite rare to see any calendars adorning the walls of local cafes. Mom's Café in Salina, Utah had three, and the breakfast was damn delicious.

Feeling much more positive about life in general, I phoned Rachel after breakfast and apologised for hanging up on her the day before.

'That's ok,' she said. 'I should have told you about Australia in a better way. I'm sorry.'

'I'm sorry too. I'm sorry for all of this. I never should have come to America in the first place.'

'Don't say that.'

'It's true. It was stupidly selfish of me. I've caused all these problems between us.'

'It's not all your fault. The timing of us getting together just wasn't ideal. I'm sure it will all work out ok in the end.'

'I really hope so. I love you.'

'I love you too'.

I drove to Arches National Park where I spent the day wandering around the park's dramatic sandstone monoliths, buttes, spires, balanced rocks, and, of course, arches that had been formed over the course of millions of years of erosion. I left feeling somewhat disappointed. If Arches National Park had been my first National Park it would have been one of the most impressive things that I had seen. But I had been completely spoiled by the beauty of America and it was almost as though I had visited the country's natural wonders in the wrong order. Having already witnessed the Grand Canyon, Monument Valley, Zion and Yosemite, a few stone arches were always going to feel like a slight let down.

The small city of Moab, Utah often describes itself as the *'Adventure Capital of the West'*. I had heard lots of great things about it. Thrill-seekers flock from all over to hike, mountain-bike, climb, abseil and go river-rafting in the surrounding area. I had high hopes as I parked up downtown to see what Moab had to offer. Nothing, in the middle of January it seems. The town was completely dead.

I picked up a copy of the local newspaper as I sat and drank a coffee in the only place open in town. The local mayor had written a feature piece for the front page of the paper:

'You're probably thinking Moab is dead this time of year,' he wrote.

Well, it's funny you should mention that, Mr Mayor, that's EXACTLY what I was thinking.

'Well, you're wrong,' he continued. 'Turn to page 32 to find out what's happening.'

Ok, so perhaps I was being too presumptuous. Maybe there is a lot going on in Moab.

As instructed, I turned to the events listing on page 32. There were two events mentioned:

YOGA CLASS – Thursdays 2pm-3pm. No need to book. Just turn up.

ROCK SOC – bring your pebbles along to Tuesday night's Rock Society to compare with others.

That was it.

As much as the lure of Rock Soc tempted me to stay for a few more days, I didn't actually have any pebbles to compare with others. So, with a heavy heart, I left Moab pebbleless and continued east and into Colorado.

Josephine had started to do the occasional juddering again like she had as I crossed the Sierra Nevada. But it would soon pass, and she would be fine for another 20 miles. I hoped to get at least as far as Denver where I could then have her looked at. It seemed that I was desperately trying to contain all my problems – both mechanical and emotional – until I got to Denver. Once I reached Denver, everything would be alright.

I arrived in Grand Junction after dark and found a cheap hostel style room at the Historic Melrose Hotel. There was no mention of what made it historic. Americans have a habit of labelling something as historic simply because it has been there for more than 20 years. I got a greasy burger at a nearby diner – there were no calendars on the wall, but it still tasted pretty good – watched some trash TV and went to bed.

I was heading towards Denver the following morning when one of my problems could contain itself no longer and unburdened its troubles on the interstate. Fortunately, it was Josephine and not me. She had a major radiator leak on I70. The temperature gauge bolted up to maximum and steam spurted out the front grill.

I was passing the upmarket ski resort of Vail at the time and was able to pull into town and park up Josephine to assess the damage. By assess the damage I mean open up the bonnet and tut quite a lot. I didn't know what I was looking for but I could tell it did not look good. I decided to leave her for a few hours to cool down while I walked around town and tried to keep my emotional state from exploding too.

Perhaps this was destiny? Maybe Josephine was supposed to break down in Vail and this would be where I would spend the rest of the winter? I could get a job as a waiter in a restaurant, do a bit of skiing, and somehow find somewhere affordable to stay for a few months. Things suddenly didn't seem so bad after all.

I spotted a restaurant called Sweet Basil. It was mid-afternoon and the place was empty apart from a couple of staff members setting tables. I knocked on the door (who knocks on the door of a restaurant?) and stepped inside.

'Hi,' said the young waitress. 'Would you like a table?'

'No thanks. I was actually looking for a job.'

'Right, ok. What sort of job are you after?'

'Anything really. A waiter?'

'Have you waited tables before?'

'Oh yes, of course. I have worked in restaurants most of my life,' I lied, having never worked in a restaurant before.

'Are you trained in silver-service?'

'Yes. Very trained,' I said, and there was an awkward pause when we just looked at each other. I was standing there in a pair of ripped jeans and three t-shirts pulled over the top of a shirt because I hadn't had a jumper since losing mine in Port Gibson. I didn't look like the most sophisticated silver-service waiter in the world.

'Ok, well I'll speak to my boss and see what she says and we'll get back to you. How does that sound?'

'Great, thanks very much.'

It wasn't until I was standing back outside the restaurant that I realised she hadn't asked me for my name or contact details, and I foolishly hadn't offered them.

I suddenly felt quite out of place in Vail. Josephine was parked up in a row of pristine black SUVs and there was something about the town that made me feel slightly intimidated. Vail was probably not for me after all.

I topped up Josephine's radiator with water and hoped that I would make it to Denver before she gave up completely. I was on the top of the Rockies and Denver was near the bottom, so in theory it should be downhill all the way.

I was listening to some random local country music radio station, as I had done for the last few months, when the music was rudely interrupted by an urgent announcement.

'WARNING!' said the stern voice on the radio. 'YOU ARE APPROACHING A ROTARY! PROCEED WITH CAUTION!'

Holy shit, what's happening? I thought. *What's a rotary?*

'ROTARY APPROACHING! SLOW DOWN NOW!' the voice said, with even more aggression this time.

Oh god, I'm going to shit myself. What the fuck is going on?

'CAUTION!'

Oh help. I can't take this. I'm going to be sick.

'GIVE WAY TO VEHICLES FROM THE LEFT. ONCE YOUR PATH IS CLEAR, PROCEED AROUND THE ROTARY IN AN ANTI-CLOCKWISE DIRECTION UNTIL YOU REACH YOUR DESIRED EXIT.'

Wait a minute? That sounds a bit like a roundabout.

And then a series of huge signs appeared on the roadside, each with more and more severe warnings about the approaching rotary, and with clear diagrams about how to navigate it.

It was at this point I realised I had driven well over 10,000 miles across America, and this was the first roundabout I had encountered. It's no wonder they were making such a fuss about it.

Despite being proven to ease congestion, being far cheaper to maintain than traffic lights, statistically safer, and much less of a blight on the landscape, America had been very reluctant to embrace the roundabout for decades. British journalist,

Stephen Beard, suggested that, *'the U.S.'s more aggressive, confrontational culture may explain why the roundabout has not been more widely adopted by Americans'*. But things are changing and there has been a dramatic increase in roundabout numbers in recent years with more and more being constructed all the time.

This particular roundabout along Interstate 70 in Colorado was presumably one of the first, which would explain why the local authorities were treating it with such caution.

Steam began spurting ferociously out of the side of Josephine's bonnet. Not because of the rotary, I should add. She coped with that marvellously. The radiator leak was more serious than I first thought, and when I reached the town of Silverthorne she spluttered to a complete standstill just off the interstate.

I phoned for a recovery truck and arranged for Josephine to be towed yet again. Whilst waiting for help to arrive, I found out that Silverthorne had a youth hostel. So after being towed to a local garage, I rented a bed for the night.

The hostel dormitory was full of people struggling with various addictions and demons, and it became clear that I had inadvertently checked myself into some sort of refuge rather than a backpacker's hostel. I had wondered why the nightly rate was so cheap. All of the others occupants of my dormitory had been there for several months and I looked more than a little out of place.

The following morning, I walked to the garage where I had paid for a diagnostics check for Josephine. The results were not good. I was hoping that the radiator could be soldered back together, or perhaps patched up with copious amounts of duct tape. But the entire thing needed replacing, as well as the water pump at a cost of $700. I was probably being greased up and screwed, but I told them to let me think about it and I spent the rest of the day moping around town feeling sorry for myself.

I considered cutting my losses and getting rid of Josephine. She had carried me all the way across America and then all the way back to Colorado. I could get a bus into Denver easily enough, and then decide whether to fly home to England, or work in a bar for a few weeks, earn some money and then either buy a new car or see some more of America by bus. That wouldn't be so bad.

But I had only recently spent time lovingly converting Josephine, and was yet to even spend a night in her. Also, the romance of the open road in America had been even more incredible than I had hoped. It wouldn't be the same on a bus. I went back to the hostel to consider my options.

I got talking to the other occupants of the hostel, many of whom were already drunk. It was 11am. They all talked about their troubled and traumatic childhoods, many having been thrown out of their homes at a very young age, or taken into care by the authorities. I heard horrendous stories of child abuse, drug addiction, violence, prison time and abandonment. It suddenly put things into perspective for me, and I realised how trivial my problems were. Paying to fix Josephine's latest ailment was not ideal, but it was hardly comparable with what these others had been through. I was in the middle of a year long holiday, and I was fortunate enough to have the money (on a credit card, at least) to pay for the repairs. I phoned the garage to give them the go ahead and I suddenly felt a lot rosier about my situation.

It would take a day or two for the parts to arrive, so I wished my roommates all the best and boarded a bus to the ski resort of Breckenridge, where one of the guys had told me there was another hostel. And this one was apparently full of 'people like me'. I wasn't sure if this was supposed to be a good thing.

28

I fell in love with Breckenridge the moment I stepped off the bus. Breckenridge is a beautiful Wild West-looking town high in the mountains. The main street is lined with wooden shops, restaurants and bars, with the majestic peaks of The Rockies all around. The town was filled with the smiling faces of skiers returning from a day on the slopes, and families heading off for drinks in the early evening sun. I later found out that the Jim Carey film *Dumb and Dumber* – set partly in the exclusive ski resort of Aspen – was filmed mostly in Breckenridge, because Breckenridge looks much nicer. The place had a wonderful feel to it, and it seemed like the perfect spot to while away a few days while Josephine was at the garage.

A few blocks away from Main Street I located The Fireside Inn; a beautiful detached pale-blue wooden building surrounded by a white picket fence. The Fireside Inn was a bed and breakfast that also had a few hostel-style dormitory rooms making it the only accommodation that sat remotely near my budget. As far as youth hostels go, it looked pretty damn perfect.

I walked through the front door and into the lounge area. A few comfy looking sofas sat around a wood-burning stove. A middle-aged lady sat on one reading her book. She looked up and smiled. To the other side, a man cooked a steak on a George Foreman grill in a small kitchen area. He too acknowledged me with a smile.

The office was located at the back of the building through another kitchen.

'Helloooo,' I called, as I cautiously knocked on the door.

'Good afternoon,' replied a very well-spoken English accent. 'I'll be right with you.'

Seconds later a man sprang excitedly into the doorway. He was in his fifties, athletically built, cropped grey hair, a broad smile, and, somewhat disturbingly, a pair of bright blue spandex leggings that left absolutely nothing to the imagination.

'Helloooo,' he said jovially. 'How can I help you?'

'Hi… I was wondering if you had a bed for a couple of nights. Preferably in one of the dormitories?'

'We certainly do. What brings you out here?'

'Car trouble,' I said.

'I'm sorry to hear that. I meant what brings you to the good old U S of A? You don't sound like you're American.'

'Oh, sorry. No I'm not. I'm from England. I'm on a road trip and I was on my way to Denver when my car broke down at Silverthorne, so I thought I would come and check out Breckenridge for a couple of days while it gets fixed.'

'Fantastic. Well welcome to The Fireside Inn.'

'Thanks! You don't sound like you're from the good old U S of A either.'

'No, no, that's correct. My wife Niki and I recently bought this place. We moved over from England with our daughter a couple of weeks ago.'

'Hello!' said another face that popped out from behind the door. 'I'm Niki, Andy's wife,' she said, shaking me by the hand.

'Hi Niki. I'm George,' I said.

'George,' said Andy. 'Good solid name that. I'm Andy.'

'Very nice to meet you both. So, what brings you both out to Colorado? Did you run a bed and breakfast back in England?'

They both burst out laughing at this point.

'No!' said Niki. 'Andy was in the army. He spent 26 years with the Royal Engineers and he retired last year so we thought we'd try something new.'

'That's right,' said Andy. 'We don't have a bloody clue what we're doing, to be perfectly honest. We have absolutely no experience of cooking or hospitality. But how hard can it be?'

'So how did you end up in Breckenridge?' I asked.

'I was based down in Colorado Springs for a while and Niki and I fell in love with Breckenridge when we used to come up to visit. When The Fireside Inn came up for sale, we thought we'd go for it.'

'Cool. How's it going so far?'

'Chaotic, but we'll get there. We're still just learning the ropes.'

'I'm sure you'll be just fine.'

'I hope so,' said Andy. 'So, is it just the two nights you wanted to stay for?'

'Yes please,' I said. But I already had a slight inkling that my stay at The Fireside Inn would be somewhat longer.

I didn't have enough money to be able to rent any skis or buy a lift pass, but I wandered down to the bottom of the slopes and stood and watched hundreds of happy people come and go, with a brilliant bright blue sky and the Rocky Mountains towering magnificently above. I could get used to this.

I thought about asking at some restaurants about work, but unless I could find somewhere to stay in town there was probably little point. Although The Fireside Inn was the cheapest place in town, staying there long term would have cost me most of my earnings. The sensible thing was to continue on to Denver where I should be able to earn some money, and then perhaps I could treat myself to a couple of days skiing.

Back at the hostel I sat on the sofa and took the time to write my diary and people-watch as the other residents came and went.

'What are you like at cooking scrambled eggs?' asked Niki, in a slightly jokey manner.

'I'm bloody good, as a matter of fact,' I said, recalling all the eggs Mark and I had eaten in Petaluma.

'How about bacon?' said Niki.

'I cook a mean piece of bacon, too. Why?'

'There was a German lad called Hans working here at the Fireside when we arrived here. He has been helping out cooking the breakfasts for all the guests each morning.'

'Yes, I think I've seen him around already.'

'Well anyway, he's decided to leave. I don't think it's because of us. Just a coincidence, I'm sure. Tomorrow is his last day.'

'Oh. Ok,' I said, still not completely sure what she was asking.

'I know you're heading off to Denver for work, but Andy and I were wondering whether you would be interested in staying on here for a couple more days to help out with breakfast, until we find someone more permanent?'

'Yes, I'd be very happy to do that.'

'The arrangement we had with Hans was…' she paused. '…non-financial.'

I gulped, expecting Niki to divulge some strange sex-slave agreement they'd had with the poor young German lad, which perhaps gave an indication about the reasons for his sudden departure.

'Oh,' I said. 'Right.'

'He helped us for an hour or so each morning with breakfast, and in return he got a free bed for the night. Plus you could help yourself to breakfast too, of course.'

'Free accommodation and breakfast in return for a couple of hours work?'

'Yes, I know it's not great. Would you be interested for a few days until we find someone to cover for the rest of the season?'

I couldn't believe what I was hearing.

'Would you and Andy consider having me stay for the rest of the season?' I said, without a second thought.

'Well, yes, of course. But what about your job in Denver?'

'Nothing has been confirmed. And I would much rather stay in Breckenridge.'

'Well we would love to have you. Andy will be delighted.'

I had only been in Breckenridge for a few hours and I already had free accommodation (and breakfast) sorted for another three months.

I bumped into Hans the German later that evening. His English was limited but he told me he had enjoyed working at The Fireside Inn. Things had definitely become more chaotic since the new owners had taken over, but he assured me that they had nothing to do with him leaving. He also warned me that I had better quickly get used to seeing Andy in spandex as it was a regular thing.

'Let me show you to your room,' said Andy. 'Well, it's not really a room. It's more of a bed. Actually, it's not even a bed. It's a mattress on the floor in a gap under the eaves. Is that ok?'

'It sounds perfect,' I said.

My sleeping quarters for the next three months consisted of a space alongside the bathroom in the upstairs dormitory. It was a gap under the eaves only suitable for storage, but it was also just wide enough to slide a thin mattress into. There was no headroom, so I had to crawl in and out, and all my belongings had to be piled up at the foot of the mattress. Harry Potter's much pitied cupboard under the stairs was a penthouse compared to this. The ungrateful little shit.

It felt just like sleeping in a small tent… but inside. I absolutely loved it. Andy and Niki stopped calling me George after the first few days and simply referred to me as 'The Cave Dweller'.

I phoned Rachel and told her all about my new job.

'So how is everything with you?' I said. 'How's life in Ireland?'

'Yeah, it's ok thanks. It's not for much longer.'

'Have you booked your flights to Australia yet?'

'Not yet. I'm still just sorting out a few things. So do you think you'll be in Breckenridge for a few months then?'

'I hope so. It all depends on whether I can get some work.'

'What sort of work?'

'I don't know really. Anything I can get. Bar work, washing up, cleaning. There are loads of bars and restaurants in town so hopefully I'll be able to get something.'

'But your accommodation is free, yes?'

'Yeah, and breakfast! But everything is so expensive out here, so I'll need to be earning money to have any chance of being able to stay here until the end of the season. And I'd love to be able to do some snowboarding while I'm here.'

'It sounds great. I'm sure you'll find some work.'

'I hope so. I really love it here. Travelling from place to place is brilliant fun but it's also nice knowing that I'm going to be in the same place for a while now.'

'It's nice for me to think of you being in the same place for a while, too.'

'How do you mean?'

'I think that's what has made this all so hard. Whenever I've thought about you I've never known where you are or what you are doing, and it makes you seem even further away than you are.'

'I guess I hadn't thought of it like that. Well now, every day about the time you are having your lunch, you can know that I'll be here cooking scrambled eggs and bacon.'

'That's nice to know. Thanks.'

I chatted to several of the other hostel guests as they came and went that first evening. Many of them invited me out for a few beers, but with Josephine's hefty repair bill looming over me, I thought I should wait until I had sourced some work before spending any more money. Tomorrow I would walk into town and go from bar to bar until I found a job. Not having any experience, or any form of work visa, was a slight stumbling block, but I was confident I could find something.

The hostel had emptied for the evening, and I stretched out on the sofa in the lounge, an 80s rom-com on the television at low volume in the corner and the fire crackling away. Life was good.

A scruffy looking man entered through the front door. He was in his late forties, with a bushy moustache, creased face, dark eyes, baggy jeans tucked inside a pair of workman's boots with no laces, and a New York Yankees baseball cap.

He was holding a pile of flyers.

'Do you work here?' he asked.

'No,' I said. 'Well, from tomorrow I sort of will.'

'Do you mind if I leave a pile of these here? They're flyers for my food delivery service.'

'I'm sure that's fine. You can leave them on top of that bookcase.'

'Thanks. Do you know of anyone with a car looking for work?' he asked.

'What sort of work?'

'I'm looking for another food delivery driver to work evenings for me.'

'I'll do it!'

'Do you have a car?'

'Yes. Well, I will from tomorrow. It's at the garage.'

'It needs to be a reliable car.'

'My car is extreeeeemely reliable. It's just in for a routine service.'

'Ok. But didn't you just say you were going to be working here from tomorrow?'

'Only at breakfast time. The rest of the day and the evenings I'm free.'

'When can you start?'

'Tomorrow?'

The man's name was James. He had lived in Breckenridge for almost ten years, working a variety of different jobs. His food delivery service was a fairly new enterprise that he was slowly building up. Rather than delivering from a specific restaurant, James had agreements with about ten different restaurants in town – none of which had their own delivery service. Customers could ring up and place orders for food from these restaurants – or multiple restaurants, if they preferred – and have the food delivered. James manned the phones, and was the middle man between the customers and the restaurants, while also controlling a team of two or three drivers. Business was going well, hence the need to employ a new driver.

29

As I walked into James's office the following evening, I shook the hands of the two other drivers scheduled for that evening's shift. They both smiled, but I could tell that behind their smiles lay suspicion. I was the new kid in town. And they felt threatened that an extra driver might decrease their workload.

A lady in her late thirties introduced herself as Maggie, because presumably that was her name. She looked me up and down but didn't seem to view me as a threat. The other driver was called Brad. He had a confident swagger about him. From the way he glared at me, I could tell he considered himself to be James's number one driver and was trying to work out if I was a rival. At this point, Brad hadn't seen the heap of shit that I called a car, or had any idea about my lack of knowledge of the town's layout. I had been in Breckenridge less than 48 hours and would get lost each time I tried to walk back to the hostel.

James explained the way things worked. He would call us on the walkie-talkie with the name of the restaurants we were to collect from, the name and address of the customer, and details of the order. We would then drive to the restaurant – it was up to us which order we visited the restaurants in (a decision which became easier once I learned more about the average cooking times at each establishment) – pick up the food in its polystyrene containers, check that the order was complete, steal a couple of fries, regret stealing the fries because we had burnt the roof of our mouth off, put the order in our delivery bags, and then deliver the food to the customer. The delivery address could be any distance between a couple of blocks or several miles up the mountain. The customer would then pay for their order in cash. At the end of the shift, we would return to James and give him the evening's takings. He would then settle up with the restaurants. Any tips collected were ours to keep.

It was a really exciting job and it wasn't long before I got familiar with the layout of Breckenridge and the surrounding mountains. There were no sat-navs or Google Maps. We had a single piece of paper with a hand drawn map of the town as our only means of navigation.

James was impressed with how quickly I learned the ropes and how many orders I could fulfil in a shift. I was never a real threat to Brad's crown. After he laid eyes on Josephine, he knew that I would never be a contender. Brad drove a sporty little Subaru 4wd, and always seemed to be on the radio waiting for the next order before anyone else. The one area in which he wasn't able to compete with me was with tips. I was leagues ahead of both Brad and Maggie. Possibly down to luck, but more likely I think due to my English accent. Most customers were American and they loved the novelty value of having a Chinese meal delivered to their remote mountain lodge by a well-spoken Englishman. They would always reward my efforts with a hefty tip. I was once given a $20 note to pay for a $6.50 pizza and told to keep the change.

Even the British customers would tip me well, presumably to show solidarity. Back at James's HQ at the end of a shift we would all compare tips. For the first few nights I was honest with my haul, assuming it to be normal. But after a very vocal display of jealousy from Maggie and Brad, I played down my tip total each night, usually hiding a couple of $10 bills in a back pocket halfway through the shift so as not to rile them even further.

Despite her shitness, Josephine coped better than I could ever have hoped with the brutal conditions. Being so high up in the Rockies, I never had to contend with rain, but snow was a major factor. And the windscreen wipers still didn't work.

Depending on the type of snow, this was obviously very dangerous. When it was particularly cold, the snow would just bounce off the windscreen and wipers would have been of little use anyway. But when the snow was wet and sticky, it would settle on the windscreen making it impossible to see. As with my navigation of the Sierra Nevada, I was often forced to stop every few metres and manually scrape away the snow with my arm.

The roads in the centre of Breckenridge were always well gritted and regularly ploughed, but up at the more remote addresses they were often treacherous.

On one occasion I delivered to an address miles from any civilisation. The house was located up a long drive, and although the snow looked fairly deep on the ground, it was too far to walk. So I put Josephine into gear and headed up towards the house. The wheels spun erratically, but she stayed on line and I made it up to the front door with no real drama. I had a stack of eight large pizzas which I delivered to a house full of about 20 young men, who all looked like they were members of a college football team.

They paid for the pizzas and included a generous tip. 'Hell, what's a crazy English dude doing delivering pizzas in the Rocky Mountains?' they said.

'I keep asking myself the same question,' I said. 'It's awesome!'

I returned to the car and put Josephine into reverse. There were no outside lights and it was very difficult to see where I was going. I realised a little too late that I was veering off course and I put my foot on the brake, but Josephine kept sliding backwards. I wasn't going fast, but the gradient of the driveway was such that the momentum caused me to keep sliding. The back wheels went up the small grass verge on the side of the road and the entire back end of Josephine disappeared into a giant snowdrift. I put her into gear but the wheels just kept spinning. She was well and truly stuck.

I was well out of range of my walkie-talkie, so had no choice but to go and ask at the house if I could use their phone to call James for help.

'Hey buddy. Everything ok? Did we not pay you the correct amount?' said the guy who answered the door.

'Oh, no, you paid the full amount. And thanks so much for the tip.'

'You're welcome. Great pizza by the way. You want some?'

'No, thanks though. I've got my car kind of stuck. I was wondering if I could borrow your phone to call my boss?'

'Where is it stuck?'

'Just near the bottom of your driveway.'

'Don't you worry. We'll get you back on the road.'

'It's well and truly buried. I don't want to disturb your pizza.'

'It's no trouble. We'll have you out in no time. BOYS!' he shouted. 'Come on out here. We've got a job to do.'

A group of about 10 of the men, all ridiculously big and muscular, followed me out of the house and down the driveway. In a matter of seconds, they had bounced Josephine out of the snowdrift and back onto the driveway. I think they could have carried her the entire way down the mountain to Breckenridge on their shoulders without breaking sweat if they had wanted to.

'Thank you so much,' I said. 'I really appreciate it. I'm sorry for disturbing your meal.'

'It was no trouble at all. We'll see you back out onto the road.'

They watched me edge back down the driveway, occasionally manhandling Josephine left or right a bit, until I was back out onto the road, and facing in the correct direction.

'You drive carefully now,' said one of them.

'Thanks again, guys. Have a good night.'

Another scary and potentially far more serious incident took place on a different peak above Breckenridge. It was always annoying to be given a job far up in the mountains. These jobs would take much longer than the deliveries downtown, and we wouldn't earn any extra money. I tried subtly suggesting to James that my car was not best suited for the unploughed mountain roads, but he wasn't having any of it. And Brad made sure that I didn't get any preferential treatment.

There was one particular address that we all dreaded going to. The first time I went there I got hopelessly lost and had to radio back to James several times for him to try and help me find the house, which was extremely difficult when I didn't know where I was on each occasion that I called him.

'What are you near?' he would say.

'Er... there are lots of trees.'

'Right. Anything else?'

'Nope. Just the road, the trees and a shit-ton of snow.'

'Can you see anything in the distance?'

'I can see the lights of Breckenridge at the bottom of the mountain.'

'Call me back when you've found something a little more distinguishable.'

'Ok.'

On this other occasion, it was a particularly stormy night. The snow had been falling since late-morning and was sitting deep even on the usually clear roads downtown. By late evening, most of the mountain roads were impassable to anything but four-wheel drives. On nights like these, calls for takeout dramatically increased as people changed their plans on account of the weather. I was given the news by James that I needed to take a delivery up to Eagle's Nest. I don't think the place was actually called Eagle's Nest, but it seems like a fitting name.

'I don't know if my car will make it,' I confessed to James.

'You'll be fine. Brad's already up at Vulture's Ridge (another made up name) on the other side of the valley, and Maggie's just dropping off an order at Devil's Peak.'

'But I've heard the roads are awful up at Eagle's Nest.'

'They are awful everywhere tonight. Just be careful and you'll be fine. If you get stuck then we can send a truck to come and get you.'

'What about that narrow bit? A truck isn't going to be much use if I go over the edge.'

'Well don't drive over the edge then.'

'Right. Thanks for the advice, James. What are the details of the next order?'

The road up the mountain was treacherous and the snow gathered deeper and deeper on the ground the further up I went. Josephine was sliding around a bit but had coped better than I expected. I reached the part of the journey I had been dreading the most. It was a section of road with a sheer drop to the left-hand side, disappearing an unfathomable distance below. To the right, the mountainside rose steeply where the road had been cut into the hillside. I was only half a mile from Eagle's Nest, and I knew if I could get through this section I would be ok.

As the road climbed up, I kept my eyes fixed firmly on the ground ahead and tried not to think about what was to the left of me. Josephine's tyres started spinning as the gradient changed and I instinctively put my foot on the brake to try and steady her. She started sliding backwards down the road and I tried in vain to correct it by pumping the brakes and putting my foot occasionally on the gas pedal in the hope of finding some traction.

To my horror, the back of the car began sliding to the left and the front end swung slowly around in a clockwise direction. The whole car was going to slide straight over the edge. I readied myself to leap from Josephine's door before she plunged into oblivion. I started to think of what I would say to James, and what I would say to Rachel about losing my car – and nearly my life – over a cliff edge.

But just at the point that Josephine was at right angles to the road, the back wheels came to rest on a small barrier of frozen snow that had formed at the roadside when snow-ploughs had cleared the road several days earlier.

The front of the car came to a standstill against the snow packed on the other side and I climbed out to assess the situation. All that separated Josephine and the valley floor below was a couple of feet of compacted snow. I couldn't risk trying to drive forwards in case Josephine slid backwards ever further. I was well and truly stuck. This time there was no group of American jocks nearby to help me out. I couldn't even see another light, let alone another person.

I reached for my radio.

'James, are you receiving? Over.'

The radio just crackled back at me. I was beyond the range of its signal.

'James! Are you receiving me? Over!' I said, with a little more desperation.

The static continued to crackle.

'James!' I shouted. 'Fucking answer me!'

Nothing.

There was nothing else for me to do other than walk the long slow road down the mountain until I could call for help. James would be mightily pissed off with me, but to be honest I was mightily pissed off with him, too. I had made my reluctance to venture up to Eagle's Nest very clear.

I picked up the delivery bag. Not with any intention of actually delivering the food, but I figured if things got really bad and I had to spend the night on the mountain, then at least I had a lukewarm portion of Surf 'n' Turf, some Cajun prawns and a portion of crispy potato wedges to look forward to.

Just at that moment, I heard a car engine further down the mountainside. There weren't any other roads on this part of the mountain, so it had to be coming my way. I could see the occasional sweep of lights through the trees as the vehicle made its way up through the switchbacks below. And then it turned the corner and the headlights shone straight into my face. As the car got closer I recognised the familiar colours and the logos emblazoned all over the hood and doors:

Dominos Pizza.

Dominos Pizza had been well established in Breckenridge for many years. They had the monopoly of food delivery in the area. When James's delivery service started up, Dominos didn't seem to care too much. But then things started to take off, and James secured deals with a couple of the other pizza restaurants in town who didn't offer delivery. Although we still weren't a threat to Dominos' domination, they had definitely started to take us seriously.

The Dominos delivery guys were all well-trained and drove modern, well-equipped vehicles to cope with the extreme winter conditions. They saw us as a bit of a joke outfit, and as I stood there, with my crappy car wedged on a cliff edge halfway up a mountain, I could definitely see their point.

We never had any direct dealings with the Dominos staff but we often passed them, either while driving, or when delivering to the same hotel or chalet complex. We would acknowledge each other, but no words were ever spoken. We were the enemy.

A young man about my age climbed out of the driver's door. I recognised him to be one of their regular drivers.

'Hey buddy,' he said. 'You having a few problems there?'

'You could say that,' I said, as he walked towards me.

'Hey, aren't you one of the drivers for that other delivery company?'

'Yeah,' I said. 'My car is not really cut out for this sort of road.'

I had given him the perfect opportunity to pass judgement, but he didn't make any criticism.

'I'm Danny,' he said, offering his hand.

'Hi Danny. I'm George. Nice to meet you.'

'Well George, I'll get you back on the road in no time. You hop in your vehicle. Put it in Drive, and when I said go, just give it a little on the gas and turn the wheel to the left until you've straightened out.'

'Ok, thanks. What are you going to do?'

'You'll see,' he said. 'Don't worry. It happens all the time up here.'

He edged his car closer until it was a couple of inches from the back right-hand corner of Josephine.

'Ok, go,' he said. 'Nice and steady now, buddy.'

I did as he had advised, and as I turned Josephine slightly to the left, I felt a gentle jolt from behind. I turned to see Danny's front bumper pressed up against the corner of Josephine's back bumper. He was pushing her up the hill. Once I had straightened out, he continued to push me until the road levelled out and I was able to finally get some traction.

'Thanks so much, Danny. You're a life-saver. Hopefully I can return the favour one day.'

He looked at Josephine and smiled sympathetically.

'You're welcome, George' he said. 'Drive safe now.'

30

Rachel and I continued to talk regularly on the phone during my time in Breckenridge. The payphone in The Fireside Inn was located at the edge of the lounge, so it was a little difficult to have a private conversation when there were always other guests about.

Australia was only occasionally mentioned. Rachel seemed quite vague about her plans and still had not purchased any plane tickets or sorted out a visa. Until that happened, I knew there was still a very small chance I could convince her to change her mind.

It was her birthday in the middle of March and, as part of her present, I sent her – in a last ditch attempt to win her over – a car key that I had cut at a locksmith in town.

I phoned her up to wish her happy birthday and she thanked me for the presents I had sent her.

'What is the key for?' she asked.

'It's for Josephine.'

'Why have you sent me a key for Josephine?'

'Because I want you to come to America to be with me.'

'And you thought sending me a key would make me come?'

'I thought that if you had your own key, then you wouldn't see it as being just my adventure. It could be OUR adventure instead.'

'I see,' she said. 'That's very sweet of you. Thank you.'

'Well?'

'Well what?'

'Do you want to come and use your car key?'

'Hmph,' she said.

'Oh god, here we go again. Enough with the hmphing.' Although, the hmphing noise sounded far more pleasant to my ears than the word 'Australia'. It carried with it a suggestion of contemplation. And contemplation meant hope.

'I'll think about it,' she said.

Life in Breckenridge was brilliant. Apart from a few scary incidents on the mountain roads, the food delivery job was great fun and still allowed me plenty of time to snowboard during the day, and socialise after my shift. I loved living at the Fireside Inn and I quickly built a reputation for cooking the best scrambled eggs in town (I didn't).

Andy and Niki were great fun and we got along really well throughout my stay. Andy was quite rightly very proud of his distinguished army career and began all of his anecdotes with the line, 'when I was in the army…' but his stories never disappointed. Niki had a habit of finishing all of my sentences for me, which I soon learned to appreciate as it meant I had to put in half as much effort when talking.

When snow was forecast, I would get up half an hour earlier to help Andy clear the pathways around The Fireside Inn before preparing breakfast. Whatever the weather, Andy would be outside in a fleece, gloves, and his spandex trousers. More often than not, one of the very first sights I would see after opening my eyes was the shiny blue Lycra-clad arse of Andy outside the front door. It was not the most welcoming view, but it never failed to amuse me.

'You should try them sometime,' he said, when he caught me looking.

'Nah, I'm alright thanks.'

'They are seriously comfortable.'

'I'm sure they are. So are my jeans.'

'No, this is a completely different level of comfort. Once you go spandex you never go back. They really contour to your body,' he said, athletically flinging a shovelful of snow over his shoulder and puffing himself out like a male peacock.

'Yes, I can certainly see that,' I said.

On one occasion I stepped outside early one morning, ready to shovel snow, and the first thing I noticed was that Andy wasn't wearing his usual spandex trousers. Instead, he was wearing a pair of leather trousers that were so tight that all of the flesh from his legs had been squashed up above his waist. He would surely need to be surgically removed from them later. They looked oddly familiar, too. I was fairly certain they were the same leather trousers his wife Niki often wore.

'Morning Andy,' I said. 'Nice trousers. Are those…'

'Niki's?' he said. 'Yes, they are.'

'Oh, right.'

'All of my leggings are in the wash.'

'And you don't have any other trousers?' I asked.

'Well, yes I probably do, but these were handy so I thought I'd just slip them on.'

'Fair enough. Did it take long to slip them on?'

'Only about 20 minutes or so. They're very comfortable though. You should try them sometime.'

As well as The Fireside's Inn's constant stream of holidaymakers, there were a few others, who – like me – had decided to stay in Breckenridge for a little longer.

Kieron and Liz were a couple from Ireland and two of the loveliest people I have ever met. Both teachers in their early thirties, they had come to Breckenridge for three months as part of a sabbatical. We shared a similar sense of humour and spent most days in each other's company. They stayed at The Fireside Inn for a couple of weeks at the beginning of their time in Breckenridge, and then rented a house on the other side of town for the rest of the season. They both did bits and pieces of work here and there, but they were mostly there for the snow.

Kirsty arrived at The Fireside Inn at about the same time as me. She was a pretty, blonde, bubbly English girl who had been in America for the best part of a year. She had spent nine months living and working with some American relatives in Sheboygan, Wisconsin. Kirsty was very loud and overly-talkative, but she had an infectious enthusiasm and a constant smile that couldn't help but make you like her. She talked incessantly about Sheboygan, Wisconsin as though it was the capital of the United States. I had never even heard of it and was convinced it was a made up place. It sounds more like the noise made by a door stop spring when flicked by a finger. It wasn't until she pointed it out to me on a map that I believed it was real. Everything we talked about came back to Sheboygan. Sheboygan, Sheboygan, Sheboygan.

'What's so great about Sheboygan?' I asked.

'Ah, it's such an amazing place.'

'What's it famous for?'

'Cheese. They make some of the best cheese in America in Sheboygan.'

'That's not very hard. America makes the worst cheese in the world.'

'You haven't tried Sheboygan cheese.'

'What else does Sheboygan have?'

'It's just great,' she said. 'I can't wait to go back. Did I mention the cheese?'

Kirsty stayed at The Fireside Inn for about a month and then moved in with her boyfriend Greasy Brian, whom I will come to later.

Soon after meeting Kirsty, I met Phil (no, not Phil and Kirsty from *Location, Location, Location*).

'Hi,' he said with a northern-English accent, after checking in to The Fireside Inn a few days after me. 'The name's Phil. Phil from Chesterfield.'

He spoke the name like a really rubbish James Bond.

'Nice to meet you Phil from Chesterfield. I'm George, George from Northampton.'

'Know anywhere good to get a beer around here, George from Northampton?' he said. 'It's been a long journey.'

'Yeah, there's a great place just around the corner.'

'Fancy a pint?'

'Sure.'

I liked Phil from Chesterfield from the moment I met him. He was a couple of years older than me but seemed wise beyond his years. He had been working for several years in a job he hated back in England and had recently split up with his long-term girlfriend. Phil had never ventured far beyond Britain, so decided to spend his savings on a few months snowboarding in Colorado.

Most nights after my delivery shift finished, I would meet up with Phil, Kieron, Liz and Kirsty and we would drink beers and whisky sours at a local bar until the early hours. I'd try to get a few hours sleep in my cave, before beginning my early morning snow-shovelling, breakfast-cooking shift.

Phil eventually moved into a house with Kieron and Liz – the Irish couple – but he still viewed The Fireside Inn as his home. Andy and Niki would occasionally have to give him a nudge at 3am when they would find him asleep on the sofa in the lounge and remind him that he was no longer a paying guest, and hadn't been for over a month.

There were many other faces that came and went during my three months in Breckenridge. Most guests would stay for a week or two and then head home, but there were a few others that lingered longer.

There was Kev from New Jersey. Kev was in his early twenties and there was something slightly mafia-like about him. In a good way, if that's possible. He was obsessed with The

Grateful Dead and was the most fearless skier I have ever seen. He tried snowboarding for a laugh one day and was an expert after just a few hours.

To save money, Kev had filled the trunk of his car with packets of instant porridge in a variety of flavours, which he seemed to eat for every meal for the couple of months he stayed at The Fireside Inn.

Susie was also from New Jersey and looked and dressed like a teenager, but I think she was in her late 40s. She and Kev had something going on together, but Kev was reluctant to admit it because of the age difference. Susie somehow landed a job as a snowboard instructor, despite not being able to snowboard.

Sean and Mason were two lads who lived up to the typical stereotype of American college students. They were loud, confident and both a complete liability.

After enjoying a few too many drinks at the end of their last ski run, Sean and Mason were both arrested for being drunk and disorderly and ended up behind bars. Without any money left in their accounts (they'd spent the last of it on beer), the police allowed them to bail themselves out using their expensive snowboards as collateral.

During the month that Sean and Mason stayed at The Fireside Inn, I don't think they ever made it upstairs to the dormitory. I found them both asleep on the sofas downstairs every single morning.

Then there was Big Stew. Big Stew was a gentle giant. He was from Fort-somewhere in Texas. He drove a big white Buick and spoke like a character from *Bill & Ted's Excellent Adventure.*

After my early start each morning to shovel snow, set the tables, cook breakfast and then clear up, I was usually finished by 10am. My evening delivery shift didn't start until about 5pm, which left me with the entire day to fill. Living at one of the best ski resorts in the world, it was not too difficult to decide how to spend my time.

I had been snowboarding a couple of times previously, and was confident enough to be able to just about get down a mountain in one piece. I was ready to go and tackle The Rockies. All I needed was a snowboard. And some snowboard boots. Some suitable clothes. And a lift pass.

'There's a pair of old snowboard boots in the lost property,' said Niki one morning. 'I don't know what size they are but you're welcome to them if they're any good. They've been there since before we arrived.'

The boots were a couple of sizes too big for me, but with a few extra pairs of ski socks – also acquired from the lost property – they just about fit. Snowboard boots are a lot softer than ski boots and allow the ankle and foot to flex. These boots had clearly seen many years on the slopes and were so flexible that they felt like a pair of slipper boots. The multiple pairs of socks made them feel even cosier.

I also obtained a pair of black salopettes from the lost property. These had previously belonged to a child and the legs stopped halfway down my shin. Still, they served the purpose better than anything else I owned so they would have to do. I also found a large ski jacket, decorated in the most revolting pattern ever imaginable. Even in the 1980s – when this jacket was probably last worn – it would have looked overly garish. It had presumably lain at the bottom of the lost property box since then. It was far too big for me and when combined with the child's salopettes I looked utterly ridiculous. But I didn't care. I was ready for the snow.

Big Stew – the gentle giant from Texas – had just got himself a part-time job at a ski rental shop. He had arrived in Breckenridge with a job lined up as a lift operator but had been fired after just three days. The circumstances of his dismissal were quite unfortunate. He had been returning to the base of the ski lift after his lunch break and was walking past a group of skiers waiting for the lift. He saw a man standing in line that he assumed to be a good friend of his. So he went up behind him and pulled the man's ski trousers down in front of the gathered crowd. Only this man wasn't his friend. It was a startled Frenchman wearing an identically coloured jacket and trousers. Needless to say, the man issued a complaint, and Big Stew was without a job.

I called in to visit Big Stew at his new place of work to see if he could do me a deal to rent a board. Even with Stew's 'mates rates', hiring a board for what could potentially be three months would not be cost-effective. It would be cheaper for me to buy one. Only I couldn't afford to buy one either.

'Do you sell any second-hand boards?' I asked Big Stew.

'Not really, bro. They sell off a lot of the ex-rental stuff but only at the end of the season, dude.'

'Ah well. I'll have to keep my eye out for something a little cheaper. Thanks anyway.'

As I was walking out the shop I noticed a fairly battered looking snowboard leaning against the wall. It was a revolting pink colour, but looked about the right size for me.

'What's this board?' I asked.

'Oh that's just a piece of shit they are throwing out. Look underneath, it's shredded to bits, dude.'

The bottom of the board did have a huge amount of deep gouges in it, but that didn't matter to me.

'How much do you want for it?'

'Seriously, dude, you don't want no heap of junk like that.'

'Why not?'

'Look at it, bro. It's been so well-used you can almost bend it in half.'

He picked up the board and pulled both ends inwards and, sure enough, the entire board could almost be doubled over.

'And that's bad, is it?' I said.

'Of course, man. You'll want a much stiffer board than that.'

'Well it's better than nothing.'

'It's all yours if you want it, dude. But you'll need some bindings for it. Actually, there's probably an old set lying out back if you're not too fussy about what state they are in.'

Big Stew returned with a pair of bindings, which, to my eyes, looked almost brand new.

'They look awesome, thanks. How much do you want for those and the board?'

'Nothing, bro, you can have them.'

'Don't be silly. How much?'

'Honestly, just take them. I'm sure my boss won't mind.'

I handed Big Stew $20 and set off with my new bindings and my bendy board, hoping that he wouldn't lose his second job in a week.

Later that evening after I finished my shift, I got chatting to Kev– the porridge-eating Mafioso – at one of the local bars. He had landed a job as a lift operator and having so far refrained from pulling any customers' trousers down, was still happily employed. Lift operators were given a free ski pass as one of the perks of the job, but Kev also told me of a scheme that would save me a huge amount of money. Lift passes were ridiculously expensive, but a discount was offered to appease the locals who lived in the surrounding area. A pass for the remainder of the ski season could be purchased by locals for about the equivalent cost of one week's tourist pass. The pass was only available to residents or people working permanently in the area. They also had to be purchased from a nearby town and were not available for sale in Breckenridge.

Andy kindly wrote a brief note on some headed paper to prove that I was 'employed' by The Fireside Inn, and after a lengthy bus trip and a payment of a couple of hundred dollars, I had a ski pass that would last me almost to the end of the season.

31

I was lucky enough to go on a few skiing holidays when I was younger. But my luck didn't extend to the resorts actually having much snow. My first two ski trips were to Bulgaria, which was just emerging from years of communist war, and the economy was still struggling. We ate pizzas on the mountain every day, my mum and dad drank lots of Bulgarian beer and wine, and I'm fairly sure they still went home with change from £10. It didn't matter that there was no snow.

Another year they splashed out and took us to a ski resort in Austria. There was so little snow at this resort that the entire mountain had to close. Each day we would have to board a bus in the town that would drop us at the base of another nearby mountain. We would then have to fight with several thousand Austrians and Germans for over an hour to squeeze into a cable car that whisked us halfway up this mountain, where we then had a two mile walk through a poorly-lit icy tunnel in our ski boots carrying our skis and poles, and our passports, to emerge at the other end of the tunnel in GERMANY. We had walked through an entire mountain into a different country. It completely blew my mind as a child, and it still seems incomprehensible today. The resort in Germany benefited from year round snow thanks to a glacier, and after just a couple of hours' skiing, it was time to repeat the arduous journey back into Austria.

The week was topped off with me accidentally changing the code to the safe in our hotel room, with our passports and my dad's wallet locked inside, on the morning we were heading back to the airport. My dad still hasn't quite forgiven me.

So my standards of what ski resorts looked and felt like was set fairly low. My first day on the slopes of Breckenridge exceeded all of my expectations. Firstly, there was snow.

Absolutely shit loads of it. The conditions were amazing. It seemed to snow every night, leaving a huge dump of powder, and the days would be bright and sunny. Then another fresh dump would arrive the following night to keep it topped up.

The vastness of The Rockies made the slopes seem remarkably quiet, too. The pistes were wide and long, and the queues for the lifts minimal. In the over-crowded European resorts, it is not uncommon to spend more time queuing than skiing.

I loved every minute of my time in Breckenridge, and used every available hour I had between my breakfast shift and my evening job to make the most of my circumstances.

Phil from Chesterfield and Kieron and Liz quickly became my daily ski buddies. My American friends – Big Stew, Kev and Susie – were too extreme for me and liked to spend their time in the board park, going off jumps and sliding along rails. I'm a bit of a wimp and preferred to keep my board in contact with the snow at all times. Kirsty didn't tend to surface before midday and then spent most of the afternoon causing havoc with Greasy Brian (don't worry, I will get to him, I promise).

Kieron was a skier with no style or grace, but was full of confidence and would happily whizz down any mountain at speed. Liz was a snowboarder and was elegant and controlled, but liked to take her time. Phil from Chesterfield could only turn one way on his snowboard, and tended to come to a stop by face-planting into a snowdrift. He was up for anything, however, and we all made a great team.

On one afternoon, halfway through my time in Breckenridge, Kieron, Liz and I reached the bottom of the mountain and realised that Phil was missing. We waited around for ten minutes but there was no sign of him. The lifts had all closed for the day and the slopes were emptying so we assumed he had come down a different slope and headed back to The Fireside Inn.

We waited back at the hostel for a couple of hours but he didn't return. We hadn't heard any sirens or seen any helicopters so thought it unlikely he had been involved in an accident. When darkness fell, and three hours had passed since we realised he was missing, we decided to telephone the local hospital and police station to see if they had any news.

Just as we were heading for the payphone, in walked an exhausted-looking Phil carrying his snowboard. Behind him in the doorway was an angry Alsatian that was snarling and salivating in his direction.

'Phil! What happened to you?' I asked.

'That fucking dog!' shouted Phil. 'That's what happened to me.'

Phil stepped inside the lounge and slammed the front door shut in the dog's face. It remained on the other side of the door, barking and snarling.

Kieron, Liz and I looked at each other with a mixture of confusion and amusement on our faces.

'What do you mean that dog? What did it do?' I asked.

'You know when we got off that last lift at the top of the mountain, and you guys shot off ahead?'

'Yeah,' we all said in unison.

'Well, I had just done up my bindings and was setting off after you, when that bloody dog came running up to me yapping away.'

'Wait, where did it come running from? What's a dog doing at the top of the mountain?' said Kieron.

'I think it belongs to one of the lift-operators. I saw it up there yesterday but it didn't seem to mind me then.'

'So, anyway. What happened?' I said.

'Well it started to follow me, and each time I tried to snowboard it would try to bite my ankles and it wouldn't stop growling.'

'So what did you do?'

'Whenever I took off my snowboard and walked, it stopped barking and trying to bite me and it just walked closely behind me growling instead.'

'How far did you have to walk?'

'The whole way down the fucking mountain!'

'Are you serious?' I said. 'Couldn't you have just put your board on and outrun it.'

'No chance. You've seen what I'm like at snowboarding. I would have panicked and face-planted 20 metres down the slope and that fucking dog would have come and chewed my face off.'

'I can't believe you walked down that mountain. How far is it?'

'It's three hours far. That's how far.'

The thought of Phil and that Alsatian kept us amused for many weeks. Phil refused to ride that particular ski lift ever again.

Now to Greasy Brian. Greasy Brian was an American who soon became Kirsty's regular boyfriend. We called him Greasy Brian – not to his face – because his name was Brian and he was very greasy looking. Even Kirsty started to refer to him as Greasy Brian when he wasn't present.

Greasy Brian was a bit of a wide-boy and although a nice enough guy, I never really warmed to him. He shared a remote cabin in the woods with a group of equally shady characters.

On one occasion, I was sitting on the sofa in The Fireside Inn just after clearing up breakfast when in walked Kirsty and Greasy Brian.

'George, man, I need a favour,' said Greasy Brian.

'Sure, man,' I said, trying to get with the lingo. 'How can I help?'

'My truck's broken down. I need you to tow me to the garage.'

'I don't have a tow bar.'

'That's ok. I've got a chain and there will be a tow point on your car that I can hook it up to.'

'Er... ok. How far is the garage?'

'Not far. It's only half a mile or so. It's just on the edge of town.'

'Alright then. I'll just go and grab my keys.'

I met Greasy Brian and Kirsty outside where Josephine was parked up. Greasy Brian's vehicle – a heavy Ford pickup – was parked on the other side of the car park so I reversed Josephine up in front of it.

'Are you sure this is going to work, Greas… I mean Brian?'

'Why wouldn't it? I've towed vehicles plenty of times.'

'But your truck is massive. Mine's a crappy old minivan.'

'It'll be fine. Trust me.'

I didn't want to break it to Greasy Brian that although I was happy to hangout with him, trusting him was something I found it hard to do.

'Ok,' I said reluctantly.

We both knelt down and inspected the underneath of Josephine. There was no sign of a tow point.

'There's got to be one here somewhere,' he said.

After another five minutes of searching we both concluded that Josephine didn't have a tow point. Her chassis was, as I had been warned, completely outta whack. I suggested that maybe he should wait for one of his friends with a more suitable vehicle to help.

'It's ok. We can just tie the chain to your rear axle,' he said.

'No, Greas… I mean Brian. I don't think that's a good idea. I've already broken one axle on this trip.'

'You won't break an axle, I promise. Those things are tough as shit. We'll take it nice and slow. It'll be fine. Trust me,' he said.

At this point I should have gone with my instinct and told him where he could stick his tow chain. But Greasy Brian had charmed me with his smooth-talking and I didn't want to be the wimpy English kid, so I reluctantly agreed. I let Greasy Brian tie the chain around the axle, and then he gave me some brief instructions about where we were going and what I needed to do.

'No sudden movements, ok? Just take it nice and slow,' he said.

'Ok,' I said.

We made it down to the main street without incident. Despite the weight of the truck, Josephine was able to roll it along behind effortlessly. We successfully navigated the town centre and were only a couple of blocks away from the garage when we came to a stop light.

After the light turned green, I edged forwards slowly, but Greasy Brian was obviously not paying attention and still had his foot on the brake. Despite travelling at a slow speed, the chain soon reached its maximum tension and broke free.

'Please be the chain and not my axle,' I said to myself, as I came to a stop in the middle of the road. I noticed that it seemed to take an awfully long time for Josephine to come to a complete stop compared to normal.

I walked to the back of the car to assess the damage. The chain was lying broken on the floor and I was relived to see that the axle still appeared to be intact.

'Sorry about that. I was just rolling a cigarette,' said Greasy Brian.

'Probably not the best time to be doing that,' I said. 'At least my axle's not broken.'

As we knelt down to re-attach the chain to the axle, I noticed something dripping from a pipe near the back wheel.

'What's that?' I asked.

'What?'

'That stuff dripping out. Is that supposed to happen?'

'Oh shit. No, that's your brake fluid. The chain must have snapped your brake fluid line when you pulled off too quickly.'

'Hey, I did not pull off too quickly, Grea… I mean Brian. I went nice and slowly when the light turned green. Just like you told me to. You were just too busy rolling a cigarette to notice.'

'Well whatever. It's not good anyway. I can stop the leak for you so that it'll get you to the garage but you'll have to get that fixed.'

'Great.'

'Don't worry. I'll pay for it.'

'You'd better, you wanker,' I muttered, out of earshot.

Greasy Brian returned to his truck and then fastened an adjustable spanner onto Josephine's leaking pipe. The dripping stopped.

'Be very careful on the brakes. No more fluid will leak out while that wrench is attached, but your back brakes ain't gonna work properly until they're fixed.'

The final few blocks to the garage were painfully slow and I was angry for letting myself get talked into what was always such a silly plan. And I was angry with Greasy Brian for being such a dick.

The repair cost me $80. Brian – the greasy bastard – never paid me a cent of it.

'George, Rachel's on the phone,' said Andy one morning during breakfast in early April.

My heart rate quickened. Rachel never phoned me. She didn't want to run up a huge phone bill on her cousin's phone in Ireland, so I always called her using pre-paid phone cards. I had a terrible feeling she was calling with some bad news.

'Hello,' I said. 'How are you?'

'Very good, thanks. Were you serious about wanting me to come to America?' she said.

'Of course I was. Why do you think I've mentioned it several times a week for the last four months? Why are you asking?'

'I think I want to come out and join you.'

'Are you serious? That's amazing. How long for?'

'As long as you want me.'

'This is just the best news ever. When can you come?'

'There's a cheap flight that gets into Denver on April 17th. How does that sound?'

'Perfect! The ski season will be pretty much over by then and my work here will have come to an end.'

'That's good.'

'Oh my god, I can't believe this. I'm so excited. I can pick you up in Denver and we can head off from there.'

'Where will we go?'

'Wherever you want,' I said.

'You mean wherever WE want.'

'Yes. Wherever we want.'

As I hung up the phone, an immense feeling of joy washed over me. I had been incredibly happy in Breckenridge, but it wasn't until that phone call with Rachel that I realised it was possible to feel even happier.

'Good news?' asked Andy, as he emerged from the office.

'Incredible news,' I said. 'Rachel is coming out to America in a couple of weeks.'

'That's brilliant news. I'm really happy for you. Does this mean we have to start looking for a new cave dweller?'

'I'm afraid so,' I said, pumping my chest with my fist. 'This cave dweller. He found mate.'

32

The following two weeks flew by. The ski season was slowly coming to an end and life at The Fireside Inn was quietening down as the visitor numbers fell. The shifts at my food delivery job had been reduced and I counted down the days until Rachel's arrival.

On April 17th, I stood in Denver airport scanning the *arrivals* board. There was no sign of a flight arriving from London at the time Rachel had said. Did I have the wrong day? Had there been a problem with her flight?

As I stood gazing at the dizzying numbers, there was a tap on my shoulder.

It was Rachel.

I threw my arms around her and squeezed her tightly.

'What are you doing here? Where did you come from?' I said. 'I thought your flight wasn't supposed to arrive for another half an hour?'

'I've been here a couple of hours.'

'I'm so sorry. I thought you said 3.40pm?'

'I did. I told you a time a couple of hours after the actual time.'

'Oh. Why did you do that?'

'I don't know. I think I just felt like I needed a bit of time to settle into America.'

'You mean like having your own adventure?'

'Yes, something like that,' she said. 'My flight even had a 45 minute stopover in Houston too, so I've travelled all over on my own.'

'Wow, you're quite the jetsetter. How did it feel?'

'It was ok. But I'm very happy I'm with you now.'

'Me too,' I said.

As we walked back to Josephine I could feel the excitement building. My American road trip had been more than I hoped. Mark and I had seen some incredible things, met some amazing people, and had a lot of fun. I'd arrived in Breckenridge and expected to stay at The Fireside Inn for a couple of nights while my car was fixed. I ended up being there for three of the best months of my life.

But now Rachel was here I felt complete. I would no longer have to endure that aching feeling during every new experience, every joke laughed at, every meal eaten or view marvelled at, that it would have been even more enjoyable with Rachel there with me.

I was also bursting with anticipation to show off Josephine and how I had converted her into a luxury campervan. I just couldn't wait to see the look on Rachel's face.

'Ta da!' I said, lifting up the boot, and displaying the neatly made bed in the back. 'Well, what to you think?'

'Um…'

'Doesn't it look great? I haven't slept in it yet. I wanted the first time to be with you,' I lied, not wanting to admit that I hadn't slept in it because I was too cold and scared.

'Er… yeah.'

'Don't you like it?'

'I do. It's just…'

'Just what?'

'Nothing.'

'Go on. It's just what?'

'I don't know. I guess it's not quite what I was expecting.'

'What were you expecting?'

'No, no, it's really nice. I just expected it to be, well, different.'

'Different, as in, better?'

'No! Well, yes, maybe a little, but it looks really nice,' she said, giving me a hug. 'Come on. Let's go and see Breckenridge.'

She walked around to what she thought was the passenger side door.

'Other side,' I said. 'Unless of course you want to drive?'

I was initially disappointed with Rachel's somewhat lacklustre reaction to Josephine. I had spent three months sleeping on a double backseat, with my feet propped up on our rucksacks. Mark and I had been cold with our flimsy sleeping bags, and the curtainless windows enabled people to peer in at any time. Compared to what it had been, Josephine was certainly now luxury accommodation on wheels.

But I soon realised that Rachel didn't have Josephine's previous incarnation to compare it to. To her, it was a rusty piece of shit on the outside, and inside it was basically still the back of a car, with a mouse-infested futon, stolen bedding from a dodgy motel and homemade curtains. When I looked at it through her eyes, I could understand her apathy.

We headed back to Breckenridge where we planned to spend a couple of days before beginning the next leg of our road trip.

As comfortable and homely as I had been in my hovel in the attic of The Fireside Inn, it wasn't the most suitable of places to share with Rachel, and I didn't think she'd take too kindly to me offering her another bunk in the dormitory. Andy and Niki kindly offered us one of the B&B rooms for a couple of nights.

My lift pass had expired but I wanted to at least show Rachel what it was like up in the mountains, even if she didn't get to do any skiing. New Jersey Kev had let me know which lifts he was working on, and when Rachel and I turned up at the bottom of the slopes the following day, he ushered us straight onto a chairlift and we were whisked up.

We sat for a few hours drinking beers at one of Breckenridge's many beautiful mountain restaurants, got severely sunburnt, and then got the chairlift back down again.

That night we met up with Kieron, Liz, Kirsty, Phil and the rest of the gang for a few beers at a local bar. Rachel was slightly overwhelmed by all my new friends, but they made her feel very welcome.

Our last day in Breckenridge coincided with Kieron and Liz's too. Phil had flown back to Chesterfield early that morning and Kirsty was heading back to glorious Sheboygan for a couple of days before her return flight to England.

I was extremely sad to leave The Fireside Inn and it was hard to say goodbye to Andy and Niki. The timing of my arrival in Breckenridge could not have been more perfect, and I think they both appreciated having me there during the first few months of their own exciting adventure. As a leaving present, Andy and Niki kindly bought me a genuine Texas Stetson. It was a very thoughtful – if somewhat impractical – gift that I could cart around America along with my guitar, my smart shoes, the large book about photography that Mark had bought me, and a snowboard and snowboard boots that I now also owned and couldn't bear to part with.

As Rachel and I had planned to head north, we dropped Kieron and Liz off at Denver airport on the way through and then it was just the three of us: Rachel, me and Josephine.

33

We left Denver on I25 towards Wyoming. I had read in my guidebook about Happy Jack Road, which was described as a '*37-mile scenic alternative to the interstate*'. It stretched from Cheyenne to Laramie, which was where we were heading, so we kept lookout for the turning.

When we eventually joined Happy Jack Road, we were a little confused as it seemed to be doubling back the way we had come. It wasn't until we reached Cheyenne, 37 miles later, that we realised we had joined it at the far end and looped all the way back to the start. So in trying to avoid the interstate, we ended up driving the Cheyenne to Laramie section of I25 twice.

Following a long stretch on I80, the needle on Josephine's fuel gauge had dipped well into the red. Happy Jack Road had not had an abundance of gas stations – at least, not ones cheap enough for me to be prepared to fill up at – and I had continued on to find fuel elsewhere.

A signpost advertised services at McFadden in 25 miles. I looked at the needle and hoped we would make it. These services never materialised. Then the sun went down, and as we continued onto another endless stretch of I80, I began to panic that Rachel's first night of her road trip was going to be spent running out of fuel on a busy interstate.

I took a gamble and pulled off at the next exit, heading off into the rural darkness towards nowhere in particular. My instinct told me that running out of gas on a quiet country road was preferable to doing it on the interstate. Memories of Josephine's transmission exploding on the New Jersey Turnpike kept flashing through my mind and I didn't want to repeat an experience like that.

Rachel had other ideas.

'What happens if we run out of petrol here?' she asked.

'We won't,' I said, glancing at the needle that had dipped even further into the red than I thought possible.

'But what if we do?'

'Then we'll either try and flag down another car, or just park up and wait until morning.'

'We might not make it till morning. This place gives me the creeps.'

The needle had dipped well below the red as Josephine eventually chugged into the tiny hamlet of Rock River, Wyoming, presumably running on fumes alone. Rock River sounds like the name of a place that a holidaying couple would stumble upon in the middle of the night in a low-budget horror film where they would meet a gruesome end. It certainly looked the part too.

Rock River had the only gas station we had seen in many miles. It was closed. There was a motel adjacent to it, but that was also closed. This was not how I had hoped the first night of our road trip would go. Judging by the look on Rachel's face, it's not quite what she envisaged either.

'I guess we'll have to sleep in the car and then hopefully the gas station will be open in the morning,' I said.

She looked around at the dark, empty forecourt, with the unlit road stretching off into the blackness in either direction.

'It doesn't look like we have much choice,' she said.

I then spotted a faint light on in a window over on the other side of the forecourt. It was a small restaurant. It too was closed but I could see someone moving around inside.

I walked over and tapped gently on the door.

'Sorry, we're closed,' called a man as he walked towards the door.

'Sorry to bother you. I know it's late, but are you in charge of the motel next door?'

'No, I'm not. Why? Is there a problem?'

'No, no problem. We were just wondering if it's possible to rent a room for the night?'

'I can give Martin a call. He owns the place. It's getting late so he'll probably be in bed by now.'

'That's alright. Don't worry about it. We'll just sleep in the car.'

'It's no problem. He won't answer if he's in bed. I won't be a minute.'

He returned a couple of minutes later.

'Martin said he'll be here in ten.'

'Thank you so much. We really appreciate it.'

'You're welcome,' he said, pulling the door to and locking it behind him. 'I'm heading off home now.'

'Thank you,' called Rachel from the other side of the forecourt.

'You have a good night y'all,' he said, tipping his hat as he walked to his car around the back.

We waited anxiously for Martin to arrive, expecting him to emerge from the motel at any moment. After nearly 20 minutes, when we had almost given up hope, we saw car headlights approaching down the road.

'Do you think this is him?' said Rachel.

'I don't know. I hope so. I wasn't expecting him to drive here.'

The car pulled up alongside us and out stepped a man. Fortunately, he didn't look like a character from a low-budget horror film.

'You must be the couple wanting a motel room?' he asked.

'That's right. You must be Martin. Sorry to disturb you. We didn't realise you had to drive here.'

'I live a few miles out of town. Sorry it took me a while to get here. How many nights are you staying?'

'Just one please.'

We felt slightly guilty about paying for only one night when Martin had had to make a special trip out. But we then discovered that he also owned the gas station and he happily switched on a pump for us and we filled up Josephine with four-star which made the journey a little more worth his while.

The motel room did not appear to have been refurbished since the 1960s, but compared to a night on the gas station forecourt in Rock River, Rachel saw it as paradise.

Martin was back in the morning when we were loading up the car.

'Thanks again for coming to our rescue last night,' I said.

'You're welcome. Did you sleep well?'

'Very well thanks. Can you recommend anywhere good for breakfast around here?'

'There's a great little diner in Rawlins. Just follow Route 30 thataway,' he said, pointing thataway.

It was not until an hour and a half later that we discovered that Rawlins was 76 miles from Rock River. It was gems like this that fuelled my love of America. In the UK, there are very few things that anyone would consider driving 76 miles for. In rural America, 76 miles is an acceptable distance to travel for a good breakfast.

Only the breakfast in Rawlins wasn't that special. Martin from Rock River hadn't mentioned the name of the diner, so we didn't expect there to be a choice. We picked a café at random – it had one calendar on the wall – and we ate a fairly decent cooked breakfast. But it was not one I would drive a roundtrip of 152 miles for if I lived in Rock River. Fortunately,

Rawlins was in the direction we were heading anyway, so we didn't have to make the return trip.

We got chatting to a lady in the diner. She asked us all about our travels and I told her where I had been and some of the other places Rachel and I hoped to see. When we asked her what brought her to Rawlins, she told us she had run away from a violent husband in Carolina. She then took another sip of her coffee and told us both to 'have a nice day'. We didn't quite know how to respond.

From Rawlins we joined Route 287 north through the brilliantly named hamlets of Muddy Gap and Three Forks; the first named after its valley location between two hills, the second named after an under-stocked cutlery drawer.

Jeffrey City, Wyoming looked quite prominent on our map. And with a name like Jeffrey City, it promised great things. In fact only about 100 people now live in Jeffrey City.

In 1957, a uranium mine was opened in the area (financed by a wealthy local named Dr Jeffrey), and thousands of people flocked there for its promise of well-paid jobs. The town thrived for twenty years with shops, a library, churches and a high-school complete with Olympic-sized swimming pool. The collapse of the uranium industry in the late 1970s caused 99% of the population to leave town. Only a couple of businesses remain, relying on the passing trade from the highway.

We made our contribution to the local economy with a coffee bought from The Split Rock Bar and Cafe. It seemed like the remaining 1% of the population of Jeffrey City were also in there. I had great admiration for their spirit and resolve.

Beyond the more heavily populated city of Lander, the road twisted and turned its way up through the Wind River Indian Reservation. The road followed the Wind River Canyon floor and we arrived in Thermopolis in the late afternoon.

Rachel was still a little apprehensive about sleeping in Josephine in rest areas or parking lots, so we booked into the mystically named Fountain of Youth RV Park for our first night in Josephine Mark II. Thermopolis – from the Greek meaning *'hot city'*- is famous for its hot springs, and tourists flock from miles around to bathe in tepid sulphur.

We took a walk into town and peered through the window of the State Bath House. As part of a treaty signed in 1896 with the Shoshone and Arapaho Indian tribes, free public bathing is provided in the bath house all year round. It looked like a small, severely over-crowded swimming pool, so we ventured back to the campsite and planned to see if it was less busy in the morning instead.

'Did I tell you we have our own hot springs on site?' said the man who ran the RV Park.

'No. You didn't.'

'It's a big outdoor swimming pool heated by the hot springs. It's apparently the third largest hot mineral pool in the world.'

'Wait... did you just say the THIRD largest hot mineral pool IN THE WORLD is on this campsite?'

'Yes, that's right. It's just over there behind those mobile homes.'

'Fantastic. How much does it cost?'

'It's free for those staying at Fountain of Youth. It's never very busy.'

'I'm not surprised,' I thought. *'Given the fact that you're not exactly quick to tell people about it.'*

We got changed and went to check out the pool. It was even better than the man had implied. It was gigantic. It measured 235 feet long, which is significantly longer than an Olympic sized swimming pool. And, unlike the indoor public pool in downtown Thermopolis, this one was completely empty. Of other people, I mean. There was plenty of water in it. 84,600 cubic feet of it, to be precise.

Seeing as we were the only people there, we were a little anxious about climbing into the water, in case it was full of toxic sulphur that was going to burn our skin off. But it was too good to resist so we climbed in and spent a glorious hour with the pool to ourselves as darkness fell.

Later that evening, we lay down in Josephine listening to the chatter of people in the neighbouring RVs. My conversion of Josephine seemed like a great success and the futon mattress with my stolen bedding felt more comfortable and cosier than any bed I had ever slept in.

'See, I told you this road trip would be fun,' I said.

'You were right. It didn't get off to the best start with us nearly running out of petrol in Rock River, but today has been pretty perfect. Thank you.'

She leaned over and gave me a kiss.

'What's that weird smell, though?' she added.

'What smell?'

'The bed smells a bit... I don't know... strange. Where did you say you got it from?'

'From my aunt and uncle. They just had it lying around.'

I decided not to divulge any further details.

34

From Thermopolis we planned to visit Yellowstone National Park, but it was still closed because of the snow. There was talk of it opening in a few days, so after spending the morning in the campsite's hot spring – again with the entire place to ourselves – we headed west towards Grand Teton National Park.

We stopped for supplies at a supermarket in Dubois that had deer heads mounted on the walls above the shelves. This was proper Wild West territory. Dubois had some motels offering cheap rooms, and we were tempted to stop, but decided to try and get a little closer to Grand Teton so that we could enter the park early the next morning.

There was a shortage of cheap motels further on, and by shortage, I mean none. We ended up renting a small wooden shed in a campsite. It had no bedding and no amenities and cost twice the price of the motels back in Dubois. This was before glamping was so trendy. Rachel and I were one of the first couples to be duped into the notion that sleeping in an empty wooden shed is considered cool.

I cooked a meal of sausages and macaroni cheese, which we ate on the porch of our little shed, wearing all of our clothes and drinking red wine from the bottle. There was nobody else on the campsite and it was a strangely romantic evening.

Grand Teton literally translates as Big Tits National Park. The area was named either by French-Canadian explorers or a Native American Sioux tribe (depending on which version of events you believe) because of the peaks' resemblance to a pair of breasts. If the National Park Service renamed it Big Tits National Park they would undoubtedly see a dramatic rise in visitor numbers, but it might perhaps leave a few tourists feeling short-changed.

Anyway, none of this mattered because the entire bloody park was closed because of the snow. That's why there had been nobody else at the campsite. We probably should have checked before we left Thermopolis, or before we rented our shed. We did get a glimpse of the Tetons through the mist from the entrance gate. They were mighty big and pert.

Despite having driven all the way to the entrance of Grand Teton, neither Rachel nor I were in the least bit disappointed that it was closed. That was the beauty of an unplanned road trip. If an attraction was closed, we would just drive on to look for something else instead. And with America as big and beautiful as it is, you are never far from something else equally good.

We continued on to Jackson Hole where we had our first encounter with Dairy Queen, the ice cream and fast food restaurant chain. I don't mean to suggest that Dairy Queen should be considered a tourist attraction, or that it is in anyway comparable to a National Park. It is of course much better.

We don't have Dairy Queen in the UK so it was something new and different for us. We spent the afternoon slowly working our way through the ice-cream menu and playing cards at a quiet table in the corner. Over the coming weeks, this became a popular way for us to spend cold and wet afternoons.

We parked up in Driggs, Idaho – a small town with little to offer except a welcoming Italian restaurant where we ate, drank and then slept in Josephine in the parking lot. It was a cold night, but infinitely more comfortable than our previous night glamping in a shed.

As the road climbed from the plains of Idaho back towards Yellowstone, the area was dusted again with recent snow. Not enough to cause any concern, though, and the sun was out and it was a beautiful day.

The local radio announced that Yellowstone had just reopened. We had timed our arrival perfectly, as visitor numbers were expected to be relatively low for the first few days of the season.

Established in 1872, Yellowstone was the world's first national park and, thanks to its abundance of wildlife and extraordinary geothermal features, it is arguably the world's most famous.

We followed the main park road through Yellowstone towards Old Faithful, pausing regularly to allow herds of buffalo to amble up the same road.

Old Faithful is Yellowstone's main attraction. Despite its commercial nature, it is impossible not to be astounded by its wonder. 32,000 gallons of boiling water erupt up to a height of 56 metres. But this isn't what makes Old Faithful so special. It is not even the largest or tallest geyser in Yellowstone – Steamboat Geyser claims that title. What makes Old Faithful so special is its reliability.

Eruptions are so predictable that it is possible to arrive at the viewing area, check the schedule and realise that you have still got 20 minutes until the next display, nip off to buy a coffee, and be certain that you won't miss any of the show.

We did just that, and enjoyed Old Faithful's display so much we hung around and watched the next one, too.

We went on several walks – sorry I mean hikes – through the snow-covered landscape to see other geysers and thermal pools; their crystal clear turquoise waters contrasting beautifully with the deep snow that lay on the ground. The pools did all look very inviting, but the frequent warning signs that told the horror stories of people who dived into these boiling pools to rescue their dogs illustrated just how deadly deceptive they are.

We stayed the night at a motel in West Yellowstone and then spent the following day exploring the northern part of the park, with many more geysers, thermal pools and the boiling river. When explorers David E. Folsom and Charles W. Cook first visited Yellowstone in 1869, they wrote up a report of their expedition, but had difficulty in convincing anyone to publish it as it was believed to be too far-fetched. And it's completely understandable why. After two days staring in bewilderment at what Yellowstone had to offer, it felt like it was all part of some sort of bizarre fairytale. I am not convinced any of it is actually real. I think it is possibly an elaborate practical joke, staged by the tourist boards of Wyoming, Montana and Idaho to increase visitor numbers in the area. Are we really expected to believe that Old Faithful isn't wired up to some electronically-timed water pump? Or that the buffalo aren't underpaid workers in costume? You're not fooling me, Yellowstone. I know your game.

It wouldn't surprise me if the Mississippi PR team responsible for the Natchez Trace Pathway follow suit soon and install some 'natural' geysers along their route, too.

From Yellowstone we drove to the town of Bozeman, Montana, which proudly boasts its claim to fame of being home to the second ever museum devoted to computers. The first – The Computer Museum in Boston – closed in 1999, so Bozeman is also able to argue it has the oldest computer museum in the world.

As much as the prospect of the museum excited us, it was unfortunately closed so we didn't get to visit. If it had been open, we would of course have thought of another excuse.

We stayed the night at a pleasant bohemian style Youth Hostel on a residential side street of Bozeman. There was only one other occupant – a Scottish man named John whom we spoke only briefly to. He told us he had tickets to watch The Grateful Dead's guitarist Bob Weir playing a special gig at a nearby venue. We went along with him but the show was a sell out so Rachel and I had a couple of beers at a bar on Bradcock and 7th street. The entire town seemed to be at the Bob Weir gig and we had the place to ourselves. The bartender told us how much he loved England – especially Ireland.

Rachel had been saying for a few days that she needed a haircut. So when we got back to the hostel later that evening, I offered to cut it for her. As she had had a few drinks, she readily agreed.

Needless to say, it was the first and last time I have been entrusted with a pair of scissors near to Rachel's hair. If I had stopped after my first circumference of her head it would have looked ok. But, because of the alcohol, Rachel seemed unable to hold her head straight. I kept being convinced that the hair on one side of her head was longer than the other. I would trim one side, and then her head would lean slightly to the other side, and, thinking it appeared longer, I would have to trim that side too. I kept trying to correct my mistakes for half an hour, before we both realised I had done a truly dreadful job and the scissors were taken away from me.

Thankfully it was very cold in Montana, so I bought Rachel a woolly hat instead.

We woke late and ate the *Best Breakfast in Town* at 4Bs restaurant. It was 4Bs that made this bold claim, not me, but as it was the only breakfast we ate in Bozeman, I have no grounds to dispute it.

We continued on to Belgrade, and then joined I15 to Montana's beautiful state capital Helena. After wandering its tree-lined streets we spent a couple of hours playing cards in Dairy Queen (it was raining, ok), before continuing on to Helmville where we accidentally joined a dirt track that wound its way through what looked and felt like the set of *A River Runs Through It.* We emerged from the spectacular Montana scenery in the village of Drummond.

We parked up in a rest area on I90, which was one of the most scenic rest areas I had stayed at. Montana is so stunning that you could build a huge multi-storey car park in the middle of the countryside and it's unlikely to detract from the view.

On the way back from the toilet, just after dark, a giant of a man was loitering by the doorway rolling a cigarette.

'Is that your Plymouth Voyager?' he asked, nodding in the direction of Josephine.

'Yes, she's a beaut, isn't she?'

He didn't answer, unsure of whether I meant it or not.

'Do you sleep in it?' he asked.

'Some nights, yes,' I said, suddenly feeling like I should not be divulging too much information to a large man outside a public toilet at an interstate rest area.

'What about you? Is one of those lorries yours?' I said.

'Lorries? I love that. It's such a cute word. Yeah, that red big rig is mine.'

'Do you sleep in that?'

'Sure do. Almost every night.'

'What's that like? Do you get lonely? Do you have family back home?'

'It's not lonely at all. I bring my wife and cat along too.'

I laughed. He didn't.

'I ain't joking. My wife and cat come on almost all my trips with me.'

'Really?'

'Sure. Come and see for yourself.'

I wandered over to his lorry with him and, sure enough, there, sitting on the cabin bed above the driver's seat was a lady with a cat on her lap.

'Annie, this young man didn't believe that you and Whisky come on work trips with me,' he said.

'Well here we are,' she waved.

'Well there you are,' I said. 'Hello Annie. Hello Whisky. I think it's amazing that you're all travelling together.'

'It certainly makes being away from home a little easier,' he said.

The following morning, we turned off the interstate just north of Missoula. A few miles later, we were stopped by a workman at some roadworks in the middle of an Indian reservation. As we were the only vehicle on the road, the workman and his *STOP* sign were positioned right next to Josephine's window for the duration of the delay.

'It's going to be about 10 minutes,' he said.

'Ok, that's fine. We're in no rush.'

I looked in my rear view mirror at the perfectly straight road behind with not another car in sight. I could see off into the distance ahead, and there were no other vehicles either apart from a lone digger, digging up a small section of the road. It was the most surreal place to be delayed.

'Where you heading?' he asked.

'Glacier National Park, in a few days,' I said. 'I'm not sure where we'll end up tonight, though.'

'No point going all the way up to Glacier,' he said. 'This here's the best place in the world.'

'Right here?' I asked, curious if he meant this particular stop sign in the middle of fuck-knows-where, Montana.

'That's right,' he said. 'You're in the Flathead Indian Reservation. Best place on the whole goddamn Earth.'

'Is that right? It looks… well… it does look nice,' I said, looking around at a vast expanse of nothingness.

'Don't just take my word for it. That dude… what's-his-name?... he said it too, many years ago. Quasimodo, that's the one.'

'Quasimodo? You mean the Hunchback of Notre Dame?'

'That's the dude. The Hunchback of Notre Dame.'

'Was he a real person? I thought he was just a fictional character.'

'Course he was real. He made all those predictions about the future, didn't he? And one of the things he said was that this here Flathead Reservation is the best place on this goddamn Earth.'

'Well I can't argue with that. Maybe we'll stick around then,' I said, as I realised that he had been confusing Nostradamus with The Hunchback of Notre Dame.

'You should. Best place in the world,' he said again. 'You have a nice day now.'

And with that, he turned his *STOP* sign to *GO* and we were free to continue on our way.

'Did you hear that?' I said to Rachel. 'He thought Quasimodo was Nostradamus.'

She didn't respond.

'I said, that man back there, he thought that Nostradamus and The Hunchback of Notre Dame were the same person.'

She just looked at me with her brow furrowed.

'I thought they were too,' she said. 'Maybe it's you that's wrong?'

'Oh Jesus,' I said. 'Not you too.'

'What? Even if they are different people, maybe the Hunchback of Nostradamus, or whatever he was called, really did claim that this is the best place in the world.'

'Well, firstly they are NOT the same person. And he might have done, I suppose, but I didn't even know the Hunchback of Nostradamus, as you called him, had been to America. But, seriously, does this look like the best place in the world to you?'

Rachel surveyed the miles and miles of grassland stretching into the distance.

'It is nice,' she said. 'But, no, let's go to Glacier National Park instead.'

We stopped briefly in St. Ignatius to visit its Mission. Built in 1891, St. Ignatius Mission is a fairly unremarkable church from the outside. It has become popular with visitors because of the 58 stunning hand-painted murals on the interior walls and ceiling. The untrained artist who created them was working as the mission's cook at the time.

I can just picture the scene at the church's monthly meeting.

'Right, next on the agenda is decorating. The walls could do with a lick of paint so we need some volunteers to help out.'

The chef puts his hand up.

'I'm happy to do a bit of painting,' he said.

'Great, thanks Malcolm. There are brushes and paint in the store cupboard. You can start today.'

Many years and 58 magnificent murals later...

'Alright already! That's enough showing off now, Malcolm. Get back in the kitchen. We're all bloody starving here.'

We passed through Paradise, Montana which – despite its name – was unable to convince enough people to move to the area. The local primary school was recently forced to close after its total number of pupils dropped to just five.

We continued onwards to the town of Hot Springs. With a name like Hot Springs, it's impossible not to call in. It would be like naming a town Free Beer. The trouble with Hot Springs was that it didn't even remotely live up to its name. The town's 'hot springs' were a grubby swimming pool owned by a hotel in town. It was closed anyway. Instead, we played cards on the shores of Flathead Lake near to the curiously named settlement of Big Arm.

We parked up later that evening outside a gas station in Kalispell and had an early night.

35

Glacier National Park is undoubtedly one of the most beautiful places on Earth. If only the Hunchback of Nostradamus had strayed just a few miles north of the reservation, he would have hastily reconsidered his dubious claims about Flathead.

Due to the snow, only 11 miles of the park's roads were open, but it meant we seemed to be the only people in the entire park.

We sat and played cards by a lake that was so still and clear it perfectly reflected the snow-covered peaks in the distance. I took off my shoes and socks and dipped my toes into the lake before unleashing a barrage of expletives that echoed around the peaceful wooded valley.

'What's wrong?' asked Rachel, assuming I had been savagely attached by an alligator or something.

'The water. It's SO fucking freezing!' I said.

'We are in GLACIER National Park. Where do you think all that water has come from?'

'I know that now. But it looked so inviting.'

We hiked a short wooded trail that looped its way through the forest. We approached a warning sign for bears. I stood in front of it to try and prevent Rachel from noticing it as she passed.

'What are you hiding?' she said.

'Nothing.'

'Yes, you are. I saw a sign or something. What does it say?'

'Nothing important. Just reminding us not to drop litter.'

'Let me see.'

'Really, it's nothing. Let's keep moving.'

'George, I'm not going anywhere until you let me see that sign.'

I reluctantly stepped to one side to reveal a bright yellow sign.

WARNING – BEAR FREQUENTING AREA

'Bears?' shouted Rachel. But she shouted it in a non-audible way, so as not to disturb the bears presumably.

'We'll be fine. I'm sure they are all still hibernating,' I said.

'But those that are waking up will be seriously pissed off and hungry.'

'Don't worry about it. Let's just keep moving.'

'We are miles from the car. What happens if we see one?'

'If it's a grizzly bear we have to play dead. Just lie down on the ground and pretend to be dead. It will soon get bored and wander off. Or is that for black bears? I can't remember.'

'What do we do for black bears?'

'The opposite. You have to shout and stamp and throw stones at it to scare it off.'

'So we do that if it's a black bear?'

'Yes, I think so. Or that might be for grizzlies. I'm not really sure, to be honest.'

'And what colour are grizzlies?'

'I don't know. Browny-blackish too, I guess.'

'Then how do we know if it's a black bear or a grizzly bear?'

'I can't remember. Look, I've never even seen a bear, let alone been forced to identify what type of bloody bear it is.'

'Well, maybe now would be a good time to remember.'

'I assume grizzly bears look more... y'know... grizzly.'

'Any bear woken from hibernation is going to look grizzly,' she snapped. 'How are we supposed to know if we should play dead or throw stones?'

'One of us could play dead, and the other could throw stones,' I suggested. 'That way, there's a very good chance one of us will survive. If we both pick the wrong method we might both die.'

'That's not even remotely funny. You are not making me feel in the slightest bit better.'

We speed-walked the rest of the way back to Josephine in complete silence. We did hear a few suspicious rustling noises through the trees, but didn't stick around long enough to find out what was making them.

We left Glacier National Park (not because of the bears) and drove through the Blackfeet Indian Reservation and then on to Cut Back, Montana, which often claims the record for being the coldest place in the entire lower 48 states. Thankfully, spring had fully sprung and I was no longer required to sleep in all of my clothes to try to keep warm. We parked up in the nearby town of Shelby on Route 2 and played pool and took advantage of the 50c beer during Happy Hour at the Montana Club, before stumbling back to sleep in Josephine.

After a breakfast of peanut butter sandwiches we headed towards Great Falls. We stopped for a short walk at Giant Springs State Park and looked at its surprisingly fascinating trout hatchery.

'There's a place called White Sulphur Springs not far from here,' said Rachel as we joined Route 87 east.

'Do you want to go there?'

'It sounds lovely. Surely they must have some hot springs.'

'But remember how crap that other place was? And that was actually called Hot Springs.'

'This one sounds better though. I like the sound of White Sulphur Springs.'

'Really? It sounds like a chemical experiment to me.'

'Pleeeease can we go,' she said.

'Fine. How do I get there?'

'Take Route 89 at the next exit.'

White Sulphur Springs was even worse than I predicted. The town did have a hot springs, but again it had been bought by a hotel, and turned into an ugly looking swimming pool.

We ate a contender for the worst meal of the trip at the Truckstop Café just outside of town. I had high hopes for the place, as two calendars were proudly displayed on the wall, but it was only because of extreme hunger, and not with a single glimmer of enjoyment, that I was able to finish my meal.

It seems to me that things have changed a great deal since William Least Heat Moon explored his blue highways, sampling the delights of the calendar cafes. Calendars are no longer a suitable way to gauge the quality of food on offer at an establishment. I found that antlers mounted on the wall are a much better indication. In all my travels in America, I never once had a bad meal at a café where a set of antlers adorned the walls.

Being a popular spot for truckers, the Truckstop Café did have a good sized car park where we parked up Josephine for an undisturbed night's sleep.

We visited the town's 'hot springs' the following morning, which were predictably disappointing, but as we had made the detour specifically for them we felt an obligation to go.

The nearby Castle ghost town again lured us in with its name and false promises. We drove around looking for it for a while and then followed a seemingly never-ending dirt track which made Josephine shake and rattle so much I thought she was going to crumble to pieces like she was made of Lego. We reached the end of the track only to discover a large sign that stated that the ghost town was on private land and we could not visit without permission.

A few miles further down Route 12, I could feel Josephine pulling to one side even more than usual. I stopped in the village of Two Dot, Montana (population 76) to investigate. I prepared for the worst, expecting it to be another axle issue or perhaps the steering column. I was somewhat relieved to find she had a flat tyre.

I sort of knew how to change a car tyre, but had never actually had to change one before. The only other time I'd experienced a blow-out was on the M1 motorway. On that occasion the roadside recovery had come to assist.

'Do you know what you're doing?' asked Rachel.

'Of course I do.'

'Do you? Last time I was with you and you got a flat tyre you had to call the AA.'

'That's because it was on the M1.'

'Does that mean you have to call for help?'

'Yes, well, I mean, probably. It seemed like the sensible thing to do.'

'Do you want me to go and ask one of those blokes over there if they can help?'

I looked up to see two men in ten-gallon hats, jeans and checked shirts leaning against a wall on the other side of the road from us. They were both looking our way.

'No thanks,' I said. 'I've got it covered.'

'Too late,' said Rachel. 'They're coming over.'

'Oh bollocks. Just what I need. An audience of real men.'

'Are you not a real man then?' smiled Rachel.

'Of course I am. You watch. I'll have this changed in no time.'

'Everything alright there, boy?' asked one of the men, as they strolled casually over to our side of the road.

'Yes, fine thanks.'

'You had a blow-out?'

'Yeah, just a slow puncture I think. Probably got it from that dirt track near to the ghost town. I'm just going to change the tyre.'

'You need a hand?' said the other man.

'Thanks, but I'm fine. Lovely day,' I said, trying to move the conversation away from the fact that I was struggling even to assemble the two sections of the jack correctly.

'Best time of the year. You sure you don't need a hand there?'

'Really, I'm fine. Thanks,' I said, locking the jack into place under the chassis and beginning to lift the car. 'So, where did the town get the name Two Dot? It's a pretty cool name.'

'From the cows,' said one of the men.

'The cows chose the name?' I asked.

'No, don't be foolish. From a local cattle rancher named George 'Two Dot' Wilson. This all used to be his land. The branding iron he used for his cows was just two dots. And the name just sorta stuck.'

'Well, I like it,' I said, successfully unscrewing the final nut and removing the wheel. I casually tried to wipe the vast amount of sweat away that was pouring from my forehead and pretend that I'd hardly had to exert myself at all.

We chatted with the men for a few more minutes about how Two Dot, Montana had once been an important stop on the Milwaukee Road – a transcontinental railway line that operated from the mid 1800s until 1980. Nowadays, very few people stop in the town. If it hadn't been for a flat tyre, we probably wouldn't have stopped either. But we were glad we had. This was the America I wanted to see.

'You done a good job there, boy,' said one of the men, as I lowered Josephine back onto the ground.

'Thanks,' I said, looking at Rachel for a sign of acknowledgement. She smiled back.

'I've never actually changed a tyre in my life,' one of the men then said.

'What? Really?'

'Yep, I've only ever had a couple of blow-outs.'

'And what happened?'

'I just called the garage in town and they came and fixed me up.'

'Same here,' said the other man.

'Anyway, it was nice to meet you both,' said the first man, as they both strolled back across the street and resumed their positions against the wall.

'Well done,' said Rachel, patting me on the shoulder. 'You did good.'

The spare tyre I had fitted was smaller than all the others. It wasn't one of those temporary tyres, designed to be lighter and take up less space. It was, as with the other tyre that Mark and I had argued about when buying snow chains, just a tyre not designed to be on this car. It seems that a previous owner – possibly that bastard Daniel whom we bought it off in upstate New York – had just bought five random tyres of differing sizes and figured they would do the job just fine.

We took it steady for the next few miles until we reached the town of Harlowton and found a garage. The tyre was non-repairable so I paid to have a new one fitted. Rather than go through the motions of switching the new one and the spare (I had already proved my manly capabilities once already), the real men in the garage took care of that.

By the time the car was fixed, Rachel and I had both lost enthusiasm for the idea of driving any further. Harlowton seemed like a nice enough town, so we decided to stick around. Just for the night, I mean. It wasn't that nice.

We ate an average meal in a roadside café and then parked up Josephine in a car park by the side of the town's Chief Joseph Park.

We spent the evening drinking beers at Oasis Bar. It was Friday night but there were only a handful of people in the bar.

'Is it always this quiet on Fridays?' I asked the barman.

'It is when it's karaoke night in Ryegate.'

'And I'm guessing it's karaoke night in Ryegate tonight?'

'Sure is. Almost the entire population of Harlowton will be there.'

'Seriously?'

'Seriously. Tomorrow night this bar will be packed. Tonight, everyone is in Ryegate. Hell, if I wasn't working, I'd be there too.'

'How far is Ryegate?' I asked, strangely tempted to head on down there and bust out my rendition of *Rhinestone Cowboy*.

'32 miles.'

'People have driven 32 miles for karaoke?

'Why sure. It's only a few towns away.'

We had a fantastic evening in Harlowton, and were thankful to the rest of the town for vacating for the evening and allowing us unlimited access to the pool table and quicker service at the bar. We ate pizza, played pool, and drank some strange cocktails – at the insistence of one of the only other people in the bar. Jack was a divorced trucker in his late 50s. He claimed to have once been the town's Chief of Police, although we had no way of substantiating this claim.

When we told him where we had parked and where we would be sleeping that night, he responded:

'You realise that most of the population of Harlowton was conceived in that park?'

'Really? We had no idea.'

'Well there ain't much to do around here. So folks are either drinking in here, or else making out over in the park.'

'Or doing karaoke in Ryegate,' added Rachel.

'Well yes, of course. But only on Fridays. Harlowton used to be a thriving town, but then the interstate came along and changed all that. People stopped passing through. And of course, cats don't drink coffee. You know what I'm saying?'

I looked at Rachel, neither of us having a bloody clue what he was saying.

'Know what I'm saying?' he repeated. 'Cats don't drink coffee!'

He elbowed me hard in the arm and laughed.

'You hear me?' he shouted. 'CATS DON'T DRINK COFFEE.'

I laughed and nodded to try and feign some understanding. To this day, I still don't know what he meant. But to be fair, he probably had a point. I have never seen a cat drinking coffee.

36

The following morning we drove to Ryegate. Not to do the karaoke, of course. Nobody does karaoke before breakfast. It happened to be in the direction we were heading anyway. Ryegate was a cute little town that gave little clue to the mass appeal it had had the previous night.

Onwards we went and stopped in the town of Roundup alongside the Musselshell River – a town that got its name for being the area where cattlemen would roundup their cows ready for the start of the cattle drive.

It had been a few weeks since we had done any laundry and Rachel and I were starting to smell. Roundup had a laundrette where we spent most of the morning. I'm sure the town had lots else to offer, but we didn't get to see much further than the inside of a washer-dryer.

The laundrette was empty apart from one other man who was sitting watching a washing machine angrily spin across from him.

'Did you know that Roundup has more bars, churches and coal per person than anywhere else in the world?' he said, not taking his eyes off the washing machine.

'No. I didn't know that. How many bars does it have?'

'Well, at least three.'

'And how many people live here?'

'Thousands.'

'Right. And it has more coal per person too?' I asked, not even sure what that meant.

'Yes sir.'

'It sounds like a great town.'

'It is. I'm a born again Christian,' he then said. 'God called me here and God will tell me when to leave.'

'The laundrette?'

'No,' he said. 'This town. Roundup'

'Oh right. Sorry.'

Rachel sniggered to the left of me.

'How will you know when God is telling you to leave Roundup?' I asked.

'I'll just know.'

We gathered up our clean washing ten minutes later and I had a sudden feeling that God was telling us to leave Roundup.

We spent the afternoon at Little Bighorn Battlefield National Monument – the site of the prominent battle of 1876. The battlefield now serves as a beautiful memorial to those who lost their lives in the battle. Originally designed to commemorate George Armstrong Custer's 7th Cavalry, the memorial now tastefully honours the Native Americans who fought at Bighorn too.

We left Bighorn along Route 212 through the small town of Busby and on to Lame Deer, which was named after the Miniconjou Lakota chief. With his contemporaries assigned powerful names such as Standing Bear, Red Cloud, Sitting Bull and Geronimo, I couldn't help feeling that Lame Deer was an unfortunate name for an Indian chief. I can't imagine he instilled too much fear in his enemy.

Soon after dark we found a pleasant but extremely windy rest area at Broadus near the Powder River, and parked up for the night.

We stopped for breakfast and coffee in Alzada on the Wyoming border, where we considered hanging around just so we could visit the brilliant looking bikers' bar Stoneville Saloon when it opened its doors later in the day. Stoneville Saloon advertised two things: *cheap drinks and lousy food.* Peering through the window, I could see hundreds of deer heads mounted on the wall. I was certain the food would be anything but lousy.

Instead, we briefly dipped down into Wyoming, before crossing another state border into South Dakota. The town of Spearfish looked like many others we had passed through, but frequent news reports on the radio about a recent murder gave the town an added edge as we drove through its streets.

We stopped for gas and I suggested to Rachel that she go and pay and ask the cashier for directions to Deadwood.

'Ok,' she said. 'But you know I'm not very good at remembering directions.'

'You'll be fine. All you have to do is just listen to what they say and then repeat it to me.'

'I'll try, but I'm warning you, I'm really rubbish at it.'

She came out five minutes later shaking her head.

'Did they not know how to get to Deadwood?' I asked.

'Yes, they did. But I can't remember what he said.'

'But it was only about ten seconds ago.'

'I know. The man had a really big beard and it distracted me so much that I couldn't concentrate on what he was saying.'

We eventually reached the town of Deadwood in the early afternoon. Deadwood became infamous in the 1870s during the Blackhills Gold Rush. When Custer announced the discovery of gold in the town, the population quickly swelled to 5000. Deadwood also became notorious for its lawlessness, and it was here, in Nuttal & Mann's Saloon, that 'Wild Bill' Hickok was shot and killed. These days, the town seems to be predominantly made up of casinos.

At the time of our visit, Kevin Costner was having some bust-up with the local Native Americans about one of these casinos. This argument was all happening behind the scenes in the law courts, by the way. I don't mean to imply that Kevin

Costner was having some sort of fist fight in the high street. Although that would have definitely made Deadwood more memorable.

We visited Saloon #10, which is the new name for the bar in which Wild Bill was killed. The original bar had a different name, was located further down the street, and burned down in 1879. Other than those minor details, it is definitely the same place.

They do have the chair where Wild Bill was allegedly sitting when he was shot (although this has never been verified) and a framed blood-splattered mock-up of the 'dead man's hand' – the cards that Wild Bill was holding at the time of his death.

Wild Bill's self-proclaimed life as a gunfighter and gambler has often been suggested to have been wildly exaggerated. He is perhaps better known as being a great storyteller. I love that this embellishment of his life even continued after his death. His 'dead man's hand' consisted of two black aces and two black eights. He was just one card away from a full house – one of the best hands in poker. Wild Bill was not the kind of person who could have possibly been shot dead holding a poker hand of 7 high.

Deadwood was moderately fun, but the whole town had a slightly Disneyland feel to it which left both Rachel and me feeling slightly let down.

After leaving Deadwood, we set our expectations very low for Mount Rushmore. The huge sculpture of the faces of the four former presidents – George Washington, Thomas Jefferson, Theodore Roosevelt and Abraham Lincoln – carved into the side of a granite mountain, is one of the most recognisable sights in all of America. We paid it a visit, just to say we had been.

It turned out to be far better than we anticipated. It was mid-afternoon when we arrived, and most of the coach parties were just departing. There were still quite a few tourists at the main viewing area, but once we started onto the footpath that leads towards the base of the cliff, we only saw a handful of other people.

People who visit Mount Rushmore often moan that *'it's much smaller than you think.'* These are people who have only looked at it from the viewing area. The viewing area is about half a mile from the monument. Things tend to look smaller from half a mile away. Even massive carved mountains.

We followed the Presidential Trail up 422 stairs (I didn't count them – it said it in the leaflet) which circled below the cliff face where you could fully appreciate its size and scale. Mount Rushmore really is a phenomenal piece of work.

The monument was originally supposed to include the presidents' bodies down to their waists, but the project ran out of money and construction ended in 1941. This premature end to the project worked in Mount Rushmore's favour, in my opinion. Hundreds of thousands of tonnes of blasted granite sit piled up on the slopes of Mount Rushmore below the monument. This gives the sculpture a fresh look as though it is still a work in progress, and the faces look as unblemished today as they did 70 years ago.

'Apparently the monument they are building of Crazy Horse just down the road is even more spectacular,' I said to Rachel.

'Why are they building a monument of Neil Young?'

'What are you talking about? They are not building a monument of Neil Young. It's Crazy Horse.'

'I thought Neil Young WAS Crazy Horse?'

'No! Neil Young had a band called Crazy Horse, but that's nothing to do with the original Crazy Horse.'

'Oh. What did he do then? Was he in a band too?'

'No. He was a famous Native American leader. Remember we read about him at the Battle of Little Bighorn site? If Mark was here he'd tell us more.'

'So you wish Mark was here instead of me?' she huffed.

'Oh don't be silly. Of course I don't. I just meant that Mark knew all this sort of stuff. If we go and visit the memorial we'll find out more.'

The Crazy Horse monument is certainly spectacular. It is larger, more intricate and more dramatic than Rushmore, but what makes it so fascinating is that it is still only partially complete.

Feeling that American history was being unfairly portrayed with the building of Mount Rushmore, Native American chief Henry Standing Bear commissioned a Polish-American sculptor named Korczak Ziolkowski to create a memorial to the iconic war leader Crazy Horse. Work began on the 195m wide monument in 1948, and there is still no end in sight. Ziolkowski died in 1982 and his wife Ruth continued to manage the project with their ten children. Ruth died in 2014 and the younger generations have all vowed to pursue their father's dream.

There is no doubt that the Crazy Horse memorial is a phenomenal project, and it is incredible to look at it and imagine how it might one day appear when complete. But the project has brought with it a fair bit of controversy. Relatives of Crazy Horse have stated that building such a memorial without first seeking the family's permission goes against their tribal culture. Questions have also been asked about the millions of dollars of donations and revenue created by the project, and what it actually funds. It is also suggested that the Ziolkowski family tend to be nepotistic with their staff, rather than offering jobs to local Native Americans.

We spent the night eating cheap junk food and sleeping in the parking lot of the Custer Taco Bell. I don't think that's what either side fought for.

37

If it wasn't for our Annual Pass, we probably would have cruised straight past Wind Cave National Park. If we had, we would have missed out on one of the most entertaining spectacles of our entire trip: a pack of prairie dogs. I'm going to look up the correct collective noun for prairie dogs shortly, but until then, a pack will have to do.

Prairie dogs, like meerkats, are ridiculously paranoid creatures. They spend their entire existence in a state of high-alert, expecting the arrival of predators at any moment. They need to lighten up a little. It would be lovely if just once you could see a prairie dog just kicking back and chilling the fuck out.

This particular pontoon of prairie dogs (still not looked it up yet) was particularly special because of one individual. Rachel named him Geoffrey for some reason. He did look like a Geoffrey, to be fair. Geoffrey was even more paranoid than most. His head constantly turned from side to side and his eyes darted all over the place looking for something suspicious. But Geoffrey had a problem in that he was either blind and deaf, or particularly stupid.

We took a tentative step towards the paranoia of prairie dogs (no, that's not it either). All the other prairie dogs disappeared beneath the ground instantly. Not Geoffrey. Geoffrey stood there with a look as if to say, 'What was that? Did I miss something?'

We stood still for a couple of minutes and all of the other prairie dogs eventually returned to their lookout duties. We took another step and they all took refuge below the surface again. All except Geoffrey, who continued to glance frantically in every direction, convinced there was something untoward, but unable to determine what.

I imagined the rest of the prairie dogs beneath the ground all calling up to him, 'What the hell are you doing, Geoffrey? Get yourself down here NOW, you maniac.'

We kept inching forwards until Geoffrey was almost in touching distance and still completely unaware. Not once did he make direct eye contact with us. Eventually we retreated back to a safe distance in case it turned out Geoffrey was acting an elaborate double-bluff, and was luring Rachel and me into his trap where he and his plethora of prairie dog (nope, not yet) friends were going to tear our faces off.

Nobody knows if you should play dead or throw stones if attacked by a coterie of prairie dogs. A coterie is the correct collective noun, by the way. I'm sure that nugget of information will come in very useful for you one day.

It is not possible to drive across this part of South Dakota without being made aware of the small town of Wall. In fact, nobody who passes within several hundred miles of Wall will be able to claim they haven't heard of it. But it wasn't always that way.

In 1931, a Nebraskan native named Ted Hustead bought a drugstore in the small town of Wall and moved to South Dakota with his wife Dorothy to run the pharmacy.

Business was slow to begin with, but then Dorothy suggested putting up signs along the highway offering *FREE WATER* to thirsty travellers heading west to Mount Rushmore. The marketing ploy was an instant success, and Wall Drug gradually developed into the huge attraction that it is today.

Billboards for Wall Drug can now be found along a roughly 650 mile section of Interstate 90, and people share photos from all over the world stating how far it is to Wall Drug, South Dakota.

It doesn't matter how hard you try, if you are passing Wall and are in no urgent rush to be anywhere else, you have to pull off the interstate to see what all the fuss is about. Rachel was extremely suspicious of visiting Wall Drug and didn't want to get sucked in by its gimmicky marketing. She tried her hardest to persuade me to keep driving. I tried my hardest to resist the temptation and stay on the interstate, but my curiosity got the better of me, and we suddenly found ourselves in Wall.

It was late evening and we (I) didn't want to rush our (my) visit to Wall Drug, so we found a cheap motel on the edge of town and booked a room.

'Are we really staying the night in a motel so you can visit a pharmacy?' Rachel asked.

'It's not just a pharmacy. They have free water too.'

'So, let me get this straight... we are staying the night in a motel so that you can have some free water tomorrow?'

'Well, yes. And there's a giant model dinosaur, too.'

'I can't wait.'

The television in the motel showed a looping slideshow of advertisements for local businesses. One such advert, which kept reappearing every few seconds, showed a menu that featured its dish-of-the-day, 'Toss Salad.' As hungry as we were, we decided to avoid it in case it involved sampling the chef's special homemade dressing.

Instead, we drove to the nearby Cactus Lounge. The kitchen was minutes from closing and they were almost out of food, but they were able to put together a tasty assortment of small dishes for us to share. It was possibly the leftovers from other customers' plates, but it still tasted very good.

We spent the following morning in Wall Drug. I don't know how it's possible to spend an entire morning in a pharmacy, but somehow we did, and the time just flew by.

I spent most of my time there desperately trying to work out what exactly Wall Drug was. It is a bizarre but fascinating concept. There are a few attractions to look at: a giant dinosaur, a fibre-glass Jackalope – which is a mythical animal (at least, I hope it is) with the appearance of a jackrabbit with antelope horns – and an art gallery. They also still offer free water and coffee for 5 cents. But basically Wall Drug is a giant gift shop selling Wall Drug tat. In the height of summer it attracts 20,000 visitors a day.

Wall Drug's popularity is a comment on the sparseness of South Dakota more than anything. If a similar attraction opened in New York City, it probably wouldn't even last a week. Although, free water and 5 cent coffee is a business model that would potentially work anywhere.

After driving through featureless expanses for mile upon mile, humans become desperate for some form of visual stimulation and Wall Drug provides this by the bucket load. Even Rachel was a convert by the end of our visit.

I never really tired of these vast areas of nothingness in America. The endless horizons and featureless vistas were mesmerising to me. Great Britain is a relatively small country, and because of our undulating landscape and predictably miserable weather, we are spoilt with lush green views for most of the year. Being able to see the horizon in every direction, with only the road we were driving on to break the scene (and the occasional '*Next Gas Station 80 miles*', or '*FREE WATER in 375 miles*' signs to look at) was still very much a novelty to us.

I can understand this emptiness might become tiresome over time, though. Even the ground itself in parts of South Dakota has got bored of its own monotony. Over the course of millions of years, billions of tonnes of rock eagerly volunteered their particles to be eroded away by wind and water, to escape to a better life somewhere else – anywhere else. Little did these particles know that, by leaving, they had in fact turned the vast featureless expanse that they once occupied into something quite astonishing.

The Badlands of South Dakota where we arrived later that day looked like nowhere else on Earth. In fact, Badlands National Park is so otherworldly it genuinely feels like you have set foot on another planet.

We spent a few hours walking around the lunar landscape, with its deep caverns and crevices, eroded buttes and sharp pinnacles – all magically created over time by erosion, surrounded by the largest undisturbed mixed grass prairie in the United States.

We also stood and watched another coterie of prairie dogs (see, I remembered) for a while, but Geoffrey had set the bar very high. Every prairie dog we will ever encounter will be a disappointment in comparison.

From Badlands we drove to Chamberlain and stopped to fill up at a gas station on Interstate 90. I went in to pay and planned to buy some bread and ham for dinner but was surprised to see a small restaurant area at the back, packed full of people. And not just the usual ensemble of truckers that you get at interstate truck stops. Entire families were sitting down to huge dinners in the gas station.

'I think we should eat out tonight,' I said to Rachel, when I returned to the car.

'Sounds good to me. Where?'

'In there.'

'The petrol station?'

'Yeah, it's packed. It looks pretty good.'

'Wow, you really know how to spoil me. Are there any antlers on the wall?'

'I didn't see any. But even so, I think we should take a chance.'

'Ok.'

Rachel and I uncharacteristically ordered a salad each.

Our diet in America had been varied and extensive, but lacking in anything green. The restaurant advertised its green salad, which included: avocados, tomatoes, cucumber, sweet corn, beetroot and a variety of mixed salad leaves.

When it arrived, it looked exactly as described, except it was covered in what appeared to be cooked mince.

'Enjoy your meal,' said the waitress.

'Thank you. Is that mince on top?' I asked.

'Sure is. It's our finest ground beef.'

'Oh, right. I didn't notice that on the menu.'

'It probably ain't on the menu. That's how the chef likes to serve the salad.'

'Ok.'

It seems that everything in middle America, whether you like it or not, is served with beef. And after demolishing my salad in minutes, I think the chef at that gas station on I90 was definitely onto something. I will ask for beef to be added to all my green salads in future.

For dessert, Rachel and I shared a portion of banoffee pie – a dish my friend claims his grandma invented. Fortunately, the chef decided against serving this with minced beef. My friend's grandma would certainly not have approved.

Despite the lack of antlers on the wall, the meal was a great success. We found a nearby rest area that was relatively quiet and parked up for the night. After writing my journal, we walked to the toilet to brush our teeth and noticed that almost every parking space in the rest area was now occupied with an RV or caravan full of the same families who had been eating at the gas station earlier that evening. It seems South Dakota is so desolate that Interstate 90 is considered a popular holiday destination.

38

There are few sights more unnerving than the blue flashing lights of a police car in your rear-view mirror when you are the only car driving along an empty highway.

'Do they want us to stop?' said Rachel, in the middle of the morning on the following day.

'It looks like it,' I said, slowing down and pulling over onto the shoulder.

'Were you speeding?'

'No. I don't think Josephine could speed even if I wanted her to. Did I tell you about the time Mark and I got stopped in Death Valley for driving too slowly?'

'No.'

'Well we did.'

'Well you weren't driving too slowly this time, were you?'

'No. I've no idea why he's stopped us.'

I watched as the officer parked up a few yards behind. He got out and swaggered confidently towards the driver's window, in the exact way you would expect an American cop to swagger. I think this walk must be taught at Police Academy.

'Good afternoon, Officer,' I said. 'Is there a problem?'

'Is this your vehicle?' he asked.

'Yes.'

'Licence and registration please.'

I reached over and retrieved the documents from the glove box and passed them to him.

'Please step out of the car, Sir.'

'Is there some sort of problem?'

'Please come with me.'

Rachel looked at me anxiously as I walked back to the police car with the officer.

'Have a seat,' he said, opening the passenger side door.

'Where are we going?'

'We're not going anywhere. I just need to have a little talk with you.'

'Ok,' I said, hesitantly climbing into the passenger side of the car. 'Could you please tell me what this is all about?'

'Your exhaust.'

'Oh, what about my exhaust?'

'It sounds quite… er… noisy.'

'Yes, it is a little noisy. Is that why you stopped us? Could you hear it all the way back down the highway?'

'Well, I guess I could, yes. You should get it checked out.'

'Ok, thanks, I will,' I lied. 'Is that all?'

'No. I see you have New York licence plates.'

'Yes.'

'Why is that?'

'Because that's where we bought the car.'

'And what are you doing all the way out here in South Dakota?'

'We're on holiday,' I said.

'Holiday?'

'Sorry, I mean vacation.'

'I know what a goddamn holiday is,' he snapped. 'Why are you vacationing in South Dakota?'

This was a question I had asked myself many times over the last few days. But I chose to answer him diplomatically.

'We heard great things about South Dakota. It's a beautiful state.'

'Hmm,' he said.

'Really, it is.'

'Are you carrying any drugs in your vehicle?' he asked.

'What?' I spluttered. 'No, of course not!'

'Is your wife or girlfriend carrying any drugs?'

'No. Neither of us are.'

'If I was to go and search your vehicle now, would I find any drugs?'

'Absolutely not. You wouldn't find any.'

'Is that because they are so well hidden?'

'No. It's because there aren't any.'

'If I was to ring my superior and get him to send a team of sniffer dogs down, would they find any drugs in your car?'

'I can assure you, the only thing that they would sniff out would be a whole lot of dirty laundry.'

'I could have dogs down here within minutes and there ain't nothing those dogs won't find.'

'Please, be my guest. Call your superior and get the dogs here. I promise you they will not find any drugs in that car.'

He sat there eyeballing me for what felt like minutes, looking for any indication that I was lying. I felt my cheeks turning red and my forehead beading up with sweat. For a moment, I almost felt like I did have drugs stashed somewhere in Josephine.

'Ok,' he eventually said. 'You can go. Enjoy the rest of your holiday.'

'What was all that about?' asked Rachel, once I was back in Josephine.

'We're from New York, so we are obviously drug dealers.'

'Is that what he said?'

'Pretty much, yeah.'

In the town of Mitchell we stopped to visit its Corn Palace. But it's not just any old corn palace. Mitchell's Corn Palace is the *'World's ONLY Corn Palace'*, according to their advertising.

The palace is not, as you might expect from its name, made from corn. Instead, it is decorated each year in huge corn murals that cover its exterior walls. It is the town's biggest attraction by far and is visited by about half a million people a year. Almost all of whom leave with the same thought: 'Meh.' The whole place is a little bit corny, if I'm honest.

Don't get me wrong, the Corn Palace is quite an achievement and is moderately interesting to look at. But you would be mightily disappointed if you had driven all the way to Mitchell especially for it. It might make a nice day trip, however, if you are vacationing on Interstate 90.

We waved farewell to South Dakota and entered Minnesota, where we joined Route 23 at Beaver Creek and headed north through the small town of Jasper (population 597) and the even smaller town of Florence (population 53) and bought the ingredients for a stir fry for dinner. The rest area near the town of Marshall that was mentioned in our guide book either didn't exist or we failed to find it, so we made our own in a lay-by on a small back road. We had run out of water so I cooked the noodles for our dinner in Miller Genuine Draft. They tasted so good that I now refuse to eat noodles unless they have been cooked in beer.

We woke late the following morning and stopped for breakfast in Marshall where we ate a *Tremendous Twelve*: 4 rashers of bacon, 4 pancakes, three eggs and a hash brown. It is not possible to have a bad day after a breakfast like that.

We turned east onto Route 19 towards Gaylord. I'm not going to pretend we just happened to pass through Gaylord. I happily admit that we spotted it on the map and pretty much planned our entire route through Minnesota accordingly.

The town is incredibly proud of its name, and so it should be. Everywhere you look the name GAYLORD is plastered in big letters – including a giant water tower that sits high above the houses, dominating the town. I was particularly enamoured by one of the town's churches which is poetically named The Gaylord Assembly of God.

Rachel sat in the passenger seat drawing a remarkably lifelike sketch of me with a ballpoint pen as we continued east. Within a couple of hours of leaving Minnesota's Midwest emptiness, we arrived at America's polar opposite: The Mall of America – the largest shopping mall in the United States.

Situated in Bloomington, Minnesota – 10 miles south of Minneapolis – The Mall of America is so big that if all of the items for sale in all of the stores were piled one on top of another, they would stretch really, really high into the sky. This is a fact.

Almost all of my time in America had been spent in places with populations of fewer than a thousand people. It was a surreal experience to be suddenly surrounded by more people than we would typically encounter in an entire week. Rachel and I walked up and down the endless floors in a daze for about an hour, feeling claustrophobic and strangely anxious. We left without entering a single store or purchasing a single item. This is something which I don't think many visitors have achieved since The Mall of America opened in 1992.

We headed back to the sanctuary of our rusty old shitmobile and into Wisconsin. After a game of pool at a small bar in Hudson, we crossed back over the state border into Minnesota to spend the night at a nice looking rest area we had passed earlier that evening.

'Where shall we aim for tonight?' I asked Rachel early the following afternoon.

'I don't mind,' she said, studying the map. 'Didn't you want to go to Sheboygan?'

After Kirsty had talked about little else for three months in Breckenridge, I felt obliged to pay a visit to Sheboygan on our way through Wisconsin.

'I do, but we won't make it as far as Sheboygan tonight.'

'Shall we just see where we end up?'

At this point, an advert came on the local radio for a comedy night at a club in Sparta, Wisconsin.

'Is Sparta anywhere near here?' I asked.

'Sparta…er… not really. It looks about 80 miles from here.'

'That's not too far. It would only take us an hour and a half.'

'It's not the way we are heading. It's directly south from here.'

'But we're not really heading anywhere in particular so we could just head south instead.'

'Ok then. Sparta sounds good to me.'

80 miles was a significant distance to travel as a detour – although we'd driven almost that far for breakfast before – but if we didn't have to drive directly east, then it was no longer a detour, it was just our new destination. I turned off the road at the next exit and started heading south towards Sparta, Wisconsin.

We arrived in Sparta at about 6pm and found a small side street alongside a park in the centre of town. It was quiet and secluded, and seemed like the kind of place we could sleep undisturbed later than night.

The comedy night took place in a large upstairs bar in the centre of town. On our arrival, we noticed that the man behind the bar – presumably the landlord – was slumped with his head on the bar next to the till.

'Is he ok?' I asked a couple of men sat at bar stools.

'Course he is. He's just having a little sleep.'

A large smiley lady behind the bar then served us both, before announcing that she was going to have to take her husband home to put him to bed. She was gone for about half an hour, and as there were no other members of staff working, the other customers just walked around to the other side of the bar and poured their own drinks. They left their money next to the till, as though this was standard procedure for a Friday night in Sparta.

The evening was hugely enjoyable. The comedy acts consisted of three comedians: one awful one, one average one, and one genuinely funny one.

Afterwards Rachel and I decided to have a game of pool at the single table at the back of the bar. I put a couple of quarters onto the table, next to two that were already there.

'You realise it's winner stays on?' said a skinny blond-haired man in his early twenties who was lining up to take a shot. He potted a striped ball into the corner pocket with way more force than was required. 'And I won't be leaving the table anytime soon,' he added, and strutted round the table with a weird snake-like swagger of his hips.

Sure enough, he confidently beat his opponent, and soon dispatched his next with ease too.

'Your turn, bro,' he said pointing to me.

'Do you want to go first?' I asked Rachel.

'No thanks. He's all yours,' she said.

I walked nervously to the table.

'Challenger breaks,' he said.

'Ok,' I said, chalking my queue.

'Where you from?'

'England.'

'What the hell you doing in Sparta?'

'We came to watch the comedy night.'

'What, all the way from England?'

'No. We heard about it on the radio as we were passing through.'

'And you thought you'd take a beating at pool while you're down here, too?'

'Nah. Not tonight,' I smiled.

He potted the first three balls with ease. His friends, who were sat alongside the wall, all rolled their eyes as he snake-danced his way around the table between shots. They were clearly bored of his arrogance.

I potted a few, before he did too, leaving him with just the black. His shot lipped out of the middle pocket, and I was able to pot my remaining two balls and sink the black to seal victory.

'I was getting a bit tired of winning,' he said, shaking my hand. 'I needed a break.'

I piled a few more quarters onto the table so that Rachel could get a game, but three others had already got in there before me.

I managed to beat the next guy convincingly – an older guy who was so drunk he could barely stand, let alone pot a ball – and then my next challenger was dispatched quickly too. I was brimming with confidence now, and there was even a gathering surrounding the table watching this young hustler from England beating all the locals. Next up was the skinny blond guy again, fresh from his rest, and eager for revenge. I played perhaps the best game of pool of my life, sinking almost impossible balls with ease. His friends were reeling in his humiliation, and I even mimicked his snake-like dance between shots which really got the crowd going. I was on top of the world, and as I potted that black, there was a look of resignation in my opponent's eyes that he had met his match.

Rachel was next up. I was anxious not to milk it too much and didn't want to appear overly cocky. Rachel had other ideas, and after a shaky start, potted five stripes in a row to leave herself a difficult black, which she somehow sank via four cushions to win the match. The crowd erupted into the biggest laughter of the night.

She then did her own snake-dance around the table to milk the applause further.

‘I think it’s time for us to leave,’ I said, downing the rest of my beer. We could still hear their laughter when we reached the street outside.

‘I was getting a bit tired of winning,’ I said, putting my arm around her. ‘I needed a break.’

‘Whatever. Loooo-seeerrr,’ she said.

39

We awoke the following morning with almighty hangovers. We staggered to a nearby café for a big breakfast and were relieved not to encounter any of the locals from the night before. We then retreated to Josephine and slept until early afternoon.

Later that day we reached the town of Seymour, Wisconsin, a few miles west of Green Bay. Seymour claims to be the home of the hamburger.

In 1885, Charlie Nagreen – now known as 'Hamburger Charlie' – was selling pork sandwiches at the Seymour Fair and unknowingly created the hamburger when he sold a meatball to a customer sandwiched between two slices of bread.

Seymour has embraced its hamburger history; it has a dedicated Hamburger Museum and an annual celebration called Burger Fest. By the time we got there, the museum had unfortunately closed for the day. We headed south and drove around the streets of Oshkosh on the shores of Lake Winnebago looking for cheap motels, but failed to find anything within our budget so continued on to Sheboygan.

Sheboygan was always going to be a disappointment. No matter how great the city, it was never going to live up to the expectations that Kirsty had set for it. Arriving tired and still suffering hangovers was not fair on Sheboygan. There could have been naked women handing out free cheese on the street, and motels offering free luxury accommodation and I would have still thought Sheboygan was a bit shit. When you have a bad hangover, everything is a bit shit. We knew it had been a bad day when the only thing we had achieved of any note was breakfast.

Unsurprisingly, there were no motels offering free luxury accommodation in Sheboygan. We couldn't even find any paid accommodation and the entire city seemed to be fully-booked. Sheboygan was clearly a popular place. We bought some Sheboygan cheese and parked up at the back of a gas station on the edge of town for another night in Josephine. It was definitely the best American cheese I had ever tasted. But that's really not saying much.

We spent the following day on the very pleasant Harrington Beach, a few miles south of Sheboygan on the shore of Lake Michigan. Even after several hours of looking out across the water, we could not get our heads around the fact that it was a lake. There was sand, small waves, and we could not see the other side. Yet it was just a lake. Our simple brains could not comprehend it.

It was at this point I realised my Leatherman pocket knife was missing. My uncle had given it to me as a gift, because – he told me – I couldn't be taken seriously as a traveller in America unless I had a Leatherman (other pocket knives are available). To be fair, it had been an extremely useful tool. I had used the screwdriver function once to adjust my snowboard bindings in Breckenridge, used the knife to slice some salami, and carved my initials into an old stick I found near Yellowstone. I don't know how I would have coped without it.

I tried desperately to think of the last time I had used it. I must have had it recently. Surely it would be in Josephine somewhere? Then I remembered using it the night before to scrape some dried dog poo off my shoe. I had trod in a pile of it in the dark by the gas station where we slept near Sheboygan. Not wanting to bring the poo-covered knife into the car, I left it by the wheel knowing that I would definitely remember it in the morning. Obviously I didn't.

'Oh well,' said Rachel. 'You can always get another one sometime.'

'But they are very expensive. I can't afford to buy another one.'

'We can't go back to get it. Sheboygan is miles away.'

'It's not that far. Only 22 miles or so.'

'And then another 22 miles back. That's 44 miles.'

'It's a really nice Leatherman.'

'Someone will have taken it by now if it's just lying there in the middle of the car park.'

'Maybe. But it was covered in dog poo, so there's a very good chance it will still be there.'

We drove all the way back to Sheboygan, with Rachel sat in the passenger seat tutting and shaking her head in despair for the entire duration. Fortunately, and to regain some absolution, the Leatherman was still there. I gave it a good wash under a nearby tap and Rachel allowed it back in the car. I don't know if she was more annoyed by me making us drive an additional 44 miles to pick up a dirty penknife, or the fact that she had to visit Sheboygan twice. We proceeded onwards towards Milwaukee.

Everything I know about Milwaukee comes from Alice Cooper's cameo in the film *Wayne's World*. The name, as Alice states, is actually pronounced *'mill-e-wah-que'* which is Algonquin for *'the good land,'* (although others claim it actually means *'gathering place by the water'*). It is also (at least it was) the only American city to elect three Socialist mayors.

We didn't stop in Milwaukee. We felt that there was nothing left for us to learn other than what Alice Cooper had already taught us. Also, we had plans to meet up with a university friend of mine in Chicago in a couple of days' time.

We spent the evening playing cards in a local diner and slept in a rest area on the Illinois border.

The hostel in Chicago which I had pre-booked online looked much better on the internet than in real life. It took us a very long time to find, and after we had seen the room we wished we had never found it. Sleeping in Josephine would have been much more preferable. But it had been a week since we had a motel and a proper wash (apart from a quick swim in Lake Michigan), and neither of us were too comfortable with the idea of sleeping in Josephine in the city centre.

We walked to a nearby bar and had a fun evening of beer, burgers and pool. The hostel room seemed far nicer by the time we returned later that night.

Rachel and I had our first proper argument of the trip the following morning. Even minutes after it started, neither of us could remember what it was about. It was too late by this point and we were both officially cross with each other.

In the space of a few months, our relationship had gone from living miles apart at different universities and talking on the telephone every couple of days, to being separated by the Atlantic Ocean for six months, to spending almost every minute of every day and night together in a hot metal box on wheels. It was a wonder we had lasted this long.

We decided to split up. Just for the day, I mean. We felt like a day apart might do us some good. I chose to spend my day visiting three of Chicago's most popular art galleries. I confess that I don't have a huge interest in art galleries, but it felt like the sort of thing I should do. I think I secretly wanted to smugly tell Rachel I had spent my day without her being cultural.

Rachel, it later transpired, spent her day visiting the same three art galleries as me, but in a different order. She doesn't have much interest in art galleries either, and I think she secretly wanted to smugly tell me she had spent her day without me being cultural.

When we met up at the John Hancock Center later that afternoon, it was like we were meeting for a first date. The spark was back and our 'trial separation' had done us both the world of good. We both also agreed that art galleries are totally overrated.

The John Hancock Center is a 344 metre, 100-storey skyscraper near to the shore of Lake Michigan. We took the elevator full of tourists who were heading for the viewing deck, but instead we disembarked at the bar on the floor above. The admission price for the viewing deck was about the same as the price of a delicious cocktail purchased at the bar. So we sat with our drinks, enjoying the peace and quiet, as we admired the identical view of those on the viewing deck below.

We got chatting to an American lady who was sitting with her husband at an adjacent table.

'Where are you heading after Chicago?' she asked.

'We are travelling east, but we don't know where else we'll stop.'

'There ain't nothing between Chicago and New York. When you get to Ohio, you should just put your foot down and drive like the wind.'

From the John Hancock Center we walked along North Michigan Avenue and tried our luck at getting a table at The Berghoff – Chicago's well known German restaurant – which had come highly recommended by several people. As it was a date night, I thought Rachel deserved more than a bologna sandwich from our cool box.

After a short wait we were given a table and had a delicious meal of schnitzel, fried potatoes and steins of German beer, before walking to meet my friend Nicky at her apartment.

Nicky was a friend from university who was living in Chicago whilst studying for a Masters in I forget what. At the time I knew her in England, Nicky was dating a guy named Nick. We also knew a few other Nicks and a couple of other Nickys, which made things very confusing. If ever we were talking about this particular Nick or Nicky, we would refer to him/her as Nicky 'Nick and Nicky' Nicky, or Nick 'Nick and Nicky' Nick. Having written that down, it doesn't seem any less confusing.

We drank wine at Nicky 'Nick and Nicky' Nicky's apartment until the early hours and chatted to her American friend Grace, before getting the 'L' back to our hostel.

We met up with Nicky again the following day and feigned interest at some more art galleries that she showed us around, before being given an archaeological tour of more of The Windy City's sights. We drank smoothies, visited a trendy second-hand clothes shop, ate deep-dish Chicago pizza, and wandered around Lincoln Park.

It was all extremely enjoyable, but we missed the open road. We missed the space, the quiet, and the endless horizons. And we missed it being just the two of us together in Josephine.

Late afternoon we said goodbye to Nicky and we said goodbye to Chicago. We followed the shore around the southern tip of Lake Michigan and parked up for the night in a quiet corner of a train station across the state border in Indiana.

Indiana Dunes National Lakeshore is a beautiful 25-mile stretch of the southern shore of Lake Michigan, managed by the National Park Service since 1966.

We spent a fun day on the beach until we were rudely interrupted by a small tornado that we could see winding its way across Lake Michigan towards us. We dashed to the car and headed under greying skies towards Detroit through the small towns of White Pigeon, Coldwater and the attractively named Cement City (I have not made any of these place names up). If we had known what a shithole Detroit was, we would have stayed in Indiana and taken our chances with the tornado.

I felt a huge amount of sympathy for the city of Detroit from the moment we arrived. When Henry Ford established Ford Motor Company in the city in 1903, other manufactures such as Chrysler, Dodge and General Motors soon followed suit and began production in the area. Detroit instantly became the indisputable automotive capital of the world.

The population grew rapidly, and by 1920 it was the fourth largest city in the United States (behind only New York City, Chicago and Philadelphia). Over the following decades, the city continued to prosper. From the 1950s, however, the city's population began to decline as the transportation network expanded and workers were able to commute from further out of the city. Car manufacturers then gradually moved production elsewhere, in search of cheaper parts and labour, and the city of Detroit went into a rapid decline.

Following its peak of 1.8 million people in 1950, Detroit had lost almost half its population by 2000. Entire streets are boarded up, thousands of buildings are left derelict, unemployment rates have soared, and the town regularly tops polls as being the most dangerous city in America. Curiously, second on most lists is Memphis, Tennessee, and I had nothing bad to say about Memphis.

Driving around the streets of Detroit didn't feel dangerous either. The city just felt painfully sad and neglected. The downtown area has some stunning buildings and the city's potential is evident everywhere you look. There is hope that one day Detroit will gradually be able to rebuild itself into something great again.

We parked up on a dark side street lined with boarded up shops and restaurants, hoping that our New York licence plates would give us some street cred and ward off any potential threats during the night.

We had an undisturbed night and when we woke up the following morning I was a year older. It was my birthday, I should add. We didn't stay in Detroit for a year. As birthday mornings go, waking up surrounded by the urban decay of Detroit was not my most memorable.

For some reason, we decided to celebrate my birthday by visiting the Henry Ford Museum. I don't know why, as neither of us had any interest in cars.

The Henry Ford Museum is split into two distinct parts. The museum itself features an impressive collection of Americana, including vehicles, steam locomotives and aeroplanes – most of which have historical significance.

The other part of the museum complex is Greenfield Village, which is an outdoor recreated community featuring noteworthy buildings from America's history. Both parts of the museum were intriguing, and there is no doubt that Ford assembled an incredible collection of artefacts. But his megalomania seemed to get the better of him, and he took the project a step too far. Henry Ford was a remarkable man whose contribution to the modern world cannot be understated, but we couldn't help feeling he was also a little bit strange.

Alongside buildings such as the Wright brothers' bicycle shop, the courthouse where Abraham Lincoln practised law, Thomas Edison's laboratory and Henry Ford's own birthplace, there are a number of buildings that seemed to be stretching the concept of nostalgia. Buildings such as William Holmes McGuffey's birthplace, whose text book Ford studied as a child, as well as the childhood homes of several other people who had influenced his career. In fact, all of the buildings in Greenfield Village would have had much more historical significance if they had remained where they had originally been built. Having them all dismantled, and then reassembled – piece by piece – in Henry Ford's model village, seemed to strip away all of their meaning.

The museum also houses some very bizarre artefacts, including a test tube containing Thomas Edison's last breath. Thomas Edison was an idol of Henry Ford's and legend has it that Ford asked Thomas Edison's son Charles to capture his father's last breath in a test tube so he could have something to remember him by.

It paints an image of quite a disturbing scene for Thomas Edison's final moments.

'I love you, Dad,' said Charles.

'I love you too, son,' said Thomas Edison, as Charles puts a test tube to his dad's mouth.

'Was that your last breath, Dad.'

'No,' croaked Thomas. 'Why?'

'I promised your mate Henry I would capture it in this test tube,' said Charles.

'That fucking weirdo,' gasped Thomas.

'Was THAT your last breath, Dad? ... Dad?'

Silence.

40

From the Henry Ford Museum we headed south through Woodhaven and Monroe and into Ohio.

I have been a big Kenny Rogers fan for most of my life. I know it's not particularly cool to like Kenny Rogers, but I really don't care. As soon as I spotted Toledo, Ohio on the map, I had to visit.

Toledo is the location of the bar in which Kenny sings about Lucille, who has just left her husband with four hungry children and crops in the field. As a child, I thought that she had left him with four hundred children and craps in the field, which is obviously much, much worse. When I discovered the real lyrics, I thought the husband should quit his whining and consider himself lucky.

John Denver also sang about Toledo. He claimed:

'Saturday night in Toledo, Ohio, is like being nowhere at all.
All through the day how the hours rush by.
You sit in the park and you watch the grass die.'

After performing the song on *The Tonight Show*, John Denver was vilified by Toledo residents and forced to cancel a concert in the town. But when he returned several years later in 1980, he performed the song at Centennial Hall to great applause, setting a new attendance record for the venue.

With only those two popular culture references to go by, we followed the shore of Lake Erie from Detroit down to Toledo.

Toledo, Ohio is the 15th most violent city in the United States. We were inadvertently doing a tour of America's most dangerous places. I sure know how to treat a girl right.

Toledo, however, was better than we expected. This was aided by the fact that we got a cheap room in a Howard Johnson hotel – our most lavish accommodation of the trip – and had a good burger, played pool and drank beer at a quiet bar near to the hotel. John Denver was right about the nightlife. The bar was empty, but it meant we were in charge of the jukebox. Much to the annoyance of the barman, we played Kenny Rogers all evening.

We followed the picturesque Route 2 east towards Marblehead, which sits on a peninsula stretching into Lake Erie. We stopped for a game of crazy golf on the way.

Crazy golf in Britain is not particularly crazy. Hitting the ball through a small opening at the base of a miniature windmill is about as crazy as the golf gets. In America, they tend to call it Adventure Golf, and it is done on a completely different scale.

We played in the shadow of a giant fibreglass mountain, with waterfalls cascading down from the high summits, buildings and obstacles taller than me to navigate, and volcanoes erupting hot lava all around us. Ok, so I exaggerated the volcano bit slightly. But after playing Adventure Golf in America, I will never be content with hitting a golf ball through a windmill ever again.

We ate a hot dog in a park and watched some mini-league baseball. This was how Saturday evenings in America should be spent. We planned to get the ferry to Kelly's Island the following morning, so parked up in the port for what we hoped was a good night's sleep.

We were woken at about 1am by a loud banging on the window.

I sat up, bleary eyed, and pulled back the curtain. A bright flashlight shone directly into my eyes and I shielded my face with my hand.

'Can you step outside the vehicle please?' said a stern voice.

'Yes, just a minute.'

I pulled back the sleeping bag that we used as a duvet and slid open the side door of Josephine.

'What's going on?' muttered Rachel.

'I don't know. Maybe we are not supposed to park here.'

I climbed out of the car and stood in front of an angry looking police officer, wearing only a pair of boxer shorts. It was me that was only wearing boxer shorts. The police officer was fully clothed.

'Is this your vehicle?'

'Yes sir.'

'I've just run a check and the driving licence registered to this vehicle has been suspended.'

'Suspended? What for?'

'Failure to pay the insurance.'

'But I have a valid insurance certificate.'

'Well, according to my details, the owner of this vehicle – a Mr Mark something – has had his licence suspended.'

'Ah, I'm not Mark.'

'But you just said that you were the owner of this vehicle.'

'I am. I was travelling with Mark and we both bought the vehicle together. His name went on the registration document, but he left the country back in January.'

'I see.'

'I have my insurance certificate here. And here's my driving licence.'

He studied the frayed bit of green paper that I handed him with the same look of confusion that all other police officers had when looking at our ridiculous driving licences.

'Ok, well perhaps you should contact the DMV and notify them that you are now the registered keeper.'

'That's a good idea, thank you. I'll make sure I do that. Are we ok to park here tonight?'

'I don't see why not. Have a good night.'

'You too. Thank you, Officer.'

'What was all that about?' asked Rachel when I pulled Josephine's side door shut.

'Mark's had his driving licence suspended.'

'Why?'

'It's a long story. Basically I think we only paid for three months of car insurance.'

'What do you mean?'

'When we set up the policy, we tried to arrange to set up payments for the other instalments, but the person sort of suggested that we didn't bother, because our certificate would show we were covered for a year.'

'So we are not insured?'

'I don't really know. This certificate says we are.'

'Has your licence not been suspended too?'

'No, apparently not. Mark's was the only name on the registration document, thank god. So Mark's a wanted man, but it looks like I'm in the clear. For now.'

We caught the 9am ferry to Kelly's Island as foot passengers the following morning. Although cars are allowed on the island, they are not recommended, so we left Josephine parked on the mainland for the day.

Kelly's Island is the largest in Lake Erie and became a target for limestone quarrying in 1830. In recent years, it is known mostly as a holiday destination.

After a big breakfast at a saloon near to the ferry port, we tried to hire some bicycles. It proved to be far more complicated than it should have been. The lady in charge of the rental place was particularly irritating.

'I'm going to need to see your driver's licences,' she said, after we had shown her our passports.

'Here you are,' I said, passing her my scrappy piece of green paper. Rachel did the same. I'm not sure why Rachel had her driving licence with her, as she had no intention of ever doing any driving.

'No, I need a valid United States driver's licence,' she said.

'I'm sorry, we don't have United States driving licences. We are British.'

'Well I'm sorry but I can't let you hire the bikes.'

'Why do we need a United States driving licence to hire a bike?' I asked.

'Because we don't accept British licences.'

'No, I meant, why do we need a driving licence to hire a bike?'

'It's for identification purposes.'

'But we showed you our passports.'

'They were British passports. So we need a driving licence instead.'

'Do you allow American citizens who don't have a driver's licence to hire a bike?'

'Of course.'

'What do they use as ID?'

'Either their passports or social security card.'

'But you wouldn't allow our passports?'

'No, because they are British passports.'

'We can't be the first non-Americans to hire bicycles on Kelly's Island?'

'Well, you're the first I've seen.'

Eventually, after much persuading, and a bit of sweet-talking by the more diplomatic Rachel, the lady agreed to rent us two bikes. She made it clear that she was doing us a huge favour, and was breaking all sorts of protocol. She also insisted on keeping our passports until we returned the bikes at the end of the day.

I'm not entirely sure where she suspected we could disappear with them to. We were on an island in the middle of one of the world's largest lakes, approximately four miles from the mainland. The only way off the island was via a ferry that departed from right next to the bike shop. It was surely one of the safest places in the world to operate a bike rental business. Still, we thanked her profusely for her immense kindness and understanding, and pedalled off on our day's adventure.

Kelly's Island was fabulous. It was still early in the season and there were very few people about. We spent the day riding up and down quiet little lanes and exploring every inch of the island. We visited several beaches, I swam in a disused quarry, we played crazy golf – this time, a more traditional (crap) British style, complete with a windmill that you had to putt through – and we ate many ice-creams.

We returned our bikes late afternoon, much to the delight of the tyrannical lady in charge of rentals, and boarded the ferry back to the mainland, before driving to a rest area further along Lake Erie.

After the scare with the car insurance, I happened to be flicking through my passport in bed when I came to my travel visa. Visitors to America are given a 90 day tourist visa as standard. To extend this trip to anything over 90 days, you need to apply for a visa. These visas – if granted – enable you to stay in the country for up to 12 months. I had applied and been accepted for my visa, which I had automatically assumed meant I could legally stay in the country for 12 months.

Studying the visa which was stuck inside my passport, I suddenly realised otherwise. The visa itself was valid over a ten year period, but there was an immigration stamp on the opposite page that had an 'admitted until' stamp with the handwritten date of April 19th. That was just six months after I entered the United States.

'Oh shit. I've overstayed my visa by a month already,' I said to Rachel.

'What do you mean?'

'It says here that I was only allowed in the country for six months.'

'I thought you said your visa was a year.'

'I thought it was.'

'Can't you just rip the page with the stamp out of your passport?' suggested Rachel.

'Er, I'm pretty sure that would be a criminal offence.'

'And outstaying your visa isn't?'

We visited a local library the following morning to use their computer, and I discovered via the U.S. immigration website that although you are entitled to stay for 12 months, it is up to the individual customs official to decide how long you can stay. Further extensions then have to be applied for during the stay. The logistics of moving from place to place and not having a mailing address made things very complicated, and there was no way I would be able to get this sorted whilst on the road.

I opened my wallet and unfolded a dollar bill that I had tucked into one of the credit card slots. This dollar bill was my contingency plan for if things turned bad. I stared at the telephone number scribbled in pencil along the top. Should I call for help?

I worked for four summers at Althorp House – the resting place of Princess Diana – near to where I grew up in Northampton. The estate was extremely popular with American tourists and during those four years I met hundreds of lovely people from all over the United States who came to pay their respects.

I had been working there for a couple of months shortly before I came to America, and I was able to proudly tell American visitors about my impending U.S. road trip.

'Make sure you look us up when you're over,' many of them would say, without telling me their name or offering any contact details.

'I sure will,' I would reply.

I chatted to one lovely man for about half an hour. His name was Nick Carter (not the Backstreet Boy). He was in his late 70s, tall, well-dressed and was travelling in England with his wife for a month.

'I used to be a very senior figure in the U.S. government,' he said. 'If you ever need anything when you're over there, or if you find yourself in any trouble, just give me a call.'

He then pulled a dollar bill from his wallet and wrote his phone number along the top.

'You keep this safe,' he said, and he handed me the note.

I have no idea who Nick Carter was, or what his position in the government involved, but having his number scrawled across the dollar bill really did fill me with confidence.

After discovering I was an illegal immigrant, I held the dollar bill in my hands for some time. I could call him. Maybe Nick Carter would be able to come to my rescue and pull a few strings to allow me to stay a bit longer. But if he was unable to help, I would be alerting U.S. immigration to the fact that I had overstayed my visa by a month and it would almost certainly result in a swift deportation. I folded the dollar bill back up and put it back into my wallet. I decided to chance it instead.

41

We considered visiting the Rock and Roll Hall of Fame, but after spending a few days in Chicago and Detroit, neither Rachel nor I were too keen on the idea of venturing into the sprawling metropolis of Cleveland. Also, I didn't think there was anything the Rock and Roll Hall of Fame could teach me. I already knew that the best one came from Tupelo, Mississippi.

We had already spent far longer in the Midwest that we anticipated, and still had the whole of New England to see. So, following the advice of the lady we met in the John Hancock Center in Chicago, we put our foot on the gas and drove like the wind through Ohio, across the north-western corner of Pennsylvania, and we were soon into New York State.

The Kazoo Co museum in Eden, New York was disappointingly closed. The factory is the only producer of metal kazoos in the entire United States and I had been extremely excited (perhaps only mildly excited) about the prospect of seeing how a museum could dedicate itself to a single, small, bloody annoying musical instrument. My curiosity will have to be satisfied another day.

From Eden, we skirted around the outside of Buffalo (the city) to Niagara Falls.

The Niagara River forms part of the border between Ontario in Canada and New York in the United States. We stood and marvelled at the hypnotic power of the most famous waterfall in North America.

Rainbow Bridge serves as a border crossing over the Niagara River gorge linking the two towns of Niagara Falls in New York with its neighbour in Canada. Pedestrians are allowed to cross Rainbow Bridge, and Rachel and I thought it would be fun to view the falls from the Canadian side while we were there.

As we made our way to the guards at the border crossing, Rachel grabbed me by the arm.

'Wait!' she shouted.

'What is it?'

'Your passport.'

'What about my passport?'

'The date stamp. It says you are only admitted until April.'

'Oh yeah. Good point. I probably shouldn't try and cross the border.'

'I think that would be a very bad idea. I don't think they would let you back in.'

'You should go,' I said.

'Really? Wouldn't you mind?' she asked.

'Of course not. You go and have fun in Canada. I'll just wave to you here from America.'

'No. I'd better not go either.'

'Why not?'

'In case I get flagged up as being connected to you – a known fugitive.'

'Fugitive?'

'Well, it's getting that way. You've overstayed your visa, no car insurance, and several run-ins with the cops. You're pretty much a man on the run.'

Even lurking near to the border crossing, I did suddenly feel a bit like a fugitive. I kept expecting one of the border guards to wander over to me and ask to do a spot check of my visa status. I took a few steps back until I had merged into the crowd.

After spending another hour viewing the falls from different vantage points on the U.S. side, we joined interstate 90 and parked up for the night in a busy but pleasant service area a few miles from Niagara Falls.

In the middle of the night I went inside to use the restroom and somehow came out with two donuts. I couldn't resist. They were a Boston Kreme and a Maple-frosted, if you are interested. I climbed back into Josephine and slowly slid the side door closed as quietly as I could.

Rachel stirred slightly and then seemed to go back to sleep. I plunged my teeth into the Boston Kreme. It didn't make a sound, but somehow The Kraken awoke. Rachel is the kindest, happiest, most thoughtful person I know... during the daytime. But when she is woken up in the middle of the night, she is horrendous.

'What the hell are you doing?' she moaned, sitting up in bed.

'Nuf-fing,' I said.

'What are you eating?'

'A doo-ut,' I said, frantically trying to swallow the mouthful. 'A donut. I bought you one too?'

'Where the hell did you get a donut from?' she asked as though I had just purchased some plutonium.

'In the service station. I only went to the toilet but felt a bit peckish. Want one?'

'No I don't want a donut. It's the middle of the night.'

I had bought two, partly as a backup plan in case she wanted one, but mostly because I wanted two.

'You are SO annoying. I was fast asleep.'

'Sorry, I'll eat them quietly.'

'You'd better. Good night.'

'Night.'

By morning I was just about forgiven, and we bought another two donuts for breakfast. This time Rachel did partake. We drove to Rochester and visited the George Eastman Museum.

George Eastman was an entrepreneur and photography pioneer who founded the Eastman Kodak Company and was largely responsible for bringing photography to the masses. The museum, set in his former house in Rochester, is the oldest photography museum in the world.

I had purchased my first SLR camera just before coming to America and was incredibly enthusiastic about photography. The museum was fascinating and we both learned a lot about an incredible man. The museum tour ended abruptly with a small sign stating that George Eastman killed himself on March 14, 1932. It didn't provide any further details.

It wasn't until reading up on him later that we found that he had been suffering from severe pain from a spinal disorder for two years. He left a note that read:

'To my friends: my work is done. Why wait?'

It had been a few weeks since I heard from Mark so I gave him a call. It was good to talk to him and he sounded like he had settled quickly back into life in the UK, and had already got a new job which he was enjoying.

I had been so immersed with the trip that I had little time to think about what would happen when I got home. I had two months' work arranged for the summer months, working at Althorp House again. But from September, I would be unemployed. I had a degree, but was qualified to do absolutely nothing. I genuinely had no idea what I wanted to do with my life. But for some reason it didn't worry me in the slightest. If anything, I was excited about the possibilities that lay ahead.

What I did now know for sure was that I wanted my future to involve Rachel. Our relationship had not got off to the best of starts, with me disappearing several thousand miles across the Atlantic. But we had managed to survive it, and travelling together in Josephine had made me realise that I wanted to spend the rest of my life with her. Rachel, that is, not Josephine.

It would be very strange to fly home and then move back to our parents' houses, having been in such close proximity for the last few months. I began to consider the idea of Rachel and me moving in together. We wouldn't be able to afford to buy a house, but if we were both able to get some form of work each – and if Rachel wanted to – then we could certainly try and rent someplace small together.

We stopped for lunch in Skaneateles, New York, at the northern edge of Skaneateles Lake – purported to be one of the cleanest lakes in the entire United States. The lake is narrow and beautiful, with its shores surrounded by very expensive-looking houses. I was desperate to go for a swim, but it didn't seem to be possible for anyone apart from these home-owners to actually get to the lake. This is perhaps why it is so clean.

I eventually gave up on the idea of swimming and we drove onwards to Cazenovia where we bought the makings of a gourmet dinner. By gourmet, I mean something that involved using our gas stove. In this case it was sausages. Most of our home-cooking involved cold foods like bread and cheese and bologna, but on this occasion we decided to cook.

We found a parking area on the shores of Cazenovia Lake. It seemed like a nice romantic location to spend the night, until I realised I was also cooking for thousands of uninvited mosquitoes who had decided to join us.

We were woken at 1am by a policeman who didn't even give me a chance to try and explain the situation with Mark and our licences. He simply said that we had to get the hell out of Cazenovia or he would have us towed. Legally, it was his problem to deal with the uninsured vehicle, but he clearly wanted to get us to move on so that we became another cop's problem instead. It was an hour and a half before we found a suitable parking area, by which point I was in a pretty foul mood.

It felt like my luck was running out. It was only a matter of time before either my licence or passport was taken away from me. Again, I took the dollar bill with Nick Carter's number from my wallet and held it in my hands. What would I say to him? I had overstayed my visa and failed to pay my car insurance. Both were things that were my own stupid fault and that I was entirely responsible for.

I couldn't sort out the lapsed car insurance because my visa situation would no doubt be red-flagged during the administration process. And I couldn't sort out my visa, because, well, it was a bit too late for that. I was certainly running on borrowed time, but there was still a good chunk of America that I wanted to see. I decided to take the simpler option. I would just ignore it.

42

The following day we visited the Secret Caverns in Cobleskill, New York, which are so secret that you can only find them by their location on a map, or by following the directions from the countless giant multi-coloured signposts all over the surrounding area.

I have always been a bit cynical of caves, feeling like if you've seen one cave, you've seen them all. But each time I set foot inside one, the childlike thrill overrides any cynicism and the experience is always incredibly exhilarating.

From Cobleskill we drove to Saratoga Springs and treated ourselves to a night in a particularly grubby motel. Even the grubbiest motel, however, can be transformed into paradise with a case of beer, popcorn, ice-cream and some trashy television.

Due to our meagre budget, our nights in motels had been strictly rationed. We tried not to pay for accommodation more than about once a week, and even Rachel had grown so fond of Josephine that nights in rest areas were often preferable to motels. Other than the obvious benefits of showers, comfy beds and television, motels also gave us the opportunity to hand-wash clothes and allow us a chance to give Josephine a general tidy up.

After too many beers the night before, we both overslept and woke up five minutes before the motel's mandatory check out time. Not wanting to risk paying for another night, we bundled everything into Josephine in a hurry, and left the motel feeling dirtier and less organised than we had been when we checked in.

We had a coffee at Caffè Lena downtown, which claims to be the *'oldest continually run folk-oriented Coffee House in the U.S,'* which is a very niche genre, to be fair. Over the years, this tiny little coffee shop has hosted some of the all-time greats of the music business including Bob Dylan and Arlo Guthrie.

The café's biggest claim to fame, however, was that Don Mclean first performed his hit song *American Pie* there. A bar around the corner – the Tin & Lint – also has a plaque on the wall at the table where they claimed Don Mclean first began writing the lyrics to *American Pie.* Presumably on the back of a napkin, or a beer mat, as all great stories go.

Mclean has since stated that, although he regularly played gigs at Caffè Lena and spent a lot of time in Saratoga Springs, he actually wrote *American Pie* in Cold Spring, New York and in Philadelphia. He first performed the song when supporting Laura Nyro at Temple University in Philadelphia.

Since Mclean set the record straight, Caffè Lena no longer boasts its claim, but the Tin & Lint around the corner is still hanging on to its version of events.

The coffee was very good, but there was very little in the way of live folk music at 10.30am on a Thursday.

'Can you go and ask for directions to Lake George?' I said to Rachel, as I filled up Josephine at a gas station on the edge of town.

'You know I'm no good at that. Remember what happened last time?'

'It'll be different this time. I can see the man at the till and he doesn't have a big beard. In fact, he doesn't look like he has any remarkable features that could possibly distract you this time.'

'I'll be useless. Why don't you do it?'

'I'm filling up the car. And besides, men don't ask for directions.'

'You're so chauvinistic.'

'Come on, you can do this. All you have to do is listen to what he says and try and remember at least the key bits. Ok?'

'Fine. I'll try.'

Rachel emerged from the gas station a few minutes later and she had a guilty expression on her face again.

'What happened?'

'I was trying so hard to concentrate on what he was saying that I can't remember any of it.'

'What do you mean?'

'I was really self-conscious that he could tell I wasn't taking in what he said, so I spent the whole time trying to make myself look like I was thinking really hard.'

'I don't understand.'

'I was worried he would think I was thinking about something else, so I was making sure I looked like I was concentrating really hard on what he was saying.'

'And what did he say? Do you know how to get to Lake George?'

'No, sorry. I don't think I heard a single word of what he said.'

'You are unbelievable. Surely it's easier to actually listen, rather than try to pull a face of someone pretending to listen?'

'Possibly. I did try.'

'What does the face of someone trying really hard to listen look like?'

'This,' she said, pulling the face that looked exactly like someone trying really hard to listen.

'Wow, that's good. Bloody useless, mind. We still don't know where we are going.'

From that moment onwards, I have never entrusted Rachel with the task of asking for directions.

Fortunately, Lake George was not hard to find. We drove along its western edge at the base of the Adirondack Mountains and crossed into Vermont. We pulled over at a roadside diner for lunch. Only all that was left was the charred remains of where a diner once stood. The only part of it left intact was a large sign saying: *Closed Wednesdays*. Unfortunately, it seemed unlikely this diner would ever open again.

Vermont contains a quarter of the world's trees. That statistic is completely made up by me. But as you drive through Vermont, it does feel like one giant forest. The thing that we noticed most within a few miles of entering Vermont was just how uncluttered the roadside was with signs and advertising. In fact, there were none whatsoever. Throughout the rest of America, you can't drive more than a few miles without seeing a big billboard or sign advertising a restaurant, bar, tourist attraction, or a drug store offering free water that is only 450 miles away. This is not the case in Vermont.

In 1968, Vermont passed a law banning all billboards in the state. This was largely due to the efforts of a state representative and environmentalist named Ted Riehle, who made it his mission to try and preserve the beauty of Vermont. The state has been billboard-free ever since.

Luckily for Vermont, there is very little in the way of tourist attractions anyway. If billboards were allowed, there would only be a small handful of them. And the vast majority of those would be advertising the Ben and Jerry's factory. Vermont's most famous tenant, the Ben and Jerry's ice cream factory, has also become one of Vermont's most visited tourist attractions. But, due to the lack of billboards and our poor map reading skills, we missed the turn off and didn't realise our mistake until we were too far past to turn back.

Still, despite its lack of commercial attractions, Vermont was spectacular to just drive through. With mile upon mile of pristine countryside, *The Green Mountain State* sure lives up to its nickname. The view from the car window was better than any ice cream factory tour.

We had an international themed evening drinking Kenyan coffee at an Irish pub in the town of Montpelier, before passing into New Hampshire and enjoying an Indian curry in the town of Lebanon, before sleeping in Josephine on a quiet side street.

From Lebanon, we joined Route 4 and headed east through Enfield before getting held up in the town of Canaan by some form of parade. We sat in Josephine at an intersection, as hoards of people stretched down the road in either direction. A man in a reflective jacket stood at the junction manning the traffic.

'What's the parade about?' I asked him.

'No idea. Folks round here always seem to be protesting about something. I'm just here to stop the traffic.'

Whatever they were protesting about, they were doing it very quietly and their message wasn't very clear. The procession eventually passed and we drove on to the town of Meredith for no other reason than it is also my middle name.

Meredith is a pleasant small town situated on the banks of Lake Winnipesaukee – the largest lake in New Hampshire, don't you know.

I felt a sense of camaraderie with the people of Meredith as Rachel and I wandered its streets. Meredith is a girl's name, so I obviously didn't broadcast the fact that it was my middle name to any of the residents. Because as much as they probably loved living there, I doubt any of the male town-folk would like to actually be named Meredith.

We headed south to Laconia at the southern tip of Winnisquam Lake (the fourth largest lake in New Hampshire, in case you were wondering), where we stopped at a small amusement park called Funspot, with its cleverly-devised slogan, *'the spot for fun.'*

Funspot had a phenomenal collection of video games machines from the 1970s and 80s. It was like stepping back in time as we walked row upon row of machines with their flashing lights, blocky graphics and retro music.

It had been a few days since we had played crazy golf and we were suffering withdrawals. Thankfully Funspot was able to satisfy our needs.

Funspot's mini golf was thoughtfully themed to celebrate *'The Famous Landmarks of New Hampshire.'* The only problem is that New Hampshire doesn't actually have any famous landmarks. Mount Washington – the highest peak in the Northeastern United States – is by far the state's most recognisable sight. But for some reason this did not make the grade to be included as one of the 18 holes. Perhaps the course's budget would not stretch to a replica mountain.

In its place were 'famous' landmarks such as train stations, churches, schools and, of course, a windmill. Despite the fact that New Hampshire doesn't have a single windmill in any one of its 9,349 sq miles, let alone any famous windmills.

But none of this detracted from Funspot's charm. A huge amount of work had gone into building this 'spot for fun' up from nothing. In 1952, at the age of 21, Bob Lawton borrowed $750 from his grandmother and used the money to open a miniature golf course and penny arcade on the second floor of Tarlson's Arcade in Weir's Beach. 12 years later, Lawton bought 21 acres of land just up the road, and Funspot grew into the amusement park that it is today, complete with ten-pin bowling, bingo and a restaurant. I was pleased to see that Funspot's hard work was rewarded in 2008, when Guinness World Records officially awarded its collection of video games the title of *'Largest Arcade in the World.'*

Our day got even better with lunch at nearby Tamarack where I had the biggest and best lobster roll I've ever tasted. Admittedly it was the only lobster roll I had ever tasted, but I have had others since and they didn't even come close to Tamarack in Laconia, New Hampshire.

We spent an enjoyable hour or so looking at the exhibits at The Loon Center, for no other reason than there was little else to do. It was a centre about the preservation of loons of the feathered variety, I should add. I was a little surprised the Loon Center didn't have a hole dedicated to it in Funspot's *Famous Landmarks of New Hampshire* mini-golf, but I later discovered the Loon Center was built decades after the mini-golf was constructed, otherwise it would have surely been a shoo-in for the coveted 18th hole.

New Hampshire had kept us amused for 24 hours, but with the Loon Centre and Funspot ticked off our list, we ventured into Maine and followed Route 25 all the way to Portland by the Atlantic Ocean.

We wandered into a bar in downtown Portland called Three Dollar Dewies. It was early evening but the place was already busy. The bar had more types of draught beer for sale than I had ever seen in one place, and it seemed rude not to stay for the evening.

'Where did this place get its name?' I asked the barman, as I ordered our third beer.

'It used to be a whore house,' he said, pointing to a painted mural on the wall. 'That should explain it for you.'

The inscription read:

'Back in the Yukon, nights were long--and lonely.
If a fellow didn't want to spend the night alone,
he might try one of the local 'houses of pleasure,'

where the ladies would smile coyly,
and point to the following list –
$1 lookie $2 feelie $3 Dewey.'

I stared at the writing for a while.

'I'm confused,' I said to the barman. 'What is a dewey?'

'It ain't pronounced due-ey,' he said. 'It's doo-ey.'

'Ah, I get it now,' I said.

'We don't offer that on the menu no more.'

'Oh well,' I said, catching a glare from Rachel sitting next to me. 'We'll just settle for two plates of nachos instead then please.'

After sampling a good proportion of the beers on offer, and two huge plates of nachos, we spent the night in Josephine parked around the corner on a back street. We had drunk far too much beer for any lookie, feelie or dewey.

The next day, we drove to Belfast on Route 3 and ate lunch at the mouth of the Passagassawakeag River estuary, where we sat considering the pressing issues of the day, such as 'how the hell are you supposed to pronounce Passagassawakeag?'

As we finished up our sandwich, another parade walked past. This was a *'walk for education'* stretching for what seemed like a couple of miles.

'Do you think they are the same people we saw marching yesterday?' asked Rachel.

'No, I don't think so.'

'Why not?'

'Because that place was over 200 miles away.'

'Oh. It's probably a different group then.'

'Yes, probably.'

'It seems that folk in New England have little else to do but march.'

We arrived at an RV park near Trenton in the early evening, hustled some teenagers on the basketball court (ok, so they were aged only 7 or 8, but we still kicked their sorry asses) and then we went to bed.

43

Acadia National Park is made up predominately of Mount Desert Island, the largest island off the coast of Maine. The rest of the park is spread over the surrounding smaller islands and parts of the mainland. This would be the furthest east we would travel, before heading back towards New York City.

Acadia National Park is a small, but perfectly formed national park. The park is dominated by Cadillac Mountain – the highest peak on the east coast of America.

After several days high-tailing it across New England in Josephine, I felt like we needed to stretch our legs and climb to the top.

'Isn't there just a cable-car or something we can get?' asked Rachel, as we walked from the car park to the start of the trail.

'No, there's definitely no cable-car,' I said.

The mountain didn't look particularly challenging from below, but I completely underestimated quite how tough it would be to climb. We were in no rush, however, so we trudged slowly up the trail as it wound its way up through the wooded slopes towards the summit of Cadillac Mountain. As we crested the tree line by late morning, the weather had become uncomfortably hot, and Rachel cursed me for convincing her to climb a mountain.

We didn't see another person the entire way up. I took this as a positive sign that we had the place to ourselves. Rachel took this as a sign that nobody else was stupid enough to try and walk up it. We hadn't brought any water with us, assuming it to be a short stroll to the top and back.

When we eventually reached the top, sweating, and completely out of breath, the place was crawling with people.

'How the hell did all these people make it up here so easily?' asked Rachel.

'I've no idea,' I said, hoping she wouldn't discover the truth.

'That lady over there is about 90 and she's got a pair of flip-flops on and she doesn't even look like she's broken sweat. I'm nearly dying here.'

'Well, appearances can be deceiving. Maybe you're not as fit as you thought.'

'I don't claim to be that fit, but I'm definitely fitter than him!' she said, pointing at a rather large man slumped on a nearby rock holding onto a set of crutches.

The view was spectacular, and well worth the trip, but we were both suffering badly from the heat and dehydration. In the distance we spotted a substantial brick structure.

'That's not a shop, is it?' I asked.

'It can't be. Can it?'

'It looks like one,' I said as we quickened our pace towards it.

'Please let it be a shop,' said Rachel.

Miraculously, it was a shop. A cold can of soda has never tasted so good, which we followed up with an ice cream.

'Hang on,' said Rachel. 'Does the lady who works in that shop have to walk up here every morning?'

'I guess so. Unless she lives up here?'

'But what about all the stock? And the money? She can't carry that up and down the mountain. You said there was no cable-car.'

'There isn't a cable car. Helicopter, maybe?'

'Don't be silly. I wonder if there's a service track for 4x4s up the mountain for staff,' she said, wandering off towards the other side of the building.

'Yes, that must be it. Don't go over there.'

'Why not?'

'Just… don't.'

'Is that… is that… a car park?' she said.

'Yes... er... well... it does look a bit like a car park. That must be where the staff park.'

'But there are about 100 cars there. There was only one lady working in that shop.'

'Maybe there's a lot of park rangers about, too?'

Rachel glared at me.

'Is there a proper bloody road all the way up to the top of this bloody mountain?'

'It appears so, yes.'

'And all these other people drove up here? So we could have driven up here too? Did you know about this road?'

I tried to speak but no words came out.

'You did, didn't you?'

'I... I... I thought it would be nicer to walk.'

After Rachel had calmed down a bit and got over my deceit, we sat and finished our ice-creams on the pink, lichen covered granite of Cadillac Mountain, gazing out over the Atlantic Ocean. It was not until this point that I realised I had successfully driven from the east to the west coast of America, and then back again.

Nearly eight months previously, I had spent the night on the beach in Ocean City, Maryland, feeling cold, alone, and apprehensive about what the following year would bring.

I had driven across the entire southern United States with Mark, all the way to the Pacific Ocean. I then had my own adventure in Breckenridge for three months, before finishing my travels with the person I wanted to spend the rest of my life with.

I gazed out at the Atlantic Ocean, feeling incredibly proud of where I had been, what I had experienced since I had last sat and stared out over this body of water all those months ago, and – more importantly – where I was now. I put my arm around Rachel.

'You have to admit, the view definitely looks better after walking up, doesn't it?' I said.

'Yes, you're right,' she said. 'It does.'

The walk down Cadillac Mountain was easy in comparison, and again we didn't pass another person the entire way. It seems that very few visitors to Cadillac Mountain walk (or hike) to the summit. But that somehow made it even more special. By the time we made it back to Josephine, even Rachel agreed it had been an extremely enjoyable hike.

We drove into the nearby town of Bar Harbor for a late lunch.

I had never ordered a whole lobster before. As we were in Maine – world-famous for its lobster – it seemed like the place to do it. We found a nice-looking restaurant by the water's edge (there are no shortage of nice-looking restaurants by the water's edge in Bar Harbor), and I ordered a lobster. Rachel played it safe with mussels.

The waiter arrived a while later and tucked a plastic bib into my t-shirt. He then placed a giant lobster on the table in front of me and handed me a metal implement that looked like a nutcracker, and a small metal hammer.

He could tell I was a lobster virgin from the weird noises I was making.

'First time, I take it?' he asked.

'Yes.'

'Would you like me to show you what to do?'

'No, thanks,' I laughed. 'I'll be fine.'

'Ok, sir. Enjoy your meal!'

'Are you sure you know what you're doing?' asked Rachel.

'How hard can it be?'

I placed one of the lobster's claws in the grip of the nutcracker and squeezed hard. A large fragment of shell flew across the table and ricocheted off the arm of a lady sitting at the next table.

'I'm so sorry,' I said, as she passed the piece of claw back to me.

She smiled a sympathetic smile.

'Is everything ok, Sir?' asked the waiter.

I was a pathetic looking sight, sitting there wearing a bib, retrieving bits of my meal from a neighbouring table before I had even taken my first bite.

'Actually, could you give me a few tips please?' I said.

'Of course, Sir.'

After a quick tuition, I understood the basics and was able to eat the rest of my lobster without disrupting any of the other diners. It took me most of the afternoon, though, and we were politely encouraged to leave by staff who had to prepare the tables for the evening bookings. Rachel sat there the entire time smiling at my incompetence, having finished her meal many hours earlier.

I enjoyed my lobster but it was far more hassle than any food should be. After walking up and down Cadillac Mountain, I was ravenous, and there's nothing more frustrating when you are hungry than having to eat a meal one molecule at a time.

To make matters worse, I had explosive diarrhoea later that day. I don't want to blame the lobster, but it was definitely the lobster.

We spent a couple of hours in the late afternoon driving the loop road around the other sights of Acadia National Park. Thunder Hole is one of the park's most visited spots, so we parked up and took a short walk to check it out.

Thunder Hole is a dramatic segment of rock which gets its name from the theatrical noise it makes as waves crash against the shore. The sea looked like a millpond during our visit. We waited for several minutes to see if anything would happen, but the only sounds we could hear were the squawk of seagulls, and the suspicious gurgling of my stomach. It was time to make a dash before I made a very public display with my own thunder hole.

We booked a pitch at a fantastic campsite within the national park boundary, surrounded by thick woodland with a very rustic feel. I successfully built a campfire and we sat and drank beer and played cards in the firelight to end a really memorable day.

Having set an alarm for 4am the following morning, with the intention of driving up to the top of Cadillac Mountain in time for sunrise, we unfortunately overslept. We didn't oversleep enough to miss the sunrise, but enough to make it a challenge to get there in time. We threw some clothes on and climbed – half-asleep – into the front seats of Josephine.

Our campsite was only a few hundred metres from the start of the road up to the summit of Cadillac Mountain, but due to the loop road around the park being one way, we had to drive almost the entire loop – 27 miles of it – just to get to the start of the summit road. We were going to be cutting it very fine, so I had to put my foot down. Based on my experience in Death Valley, park rangers like you to drive as fast as physically possible through national parks, so I knew they would be proud of what I was doing.

We made it to the summit car park with minutes to spare, and were surprised to find it even busier than it had been the previous day. Cadillac Mountain is the first place in the United States to see the sunrise. Well, for six months of the year it is, and admittedly not during the month we visited (between March and September – because the sun rises slightly further to the north during these summer months – this accolade goes to Mars Hill near the Canadian border). But this didn't stop hundreds of people making their pre-dawn trip to the summit.

We parked Josephine in the car park and made our way to a rocky outcrop. Despite the number of people, there was still plenty of space to get some solitude. Many visitors didn't stray further than the car park. Some even watched the sunrise from the warmth of their cars.

It was an even more beautiful sight than we had witnessed the day before. The Atlantic Ocean – the second largest body of water on Earth – was still tucked up neatly in bed under a thick blanket of cloud. It was surreal to think of everything that lay beneath it – all that power, all that life – yet the cloud gave the impression it had been able to tame it.

The sun eventually made an appearance and we all made the appropriate sunrise 'ooohs' and 'ahhhs' and were delighted we had made the effort to get to the summit in time.

As the car park slowly emptied, we couldn't face joining the queue of vehicles back down the mountain, so instead we climbed into the back of Josephine and slept solidly for three more hours.

We headed into Bar Harbor later that morning for breakfast (I didn't order lobster this time), and then on to a nearby beach.

I have never been one for lying on a beach relaxing, so while Rachel sunbathed I followed the Great Head Trail for a couple of miles up to a nearby peak. From the top I could just make out Rachel on the beach below and Josephine parked in the nearby car park.

I made my way back down to join Rachel on the beach before driving that sodding loop road once more and heading out of Acadia National Park.

44

We found a rest area back on the mainland, and it wasn't until I had setup the cooking stove and put a pan of water on to boil for some pasta that we realised just how bad the mosquitoes were. I had left the boot of Josephine wide open while I prepared dinner and the inside had already filled with the devil's spawn.

What followed was one of the most horrendous nights of my life. Mosquitoes love me. I don't know why. I must be particularly tasty – or perhaps just incredibly pungent – because they can't get enough of me. I spent the entire night, wide awake, listening to the terrifying screech of those tiny little demon bastards as they took it in turns to dive-bomb me. What is worse than the noise they make is the sound of the silence which follows their attack. Because this silence means that they have landed somewhere. And that somewhere is usually on a part of my body.

At this point I would flail around manically armed with a rolled up Rand McNally road map, frantically trying to swat the fuckers illuminated in the fading beam of my torch. Often they would come to rest on the curtains where I could easily score a direct hit. Throughout the course of the night, I decorated Josephine's curtains and roof with my own rendition of a Jackson Pollock.

Every few minutes, Rachel would awaken from her slumber and sit bolt upright as I did a fist-pump after I had successfully reduced the world's mosquito population by one. But the amount of my blood now splattered around Josephine was a clear enough indication that the mosquitoes had already won the war.

By morning – which I decided was the very second the sun had risen – the inside of Josephine looked like a crime scene.

Every part of my body was covered in bites, and my skin was swollen and terribly itchy. Rachel was virtually untouched.

We drove to Old Orchard beach, which is a very touristy but quite pleasant little town south of Portland, Maine. We had a quick walk around but I was in no mood for sightseeing, so we decided to cancel the rest of the day. As it was still very early in the season, motels were offering very good deals. I couldn't face a second night in Josephine in case any of the mosquitoes had survived the night, so we booked a room, bought beer, takeaway pizza, ice-cream, insect repellent (a little too late) and then watched TV for 12 hours straight.

We spent the following morning having a look around the pretty town of Kennebunkport, which incidentally sounds like early settlers couldn't decide on a name so just joined together three random words.

'We need a name for this town,' said Kenny.

'How about John… lamp… shoe?' said John, looking around the room for inspiration.

'Johnlampshoe? That's rubbish,' said Kenny.

'Barryfloormilk?' suggested Barry.

'Crap,' said Kenny.

'Johnnywindowbeer?'

'That's even worse, John,' said Kenny. 'I know. How about Kennybunkport?'

Barry and John stared at each other with a look of apathy.

'Fine, Kenny. Let's go with that then.'

After using the internet in the town's library, we continued south and into Massachusetts. Boston is a city I had always wanted to visit, but we had run out of both time and money to do it justice. We didn't want to rush our visit to Boston so decided to leave it for another trip.

Rachel fell asleep as I tried to navigate my way through the city. When she awoke she looked at the map and told me how excited she was about visiting Salem.

'Ah, sorry, we passed the turning for Salem about half an hour ago.'

'Can't we just turn around? I really want to see it.'

'Really?'

'Yes, I was totally obsessed with the Salem Witch Trials as a teenager and I've always wanted to go.'

'There will be other chances, I'm sure. It's at least 30 miles back.'

'You drove 76 miles for breakfast a few weeks ago.'

'That wasn't my idea.'

'You took a hundred mile detour for a comedy night.'

'That was your idea too.'

'You made us drive 44 miles for a pooey penknife.'

'It wasn't just any old penknife.'

'Oh come on. Please! It's only half an hour.'

'Fine,' I said, pulling into a gas station forecourt and turning the car around. 'But it better be bloody good.'

Salem has a very significant place in American history. The area was first settled by Europeans in 1626 by fishermen from Cape Ann, and soon became a prominent port on the east coast.

Salem is most famous for its Witch Trials that ran between February 1692 and May the following year. Belief in the supernatural was widespread at the time, and mass hysteria broke out about certain individuals being associated with witchcraft. During those 15 months, 19 people – 14 women and 5 men – were hanged, and one was pressed to death. The trials only ended when Governor William Phipps disbanded the court after his own wife was accused of being a witch.

We made it back to Salem at 6pm, just as all of the museums and historic buildings had closed. Rachel wasn't too disappointed, and it was fascinating to wander the town and have a look at some genuinely old American buildings, rather than having to read plaques to mark where they once stood.

Later that evening, we hit the road again and I had to navigate Boston for the third time. We parked up in a service area off the interstate about 40 minutes from Cape Cod.

We were a little over a week away from the end of our trip. With flights booked out of New York, we would soon have to get back to the city to allow a few days to try to sell Josephine before heading home.

We knew little about Cape Cod other than it was a popular holiday destination on the east coast. For that reason, as soon as we crossed onto the peninsula, we felt like we were on vacation. Cape Cod would be our holiday destination for the next few days, before making a beeline to New York City.

Funds were low, and Cape Cod's accommodation was well over our budget, so we pulled into the car park at a Park and Ride close to the Sagamore Bridge which connects Cape Cod to the mainland. We parked up and decided to call it home for a little while.

That evening, as we lay together in the back of Josephine, I decided that now was as good a time as any to broach the subject of our future.

'I've been thinking about what will happen when we go back home,' I said to Rachel.

'What about when we go back home?'

'It will be strange when we've been with each other all day every day, and then you move back in with your parents and I move back in with mine.'

'Yes, it will be weird. I hadn't really thought about that.'

‘I hadn’t either until the other day. But I’ve been thinking about it a lot now.’

‘What do you think will happen?’ she asked.

‘I was wondering how you would feel about you and me moving in together?’

‘You mean into our own house? Just the two of us?’

‘Yes, well, I don’t think we would be able to afford a house. It would probably be a small flat. But it would still be fun. What do you think?’

‘I think it sounds like an amazing idea. I would love to do that very much.’

‘I would love to do that very much, too,’ I said. ‘This is the first time I’ve actually felt excited about going home.’

‘Me too.’

We spent four nights in that Park and Ride car park. Having that consistency really did make us feel like we were on holiday. Each morning we would wake up, have a wash in the bathroom of Dunkin’ Donuts next to where we had parked, followed by coffee and a couple of donuts each for breakfast. We would then either catch the bus, or drive Josephine to explore a different part of Cape Cod.

Provincetown – or P-town as the locals call it – at the far tip of Cape Cod was originally inhabited by the Nauset tribe before being colonised by European settlers in the 1600s. For many decades now, P-town has been an extremely popular holiday destination for the LGBT community; the town has the highest rate of same-sex couples in the United States. Even though it was only May, the place was in full summer vacation mood.

We spent a memorable couple of days walking around the harbour in P-town, sitting on the beaches, people-watching, and sampling the incredible burritos from Big Daddy’s. Rachel and I appeared to be the only couple in the entire town not to be wearing a small dog in a baby-carrier on our fronts. We did consider trying to rent one just to blend in.

We played several games of crazy golf during our time on Cape Cod; we walked the streets of Hyannis and had an enjoyable Indian meal one night; we visited a proper American drive-in movie theatre where we watched a bizarre double-bill of *The Mummy* and *Crocodile Dundee*; we visited many different beaches, viewed Martha's Vineyard across the water (we couldn't afford to visit), and explored the perimeter of a disused quarry filled with beautiful crystal clear water. I couldn't resist diving in, and then regretted it after we passed a warning sign about dangerous algae on our way out.

A rash appeared on my chest and shoulders later that evening. I spent the following day feeling faint, convinced I'd caught some waterborne disease or had contracted yellow fever or dengue fever from the mosquito bites a few days previously.

My days were numbered and I was going to die a slow lingering death in a parking lot outside Dunkin' Donuts. I even suggested to Rachel that she go and buy a test tube to try and preserve my last breath to have something to remember me by.

'I don't think so,' she said. 'I can still smell that curry you ate last night.'

Later that afternoon, I had somehow come back from the brink and shaken off whatever tropical (or imaginary) disease I'd been infected by and I was raring to go again.

We left Cape Cod and parked up in what I thought was a quiet corner of an interstate service area. We both climbed into the back and Rachel was asleep within minutes. I followed soon after.

I woke in the middle of the night to a strange sound.

'Can I take your order please?'

'Yeah, can I get a Whopper meal, bacon double cheeseburger with extra cheese, and a Diet Coke.'

'Sure. Anything else?'

'Nah, that's all.'

'Please proceed to the second window.'

What is going on? This is some damn freaky dream, I thought. But I felt sure I was awake.

It went silent for a couple of minutes and I drifted back to sleep.

'Can I take your order please?' the voice said again.

'Can I get two whoppers and a large Dr Pepper.'

'Anything else?'

'That's it.'

'Please proceed to the second window.'

I had experienced some pretty weird dreams in the past, but I had never had such a vivid dream of being in Burger King. But I was definitely wide awake now, and those voices in my head hadn't stopped.

'…bacon double cheeseburger…'

'…large fries…'

'…side of onion rings…'

'…large Coke…'

The voices were real. I peered out of the window and discovered I had unknowingly parked next to the ordering point of a Burger King drive-thru. Rachel was still fast asleep, and, as I am able to sleep through most things, I decided to try and ignore it and go back to sleep.

But I couldn't ignore it.

Not because the noise was bothering me, but because the thought of all of that food had made me ridiculously hungry. Moving the car would not solve the problem now. There was no way I could get back to sleep when my stomach was sending me urgent messages about food. We had some stale bread and a couple of apples in the car, but that would not suffice. It had to be Burger King.

I pulled on some clothes and quietly climbed into the front seat, before leaving Josephine stealthily via the passenger door.

I walked up to the entrance of Burger King. It was closed. Most of the lights in the restaurant section were off, and there was nobody seated at the tables inside. I could see staff busy in the kitchen and realised it was only the drive-thru that was open.

I was already parked up so it seemed a little impractical to use the car. I was just about to walk up to the order point when another car appeared. I gestured for them go first and queued patiently behind them on foot while they placed their order. Another two cars joined the queue behind me, but I held my ground so that they didn't steal my place.

Then it was my turn.

I walked up to the speaker.

'Hi,' I said. 'Could I have a Whopper meal with a coke, and a side of onion rings, please?'

'Do you have a car?' said the female voice from the order post.

'Yes I do, but it's parked up. My wife is asleep.'

'I'm afraid we can't serve customers on foot at the drive-thru.'

'But I'm only at the drive-thru because the restaurant is closed.'

'I understand that, but we are not allowed to serve customers on foot.'

How did she even know I was on foot? I considered making a revving noise to try and convince her that I was actually in a car. Then I spotted the tiny camera lens above the speaker and realised she and her colleagues were probably watching me pathetically standing there trying to order a Whopper at 2am. I gave her a cheery little wave, hoping to win her over.

'I'm sorry. It's to do with health and safety.'

'Ok, fine,' I conceded, climbing across a small flowerbed to where Josephine was parked.

I considered asking someone else to place my order for me, and then giving them the money. But I only had a $20 note. That would have been too complicated to work out my change. There was only one solution.

I pulled back the curtain divider between the front seats and the back of Josephine. Rachel was still fast asleep. I turned the key in the ignition hoping that Josephine would miraculously start up in stealth mode, but as usual she woke up like an angry rhinoceros.

'What are you doing?' groaned Rachel.

'I'm just putting the heaters on for a few minutes,' I said. 'Go back to sleep.'

She rolled over and seconds later was breathing heavily.

I slipped Josephine into reverse and slowly turned the car around so that I could enter the drive-thru.

'Can I take your order please?'

'A Whopper meal with a Coke and a side of onion rings, please?' I whispered.

'Sorry, was that a Whopper meal?'

'Yes please.'

'What drink would you like?'

'Coke.'

'Was that a Coke?'

'Yes, please. Coke,' I whispered again.

'Sorry, it's hard to hear you. Did you say Coke?'

'Yes. Coke please.'

'Will that be all?'

'And a side of onion rings please.'

'Thank you. Please proceed to the second window.'

'What's going on?' said Rachel from the back.

'Nothing, go back to sleep.'

'What are you doing? Where are we?'

'We are still in the car park. I'm just moving the car to a better spot.'

I looked back and could see her pulling the curtain back and peering out of the window.

'Are we at Burger King?'

'What? No… well… sort of… yes.'

'There you go,' said the Burger King lady, handing me my food. 'Enjoy your meal. Have a good night.'

'Thank you,' I whispered.

I thought perhaps I had got away with the staff not realising I was the same man who minutes earlier had tried to walk through the drive-thru, but the smile on the lady's face as she handed me my meal, and the mock cheery wave she gave me, suggested otherwise.

'Have we just been through a drive-thru?' snapped Rachel.

'Drive-thru? No, no, of course not. It's 2am. Go back to sleep.'

'What's that I can smell?'

'I don't know,' I said, parking the car a safe distance from Burger King and turning off the engine.

'It smells like onion rings.'

'Gwo bwack to sweep,' I said, my mouth full of onion rings.

'You're eating onion rings, aren't you? Why would you do that?'

'I'm really sorry. I couldn't sleep because all I could hear was people ordering food and it made me so hungry.'

'Couldn't you just have eaten a banana or something?'

'No. It had to be a Whopper.'

'A WHOPPER?' she barked. 'I THOUGHT YOU SAID IT WAS ONION RINGS?'

'It is onion rings. And a Whopper. And fries. And a Coke.'

‘Oh my god. You are SO annoying. Couldn’t you have gone and eaten it inside, rather than stink the car out while I’m trying to sleep?’

‘I tried to. But it was closed, and they wouldn’t serve me at the drive-thru without a car.’

‘You didn’t try did you?’

‘Yes,’ I said sheepishly.

‘You really are a weirdo,’ she said, but I could detect a hint of laughter in her voice.

‘Sorry. Would you like a bite of my Whopper?’

‘Is that supposed to be some sleazy chat-up line?’

‘No, it was a genuine offer. Onion ring?’

‘No thank you. Good night.’

And with that, she fell silent, and I sat and enjoyed the rest of my meal in peace.

45

I woke in the morning feeling quietly content after my midnight feast. We had a long drive ahead as we hoped to be in Manhattan by the end of the day.

We had two days to spend in New York before catching our flight home. Rachel had never been to the Big Apple before so was keen to cram in as many of the sights as possible during our brief visit. Unfortunately, I had the small matter of trying to sell Josephine to take care of.

I wrote a couple of *FOR SALE* adverts that I pinned to the wall in our hostel, and another hostel located nearby.

PLANNING A ROAD TRIP?
1989 Plymouth Voyager / Dodge Caravan
Has just driven around America – ready to go again!
New (ish) transmission
New (ish) tyres
New (ish) radiator / water pump
Back area converted into large sleeping area
$1000

All the necessary paperwork that would be required to transfer Josephine to a new owner had been mailed to the post office box Mark and I had rented in upstate New York, several hundred miles away.

I contacted the DMV and explained the situation and, for a fee, they said they could mail a replacement to me. I explained that I needed it urgently, and they said that for an even larger fee, it could be couriered next day delivery.

On our first full day in Manhattan, Rachel and I did a whistle-stop tour of the Empire State Building, Times Square and Central Park, before returning to the hostel later that afternoon.

A slightly annoying English guy named Matt asked me a few questions about Josephine. He suggested that he and his slightly annoying friend Chris were interested. Unfortunately, Matt had overhead my frantic phone call with the DMV earlier that morning, and was therefore fully aware of the rush I was in to sell Josephine.

'I'll give you $100 for it,' he said.

'No, she's worth much more than that. I've spent thousands on her in the last year. The transmission, tyres, radiator, water pump have all been replaced within the last eight months. She needs no work.'

'$200,' he said, sensing I was desperate.

'I'm not taking less than $800,' I said.

'Oh well,' he said and he turned and left the room.

'Why don't you just sell it to him for $200?' said Rachel.

'Because the guy's a dick. He's just trying to take advantage of me because we are in a rush. Even $800 would be a bargain. I've spent over $4000 on repairs for Josephine and she's in a much better state now compared to when Mark and I bought her.'

'Still, $200 is better than nothing.'

'I think I would rather just leave Josephine to rust in the parking lot than get greased up and screwed by Matt from Oxford.'

'What are you talking about?'

'Oh, sorry, nothing.'

Rachel and I did some more speed-sightseeing the following morning, and then sat around in the hostel's lounge all afternoon waiting for the FedEx delivery to arrive. By 5pm, the time slot had elapsed, and there was still no sign of my documents.

I approached the man who was manning the hostel's office. He was in his late teens and sat slumped on a small sofa in a little office room watching TV. He seemed to be permanently stoned.

'Hi, you haven't seen a FedEx delivery have you?'

'Yeah, man. The guy came an hour or so ago.'

'Oh, why didn't you tell me? Remember I said I was waiting for a delivery and would be in the lounge all afternoon?'

'Yeah, man. I thought you'd gone out. Sorry.'

'Did he leave you anything?'

'Yeah, man, he did,' he said, rummaging through a pile of papers on his desk. 'Here you go.'

He handed me a *'packages not delivered'* slip and my heart sank.

'I've been sitting just through there all afternoon!' I said.

'Sorry.'

The note said I could collect my package from 10am the following morning, from a depot that was located on the other side of Manhattan. It was going to be cutting it incredibly fine to get there and back before we had to leave to catch our flight. It was looking more and more likely that I might have to leave Josephine to rust in the hostel's parking lot after all.

Matt the twat approached me later that evening as Rachel and I headed out for a few beers on our last night in America.

'Thought any more about my offer?' he said. 'I'll still give you $200 for the car.'

'Sorry, Matt. The price is $800.'

'Don't you have a plane to catch tomorrow?'

'Yes.'

'Then you'll surely want to sell it before you leave.'

'Not for $200, I won't.'

At breakfast the next morning Matt passed me again.

'$300?' he said.

'Matt, come on mate, you know she's worth much more than that. I tell you what, how about $700, and I'll throw in our gas stove, blankets, cool box, pots and pans and a few other bits.'

I had planned to include these with the sale anyway, but Matt didn't know that. He looked over at his friend Chris who was eating a bowl of cereal at a nearby table. Chris nodded.

'Deal,' said Matt, with his hand outstretched.

I shook it.

'Deal,' I said.

'Is there some paperwork we need to sign?'

'Ah, yes, there is. I've got to sort that out this morning. Can we meet back here at midday?'

'Ok.'

I left Rachel at the hostel to clear out all our belongings from Josephine, and I made a mad dash for the subway where I raced across Manhattan, joined a frustrating queue that snaked out of the FedEx doors, and then eventually received my documents. I then jumped in a cab and got back to the hostel at 12.30pm. Fortunately Matt was still there.

'Sorry I'm late,' I said. 'I've got everything we need now.'

We completed all the paperwork and I showed Matt and Chris how to operate Josephine's quirky ignition. I had already explained that the windscreen wipers didn't work. Matt looked at the blue sky and optimistically said, 'It doesn't rain in America, does it?'

I was already starting to like Matt a little more.

I also explained the blood splatter all over the curtains and ceiling and the fact that although it said it was a Plymouth Voyager, it was technically a Dodge Caravan.

'Take good care of Josephine,' I said.

'We will do, I promise.'

'I hope you have a brilliant adventure. Where are you heading first?'

'Who knows?' he said. 'We'll see where the road takes us.'

I shook Matt and Chris by the hand and then gave Josephine an affectionate stroke, lingering for an uncomfortably long time.

'George, we've really got to go,' said Rachel. 'We will miss our flight.'

'Ok, sorry. Let's go. Goodbye Matt and Chris. Goodbye Josephine. Happy travels.'

We heaved our backpacks on and I grabbed my stupid guitar that I had taken out of its case only half a dozen times in eight months, put my Stetson on, and slung my snowboard in its bag over my other shoulder and we dashed from the hostel.

We reached the end of the block, turned the corner and then descended down the steps to the subway. As we stood on the platform waiting for the train to arrive, I checked my pockets in the way I nervously do every five minutes when I'm heading to an airport.

Got my wallet. Got my boarding pass. Got my passport. No, wait, I have A passport, but I was supposed to have two. Shit, this one is Rachel's. Where the fuck is mine?

'Do you have my passport?' I asked Rachel.

'No. You had them both. Have you lost them?'

'I've got yours. But mine has gone.'

'When did you lose it?'

'I definitely had them as we left the hostel. I checked. I've managed to lose it between the hostel and here.'

'Do you think someone stole it?'

'No, it must have fallen out when we were running. You wait here and I'll go and see if I can find it.'

'If you've lost it out on the street then it will be gone for good.'

'Well, it's worth a try. I don't know what else I can do.'

I dumped my bags on the ground, sprinted back across the platform and up the steps to the street above. Of all the places in the world, a sidewalk in downtown Manhattan must be one of the stupidest places to lose a passport.

I emerged at street level and scanned the area at the top of the stairs, but there was no sign of it. I made my way into the throng of people bustling up and down one of New York City's busiest streets and began to retrace my steps towards the hostel. The sidewalk was so busy that I could only see a small section of ground around my feet, as I frantically searched for my passport.

I had survived eight incredible months in America. But now my luck had finally run out. And it was only me that could be held accountable.

My mind whirred. I didn't know what to do. I would have to contact the British Embassy and try to arrange for a new passport or some sort of emergency replacement. But that could take days. Or even weeks. And what would happen when they discovered I had outstayed my visa?

I was furious with myself for being so careless. But I tried to remain grateful about what an amazing experience I had had up until this point. I thought about the first time I had emerged alone and naive from the subway in Manhattan eight months previously, and everything that had happened between then and now. My travels across America had exceeded all of my expectations. Its cities were bigger, its mountains higher, roads straighter, rivers wider, lowlands sparser, buildings taller, lakes greater, winters colder, gas cheaper, portions larger, canyons grander, badlands badder, deserts desertier, desserts dessertier, taxis yellowier, Halloweens scarier, bears grizzlier, corn palaces cornier, ski slopes snowier, Brians greasier, prairie dogs dafter, walks hikier, bacon crispier, green salads beefier, park rangers speedier, mechanics wackier (and sometimes grease-you-up-and-screwier), crazy golf crazier, drive-thrus noisier, and its people friendlier than I could have ever possibly imagined.

The United States is a country full of wonderfully kind, generous and welcoming people. What I admired most was how Americans were, without exception, lovingly patriotic about their country, and, more noticeably, their home towns. From Eureka, Nevada, to Two Dot, Montana, each and every person I met was immensely proud of the small piece of the American jigsaw that their home town formed.

And what a stunning jigsaw it is.

The country can be big and brash, loud and arrogant, but it can also be incredibly modest and understated. It is a country that is a world-leader in commerce, technology, and human achievement, yet its countless deserts, mountain ranges, lakes, wilderness areas and even its spectacular cityscapes, make it one of the most stunningly beautiful countries on Earth.

It shouldn't need to erect signposts to commemorate waterfalls that are no longer there, or celebrate areas where pigeons used to roost, or label a building 'historic' just for the sake of it. America has more than enough splendour in every direction you look. In the eight months I spent travelling its back roads, I covered many thousands of miles, and visited 35 of America's 50 states, yet I still felt like I had not even scratched the surface of such a truly remarkable country.

I had taken a big gamble by heading off to America without Rachel. It hadn't been easy, and our relationship was heavily tested while we were apart. But we got through it, and the months we spent in each other's company driving across the northern States brought us even closer together. Having spent so much time with Rachel, cooped up together in Josephine, I now couldn't imagine ever living apart from her. When we returned to England, we would find a place to rent. Somewhere we could begin the next stage of our lives together.

My relationship with Mark was stronger as a result, too. We had gained a wealth of shared experiences that we could recount to each other until we are old and grey.

I arrived in America as a bedraggled looking student-type, and I would be leaving as a man. Actually, that's not true. I was far more bedraggled-looking and significantly worse off financially than when I arrived. But I did feel like I had matured, even if only slightly, during the course of my travels.

There had been many challenges along the way; mechanical, emotional, physical and administrational. All of which I somehow overcame, or successfully ignored. And I hadn't needed to phone Nick Carter for help.

I still keep his dollar bill in my wallet, though. Just in case.

It was then that I saw it.

My passport.

Lying there on a dirty sidewalk, on one of the busiest streets in one of the busiest cities in the world. I shrieked with delight, which made the man in the grey suit walking alongside me quicken his pace to get out of my way.

I bent down to pick it up and flicked quickly through the pages to make sure it was all intact. I clutched it tightly to my chest, turned around, and jogged back to the subway station.

'Oh my god,' said Rachel, as I ran towards her waving the passport and smiling the biggest smile I have ever smiled. 'Where was it?'

'Just lying on the pavement up there.'

'You are incredibly lucky.'

'I know I am,' I said, taking her hand and squeezing it tightly. 'Let's go home.'

Acknowledgements

Thank you to Mark for allowing me to gatecrash your trip to America. It was even more brilliant than I hoped.

Thank you to Rachel for your help with the editing of this book and, far more importantly, for standing by me when I stubbornly went to America without you, and for standing by me ever since.

Thanks to Tim Windram for your proofreading help. Special thanks, to Becky Beer, for putting up, with, my excessive use of, commas. And for accepting that it's ok to start a sentence with the word 'and'.

Thank you to all of the hundreds of kind people who made me feel so welcome throughout my time in America. I hope to be back one day soon (if US immigration allows me).

This was the first book I ever wanted to write. I kept a diary during my time in the USA with the intention of writing my very own American travelogue once I returned home. Then real life got in the way and I convinced myself that nobody would ever want to read a book of mine. So lastly, and most importantly, huge thanks to you for choosing to spend your time reading a book of mine. It really means a lot.

If you enjoyed reading my book, I would be extremely grateful if you would consider posting a short review on Amazon. Reviews are so important for authors, so any way in which you can help spread the word is incredibly helpful. Thank you.

There will be photos from the trip added to my Facebook page shortly so please LIKE that to keep up-to-date.

www.facebook.com/georgemahood

I also have a useless website that I don't update at all, but there is a mailing list sign up page if you would like to join and be one of the first to hear of my new books.

www.georgemahood.com

I am also on Twitter for general ramblings:

@georgemahood

Or you can drop me an email with any comments, feedback or criticism. It's always great to hear from readers.

george@georgemahood.com

I have written a few other books too, so please take a look…

FREE COUNTRY:
A Penniless Adventure the Length of Britain

'...spent last night laughing so much my coffee came out my eyes...'
'...this book is quite simply the best I've read in years...'
'...a completely bonkers challenge and a brilliantly funny read, I couldn't put it down...'

The plan is simple. George and Ben have three weeks to cycle 1000 miles from the bottom of England to the top of Scotland. There is just one small problem... they have no bikes, no clothes, no food and no money. Setting off in just a pair of Union Jack boxer shorts, they attempt to rely on the generosity of the British public for everything from food to accommodation, clothes to shoes, and bikes to beer.

During the most hilarious adventure, George and Ben encounter some of Great Britain's most eccentric and extraordinary characters and find themselves in the most ridiculous situations. Free Country is guaranteed to make you laugh (you may even shed a tear). It will restore your faith in humanity and leave you with a big smile on your face and a warm feeling inside.

Free Country is available on Amazon.

OPERATION IRONMAN:
One Man's Four Month Journey from Hospital Bed to Ironman Triathlon

"…George's books just keep getting better…"
"…laugh out loud funny (note to self, don't read it on the tube)…"
"…it won't fail to entertain, enthral and motivate…"
"…hilarious and heart-warming…"
"…inspiring, poignant and humorous…"
"…I laughed, I cried, and am proud of a man I have never met…"

Operation Ironman follows George Mahood's inspiring and entertaining journey from a hospital bed to an Ironman triathlon. After major surgery to remove a spinal cord tumour, George set himself the ultimate challenge –
a 2.4 mile swim,

a 112 mile bike ride,
and a 26.2 mile run,
all to be completed within 16 hours.

He couldn't swim more than a length of front crawl, he had never ridden a proper road bike, and he had not run further than 10k in 18 months.

He had four months to prepare.

Could he do it?

Operation Ironman is available on Amazon.

EVERY DAY IS A HOLIDAY

"...laugh out loud moments on nearly every page..."
"...had me laughing from beginning to end..."
"...loved the book – funny and engaging..."
"...read it, love it, recommend it..."

George Mahood had a nice, easy, comfortable life. He had a job, a house, a wife and kids. But something was missing. He was stuck in a routine of working, changing nappies and cleaning up cat sick. He felt like he was missing out on a lot of what the world had to offer.

He then discovered that it was Bubble Wrap Appreciation Day. The day after that was National Curmudgeon Day, and the day after that was Inane Answering Machine Message Day. In fact, the calendar is FULL of these quirky, weird and wonderful events. He realised that somebody somewhere had created these holidays, believing that they were important enough to warrant their own official day. Surely he should therefore be more appreciative of their existence? So he decided to try and celebrate them all. As you do. He hoped that at the end of the challenge he would be transformed into a happier, more intelligent and more content person.

Follow George on his hilarious, life changing adventure as he tries to balance his normal life with a wealth of new experiences, people, facts and ridiculous situations. It's a rip-roaring, life-affirming, roller-coaster of a ride, where every day is a holiday.

Every Day Is a Holiday is available on Amazon.

Thank you all again.
BIG love,
George

www.facebook.com/georgemahood
www.twitter.com/georgemahood
www.georgemahood.com

Printed in Poland
by Amazon Fulfillment
Poland Sp. z o.o., Wrocław